Treasures of the Vieux Carré

Ten Self-Guided Walking Tours of the French Quarter

Frank Perez

Treasures of the Vieux Carré
Ten Self-Guided Walking Tours of the French Quarter

ISBN: 978-0-9574726-7-9
Paperback version
© 2014 by Frank Perez

Published in 2014 by LL-Publications. P.O. Box 542,
Bedford, Texas 76095
www.ll-publications.com

Edited by Billye Johnson
Proofreading by Janet S.
Book layout and typesetting by jimandzetta.com
Cover photo: George P. Marse
Tour Photographs: George P. Marse
Author Photograph: Larry Graham
Maps © OpenStreetMap developers, www.openstreetmap.org
Map data available under the Open Database License,
opendatacommons.org

Printed in the UK and the USA

All rights reserved. No part of this publication may be copied, transmitted, or recorded by any means whatsoever, including printing, photocopying, file transfer, or any form of data storage, mechanical or electronic, without the express written consent of the publisher. In addition, no part of this publication may be lent, re-sold, hired, or otherwise circulated or distributed, in any form whatsoever, without the express written consent of the publisher

PRAISE FOR *TREASURES OF THE VIEUX CARRÉ*

"My wife and I have visited New Orleans for years and we're familiar with the city but this book opened our eyes to places and things we never knew about. An outstanding guide book!"
— Joseph McCann, Atlanta, Georgia

"I learned so much from this book—including where to eat like a local!"
— Jeanette Hauser, Eugene, Oregon

"Frank Perez' extensive knowledge of the French Quarter puts this book in a class all its own."
— Steven Garcia, Historian

"Frank's unsurpassed depth of historical knowledge and local lore, keen understanding of what makes a good walking tour, and endless catalog of obscure facts that you may - or may not - want to know about the French Quarter, make Treasures of the Vieux Carré *a go-to resource for visitors and tour guides alike. It's already an essential part of my reference library for specialty tours."*
— Grey Sweeney Perkins, New Orleans Tour Guide

"As a tour guide, I would recommend this book to visitors to explore the Quarter's rich diversity as a cultural landmark. For tour guides, it can serve as a source to amplify your appreciation and presentations."
— Ron Joullian, New Orleans Tour Guide

"When I became a tour guide in New Orleans the best advice I received was from Frank Perez-'Talk about what's in front of you.' Well, easier said than done! The beauty of this book is that it allows one to see what Frank sees! There isn't an inch of the Quarter's brick-lined streets and alleys that he hasn't walked, rambled, sauntered and second-lined! He knows their stories and secrets and the tales behind the tales where the true treasures lie! And he carries this knowledge as lightly as he wears his ever-present wide brimmed hat! And here he generously shares it all with readers!"
— Michael Naughton, New Orleans Tour Guide

"This book captures the history and culture of New Orleans in a variety of ways. Treasures of the Vieux Carré is not only helpful to visitors, it's also a great reference book for locals and even tour guides."
— Robi Robichaux, New Orleans Tour Guide

"An invaluable resource for tour guides and tourists."
— Jeff Palmquist, Three Time GAA Bartender of the Year, New Orleans

Acknowledgments

Much of the research for this book was conducted at the Williams Research Center of the Historic New Orleans Collection, and I am grateful for the assistance and guidance its staff afforded me. I would also like to thank the staff at the Louisiana State Museum as well as the volunteers and docents that constitute the Friends of the Cabildo. Finally, I wish to express my gratitude to my fellow tour guides, several of whom have become not only professional colleagues but also good friends.

Dedication

For Paul Cassella, whose love of New Orleans rivals my own
and whose friendship means the world to me.

Table of Contents

Introduction 9
Historical Overview... 11
Notes on Maps, Streets and Directions 21
Notes on Safety and Etiquette 22
Notes on Street Names in the French Quarter 23
Topical Organization Codes 26

The Tours
General Walking Tour: Highlights of the French Quarter 27
African American Heritage Walking Tour 57
Architectural and Historic Homes Walking Tour 78
Culinary Walking Tour... 100
Gay Interest Walking Tour.. 124
Ghosts and Spirits Walking Tour 145
Hollywood South Walking Tour 161
Jazz and Musical Heritage Walking Tour 179
Literary Walking Tour... 202
Vice and Crime Walking Tour 220

Recommendations for Guided Tours 236
About the Author.. 237
Index 238

Introduction

Welcome to New Orleans! If you're a returning visitor, it's good to have you back. If this is your first time here, you're in for an experience you'll never forget. You will eat some of the best food on earth, hear some of the most inspired music ever created, meet the most interesting characters anywhere, and be seduced by a truly unique city that has been marinating for almost 300 years. New Orleans is a sensuous city, and the best way to experience it is on the streets. As you wander around the French Quarter, you will be surprised and delighted and maybe even amazed by just how culturally rich this little neighborhood is with history, art, music, food, architecture, and characters. There really is no other place quite like it. If you talk to enough locals, which is something you should certainly do, you will surely meet someone who once visited here, fell in love with the city, and never left. New Orleans has a way of doing that.

After Hurricane Katrina, local writer Ian McNulty observed, "People don't live in New Orleans because it is easy. They live here because they are incapable of living anywhere else in the just same way." That's about as good as anyone has ever put it, but McNulty's observation begs the question—just what exactly makes living in New Orleans different than living anywhere else?

It's stepping outside your door to get some fresh air only to find a brass band leading a second-line parade down the street; it's being chased by The Big Easy Roller Derby Girls as they skate past you and whack you with a pool noodle during the New Orleans' version of the Running of the Bulls; it's walking past the window of GW Fins and seeing an elderly man in a seersucker suit eating baked oysters; it's dancing in the street to the To Be Continued Brass Band playing at the corner of Canal at Bourbon on a Tuesday evening; it's catching some beads from Pete Fountain on Mardi Gras morning as his Half Fast Walking Club marches past you; it's being able to find a cocktail at 4:00 in the morning and then walking down the street with it; it's having your waiter at Galatoire's serve you turtle soup and whisper in your ear, "The turtle's name was Fred"; it's taking forever to run what should be a ten-minute errand because there are so many bars between your home and wherever you're going and in each one is someone you know; it's hearing members of the local opera company sing arias in the lobby of the hotel where the French Opera House once stood; it's having perfect strangers pin money to your shirt on your birthday; it's dressing your dog in a silly costume for the Barkus Parade; it's breathing in the scent of thousands of used books at the Dauphine Street Book Shop; it's sinking your teeth in a homemade lamb sausage po-boy in the back room at the Erin Rose; it's having Ashley the Traffic Tranny blow her whistle at you as she directs traffic at St. Ann and Bourbon; it's eating a fluffy omelet at the Clover Grill at 3:00 a.m.; in short, it's waking up every day and feeling like you're getting away with something.

Yes, we live here differently and we live here well. That's not to say New Orleans is without her problems—poverty, crime and corruption chief among them, to say nothing of the constant threat of another Hurricane Katrina. And yet, here we are, still here, determined to let the good times roll. Why? Well, that question was best answered by Lafcadio Hearn, a visitor to New Orleans in 1877: *"Times are not good here. The city is crumbling into ashes. It has been buried under taxes and frauds and maladministrations so that it has become a study for archaeologists . . . but it is better to live here in sackcloth and ashes than to own the whole state of Ohio."* Hearn ended up staying in New Orleans ten years. Now, when did you say your departing flight is? If you miss it, you wouldn't be the first.

Historical Overview

The French Quarter is the heart of New Orleans and the site of the original city, which was founded in 1718. In the seventeenth century, as the nations of Europe began jockeying for position in the New World, it soon became apparent that controlling the mouth of the Mississippi River was crucial to colonial success. The Spanish explorer Hernando de Soto was the first European to discover the Mississippi River in 1541. In 1682, the French explorer René-Robert Cavelier, Sieur de la Salle erected a cross on the banks of the Mississippi River near its mouth and claimed all the land drained by the mighty river for King Louis XIV of France. At that time, a number of Native American tribes resided in what we now call South Louisiana. These included the Choctaw, Biloxi, Bayougoula, Houma, Chitimacha, and Atakapa. The site of the French Market was an important commercial trading center for several Native American tribes prior to the arrival of the Europeans.

When LaSalle claimed all the land drained by the mighty river for France, he most likely had no idea just how vast his claim was. Beginning in Minnesota, The Mississippi River, the fourth longest river in the world, snakes its way 2,530 miles (4,070km) south to the Gulf of Mexico. The river drains all or parts of thirty-one states and two Canadian provinces. Claiming the land was one thing but settling it was quite another. Seventeen years after LaSalle's claim, two brothers from Montreal—Pierre Le Moyne d'Iberville and Jean-Baptiste Le Moyne, Sieur de Bienville—explored the lower Mississippi and Gulf coast. The first permanent settlement in the French colony of Louisiana was at Ocean Springs near Biloxi in present-day Mississippi. In 1702,

Iberville and Bienville founded Mobile in present-day Alabama. Bienville founded New Orleans in 1718.

The sharp bend in the river where Bienville chose to locate the colony's capital was not without controversy. Some people argued Biloxi, on the coast, should be the capital while others advocated for Manchac, further upriver. Still, others favored Baton Rouge. Each site had its merits as well as its faults, but in the end, Bienville's "beautiful crescent" won out in no small part because of its strategic proximity to Lake Pontchartrain. The lake is roughly five miles from the river (where it bends at the French Quarter) and offered sailing vessels an alternative access route to the city via its neighbor Lake Borgne, which is actually a bay accessible from the Gulf of Mexico. From Lake Borgne, ships could enter Lake Pontchartrain through an eight-mile straight called the Rigolets. Instead of having to fight the strong Mississippi River current for 110 miles, ships and boats could easily and more safely access the city through the back door. From the lake, Bayou St. John flowed to within about two miles of the city. From that point, the riverfront was accessible by an old Indian portage, which the Native Americans had shown Bienville years earlier.

The very first buildings and homes in New Orleans were wooden huts and shacks, most of which were blown down in a hurricane in 1721. The streets of the French Quarter we know today were laid out in 1722. The city's initial residents were involuntarily sent to Louisiana and consisted mostly of convicts from Paris (chiefly thieves and prostitutes) and peasants. An influx of African slaves (primarily from the Senegambia region of West Africa) and German immigrants followed. Until 1731, the Company of the West (later the Company of the Indies) administered the colony. France had hoped Louisiana would become a great tobacco colony, but Louisiana tobacco proved to be far inferior to the tobacco being grown in the British colonies on the Atlantic Seaboard. In 1729, the Natchez Indians attacked the Fort Rosalie settlement at present-day Natchez, Mississippi, killing over 230 settlers and burning their tobacco fields. Disappointed and dispirited, the Company of the Indies retroceded to the French Crown its exclusive Louisiana monopoly in 1731.

Imperial neglect marked the next thirty years. A number of European conflicts preoccupied France while the Louisiana colony dealt with a series of problems with various Native American tribes. Some tribes had allied with the English, who were firmly established on the east coast while others had alliances with the French. British encroachment into the Louisiana territory was a perennial threat. Supply shortages were also common. During this period, plantations shifted their production from tobacco to indigo. Illegal trading and smuggling became commonplace, and in many cases, necessary for the colony's survival. It was also during this period that a distinct Creole culture began to emerge. Originally, the term Creole simply meant native born, or born in the colony. The French colonial period lasted until 1762 when King Louis XV ceded Louisiana to his cousin, King Carlos II of Spain.

The transfer of Louisiana from France to Spain was the result of the Seven Years War—a global conflict involving France, Great Britain, Austria, Sweden, and Prussia. The North American theatre of this war is commonly referred to as the French Indian War. In order to prevent England from gaining control of Louisiana and specifically New Orleans, France gave to Spain all of its territory west of the Mississippi River and New Orleans. The Spanish colonial period lasted from 1762 to 1803, when Spain retroceded Louisiana back to France.

Although the secret transfer took place in 1762, the first Spanish governor, Antonio de Ulloa y de la Torre-Girault, did not arrive in New Orleans until 1766. The French colonists were surprised to learn they were suddenly subjects of the Spanish Crown. It did not take long for their surprise to turn to anger, and in 1768, a group of leading colonists rebelled and expelled the Spanish governor from New Orleans. Restrictive trade regulations imposed by the Spanish Crown were the main cause of the insurrection. The King of Spain responded to the rebellion by sending an Irish mercenary to take control of the colony on behalf of Spain. Alejandro O'Reilly arrived in 1769 with over 2,000 troops and promptly executed the leaders of the insurrection. Since then, he has been known as Bloody O'Reilly in the annals of Louisiana history. Frenchmen Street, now famous for its live music venues, was named in honor of the executed French loyalists.

Throughout the Spanish Period, New Orleans remained a thoroughly French town. Spanish governors, soldiers, and bureaucrats married French women, thus ensuring the survival of the French language and culture. Spain's most enduring legacy in New Orleans is perhaps architectural. In 1788, a great fire swept through the little town and destroyed over 800 structures. Six years later, after another fire destroyed over 200 buildings, the Spanish adopted a fire / building code which required, among other things, buildings to be built flush up against the sidewalk. The Cabildo and the Presbytere, the handsome buildings that flank St. Louis Cathedral in Jackson Square, are fine examples of Spanish colonial architecture (except for the French Mansard roofs, which were added later). The Spanish also created the French Market in an effort to consolidate the city's many food vendors. It was also during the Spanish Period that the Acadian exiles from Nova Scotia arrived in Louisiana. The Cajuns, as they would come to be called, settled the area south and west of New Orleans. Unlike the French, the Spanish were meticulous record keepers and were very experienced in colonial administration having already spent centuries in Latin America when they acquired Louisiana.

Yet another significant contribution of the Spanish in Louisiana dealt with slavery. The French had instituted a set of laws governing the treatment of slaves called the *Code Noir* in 1724. The Spanish kept most of the principles of the *Code Noir* but also added important provisions, the most significant of which was the law of *coartacion*. This law gave slaves the right to purchase their own freedom. Some 1,500 manumissions were granted during the Spanish Period, thus contributing to the growing population of free people of color. The slave trade expanded under the Spanish, and by the turn of the eighteenth century, New Orleans was home to slaves from a variety of African nations.

In 1791, the slave population in the French colony of Saint Domingue, inspired by the French Revolution of 1789, rose up and, in a violent insurrection, overthrew their masters. The conflict lasted thirteen years. The Haitian Revolution had a profound influence on New Orleans. Many of the refugees from Saint Dominque came to French-speaking New Orleans. At one point, 1/3 of the population in New Orleans was from Saint Domingue. Also, the fall of France's leading sugar colony enabled the sugar industry to boom in Louisiana. But even more importantly, the Haitian Revolution paved the way for the United States to purchase Louisiana.

In 1800, Napoleon Bonaparte persuaded Spain to give Louisiana back to France in exchange for the Italian region of Tuscany. Embroiled in war in Europe, Bonaparte did not immediately take possession of Louisiana. Also, the staging point of France's repossession of Louisiana was to be Saint Domingue. When Saint Domingue finally fell and became the Republic of Haiti, Bonaparte abandoned his dream of a

North American empire and became willing to sell Louisiana to the United States.

In 1803, the United States purchased Louisiana (over 800,000 square miles) for $15 million—or about four cents an acre. The territory effectively doubled the size of the United States and consisted of parts or all of what would later become fourteen states. Louisiana was admitted to the Union as a state in 1812. As was the case during the Spanish Period, New Orleans remained a thoroughly French town during the early American Period. As Americans poured into the city, they were viewed with suspicion by the Creoles, who regarded the Americans as uncultured Protestant foreigners. A rivalry developed between the two groups and the Americans settled along the river south of Canal Street.

The Creoles and Americans set aside their differences briefly in 1815 when the British attempted to invade New Orleans. The Battle of New Orleans took place on January 8, 1815, a few miles downriver in present-day Chalmette. In one of the greatest upsets in American military history, General Andrew Jackson routed the British in a decisive victory. Some historians have argued the Battle of New Orleans was irrelevant since the Treaty of Ghent, which ended the War of 1812, had already been signed. While it is true the treaty had been signed, it is important to remember it had not yet been ratified at the time of the battle.

The decades that followed up to the Civil War (1861) were New Orleans' golden years. This was the age of steamboats, of cotton and sugar and the flowering of plantation culture. The city grew tremendously as the port became one of the busiest in the world. Immigrants from a multitude of nations (especially Ireland and Germany) poured into the city and the town began to expand outside the original bounds of the French Quarter (or *Vieux Carré*, as it was then called).

During this era, New Orleans took on the cosmopolitan vibe it retains today. Along with great financial prosperity, the city also experienced a building boom during this era. In the French Quarter, 956 buildings were constructed between 1820 and 1850. Jackson Square was rejuvenated between 1849 and 1855 with the construction of the Pontalba Buildings and facelifts for the cathedral, the Cabildo, and the Presbytere.

Despite all the wealth and affluence New Orleans attained in the first half of the nineteenth century, life was not all merriment and money signs. The city was under the constant threat of plagues and diseases, to say nothing of hurricanes. Yellow Fever epidemics broke out every few years with alarming regularity; 10,000 people died of it in 1853 alone. Cholera was also a perennial problem. Sanitation was virtually non-existent. Streets were often muddy as well as filthy with trash, excrement and animal carcasses.

But the times were not all misery and heartache. The period before the Civil War saw the birth of modern Mardi Gras in New Orleans. The Shrove Tuesday celebration was brought to New Orleans by the French explorers and celebrated in southern Louisiana as early as 1699. The holiday, which has its roots in Roman Catholicism, has always been celebrated in New Orleans, but it wasn't until 1838 that the first parade occurred. This consisted of a walking procession of masked figures. Float parades were introduced in 1857. In that year, Mardi Gras in New Orleans was on the verge of extinction. The annual celebration had become a drunken, chaotic, and increasingly violent street party. The revelry and disorder that characterized the day offended puritanical American sensibilities and there was serious discussion of permanently canceling the event. A group of businessmen then suggested that instead of canceling Mardi Gras, a sense of order should be imposed upon the celebration. They proposed a float parade with a theme and masked riders. Thus, the Mistik Krewe of Comus was born, and with it, the custom of float parades on Mardi Gras. The idea of imposing order on a day defined by disorder and misrule violated the essential spirit of Mardi Gras; nevertheless, the float parade was a practical solution that proved very popular. Today, there are numerous float parades throughout the New Orleans area in the weeks leading up to Mardi Gras.

In 1861, Louisiana seceded from the Union and joined the Confederate States of America. Defending New Orleans from a Union naval invasion during the Civil War were Forts Jackson and St. Philip, about seventy miles downriver. The two forts proved no match for the Union forces, and on April 25, 1862, New Orleans surrendered without incident to Admiral David Farragut. If there had been a battle, much of the French Quarter we know today would have probably been destroyed. The first eight months of Union occupation were directed by military governor General Benjamin Butler, or "Beast," as most of the local population referred to him. Universally despised by locals, the Beast did enact some positive changes to the city, specifically in the areas of sanitation and assistance to the poor. New Orleans remained occupied by Union forces until 1876.

As the nineteenth century came to a close, the French Quarter was beginning to show its age and by the early 1900s was a run-down slum housing mostly Sicilian immigrants. The riverfront, so picturesque and visitor friendly now, was all wharves and warehouses. Restoration efforts to save the dilapidating buildings throughout the Quarter began in earnest in the 1920s and 1930s, thanks largely to the work of Lyle Saxon, Elizabeth Werlein, and other preservationists. Saxon championed the Quarter as an artist's haven and advocated for the preservation of historic buildings. In the 1920s, something of a writer's colony coalesced around

Saxon, and for a while, the Quarter played host to William Faulkner, Sherwood Anderson, John Steinbeck, John Dos Passos, Carl Sandburg, and Gertrude Stein among others. Werlein was instrumental in the creation of the Vieux Carré Commission, an agency still charged with preserving the architectural and historical authenticity of the Quarter.

By mid-century, the upper part of Bourbon Street had fully transitioned from a residential street to the neon strip it remains today. This transformation laid the foundation for the modern tourist industry, which matured in the 1970s and 1980s with the metamorphosis of the riverfront and Decatur Streets from wharves and seedy sailor bars into visitor-friendly venues. When the local oil industry busted in the 1980s, tourism became the second most important industry in New Orleans; only the city's port activity had a more significant economic impact. Since then, the growth of tourism has been steady, interrupted only by the flooding of the city after Hurricane Katrina.

On August 29, 2005, Hurricane Katrina made landfall east of New Orleans. The hurricane caused a storm surge in Lake Pontchartrain, which rushed up many of the man-made canals connecting the lake and the river. The force of the surge caused the levees to fail, and before the day was over, 80% of New Orleans was flooded. The French Quarter did not flood. Much of the city is just at or slightly below sea level; the Quarter, because of its proximity to the river, sits on some of the highest ground in the city, roughly eleven feet above sea level at the foot of Jackson Square. Because the levees that collapsed were (and are) constructed and maintained by the U.S. Army Corps of Engineers, many locals refer to the flood as a man-made, not natural, disaster. If the levees had held, August 29, 2005, would have been just another windy, rainy day in New Orleans.

Today, the French Quarter is a truly unique neighborhood and has been designated a National Historic Landmark by the federal government. Roughly 5,000 people live and work in the Quarter and millions visit it each year. The Quarter is many different things to many different people—residential neighborhood, outdoor shopping mall, architectural wonderland, living museum, adult playground, a haven of eccentric characters—but to all who have spent time here, it is a place of special memories. Once you walk its streets, discover its mysteries and meet its people, it will mean something special to you as well.

Notes on Maps, Streets and Directions

The French Quarter is laid out in a grid pattern and is bounded by the Mississippi River, Canal Street, North Rampart Street, and Esplanade Avenue. The French Quarter is sometimes called the Vieux Carré (French for "old square") but is more commonly referred to as simply "the Quarter." The total area of the Quarter is 0.66 square miles and comprises roughly 85 city blocks. Because the Mississippi River flows north at the Quarter, traditional compass directions are rarely used; instead, locals use the following reference terms: riverside, lakeside, upriver, and downriver. This can sometimes lead to confusion among visitors. For example, even though Esplanade Avenue is north of Canal Street, it is downriver. Neighborhoods along the river on the south side of Canal Street are collectively referred to as Uptown because they are upriver even though they are south of the Quarter. If you find yourself disoriented in the Quarter, just look down the street for the tall buildings; Canal Street is in that direction. Blocks are numbered in increasing order away from Canal Street; for example, the block between Canal Street and Iberville street is the 100 block.

For the purposes of using the maps, you'll see directions like '*away from Canal Street*', or '*towards the river*'. Use this directional guide when looking at the maps to help you with direction.

Notes on Safety and Etiquette

Many of the streets and sidewalks in the French Quarter are very old and uneven in places due to heat buckling, age, and potholes. Trips, stumbles, slips, and falls are not uncommon. Please take caution not to trip and fall.

Just like any other city, New Orleans has its fair share of crime. During the day, the French Quarter is generally safe, although it's always a good idea to keep your guard up. At night, it's wise to stay between Bourbon Street and the river; the other side of Bourbon Street can get a little dicey. At night, it's always safer to walk in groups rather than alone. Keep valuables in your hotel room and keep expensive smart phones in your pocket or purse. Don't flash money on the street and make sure no one watches you if you use an ATM. Be aware of your surroundings and avoid dark, deserted streets at night.

Beware of anyone who randomly approaches you in an overly friendly manner. Such people are probably scam artists, panhandlers, or time-share marketers. I suggest you politely ignore them by saying, "I'm not interested." If they persist, be firm and don't feel guilty about it.

If you take a picture of a street performer or pause to listen to a street musician, it is customary to tip the person.

Police patrol the French Quarter on foot and horseback, and it's usually not hard to find an officer. The police station is at the corner Royal and Conti Streets. The non-emergency police phone number is 504-821-2222.

Notes on Street Names in the French Quarter

Canal—Named for a drainage canal that was planned but never built

Iberville—Named for the French Canadian who explored the lower Mississippi and Gulf Coast

Bienville—Named for the founder of New Orleans, brother of Iberville

Conti—Named for the Prince de Conti

St. Louis—Named for Louis IX, the Patron Saint of France

Toulouse—Named for Louis XIV's illegitimate son, the Duc d'Toulouse

St. Peter—Named for the Roman Catholic and Patron Saint of the House of Orleans

Orleans—Named for Philippe II, Duc d'Orleans, Regent of France when the city was founded

St. Ann—Named for the Roman Catholic and Patron Saint of the House of Orleans

Dumaine—Named for Louis XIV's illegitimate son, the Duc d'Maine

St. Phillip—Named for the Roman Catholic and Patron Saint of the House of Orleans

Ursulines—Named for the Ursuline Nuns

Gov. Nicholls—Named for the Civil War hero and Louisiana governor

Barracks—Named for the building that housed troops

Esplanade—Once considered "millionaire's row" for the Creole aristocracy

Decatur—Named for Stephen Decatur, U.S. Naval Officer; formerly Levee Street

Chartres—Named for Philippe II, Duc d'Orleans' son

Royal—Named in honor of the Royal family of France

Bourbon—Refers to the Royal House of Bourbon; specifically, the Duc d'Bourbon

Dauphine—Named for either the Dauphiness or the French Province

Burgundy—Named for King Louis XV's father, the Duc d'Burgundy

North Rampart—Refers to the wall that was meant to protect the colonial city

Exchange Place—Refers to the Exchange at the old St. Louis Hotel to which it once led

Pirate's Alley—Named in honor of the role pirates have played in the city's history

Père Antoine Alley—Named for Antonio de Sedella, a beloved Capuchin priest

Madison—Named for the Secretary of State who signed the Louisiana Purchase Treaty

Wilkinson—Named for the Territorial Governor of Northern Louisiana after the purchase

Dorsier—Named for Eugene Dorsier

North Peters—Named for Samuel J. Peters, a city official in the 1830s

Topical Organization Codes

Some points of interest fall into more than one category. Therefore, each stop's entry is followed by a series of letters indicating the site's relevance to particular topics. The letters and topics are as follows:

A = Architecture
AA = African American
C = Culinary
F = Film
FC = French Colonial Period
G = General Interest
H = Haunted / Ghost
L = Literary
M = Music
Q = GLBT
R = Religious
SC = Spanish Colonial Period
V = Vice

General Walking Tour: Highlights of the French Quarter

"My advice to you is to stay for a while in the old section of the city, sit for a time in Jackson Square and let the old world charm you. Give the atmosphere a chance to lull you. Take your time and wander slowly; look twice at the old houses, they are worth it. Talk to the beggars in the street; talk to any one you chance to meet. The natives of the Quarter are pleasant people and they will gladly tell you anything they happen to know."
— Lyle Saxon, *Fabulous New Orleans*, 1928.

Sherwood Anderson called the French Quarter the most civilized place in America. To that distinction, we could also add unique, gritty, inspiring, beautiful, decrepit, strange, cruel, kind, sad, haunted, lazy, and timeless. The place is literally drenched with history and is perhaps best described as a living museum, not only of historic buildings and significant events and colorful characters, but also of an attitude—a lazy, care-free, *joie de vivre* spirit that is utterly unconcerned with time, responsibilities, and morality. The architectural charms are obvious as are the Caribbean atmosphere, the lax liquor laws, and the numerous street performers. What may not be so obvious is *the real* Quarter, the one hiding just behind the tourist veneer. The only way to get to know *the real* Quarter is to take Lyle Saxon's advice and talk to the locals. When you do, you will notice how striking the sense of place is here. Many people who live in the Quarter wouldn't dream of living anywhere else.

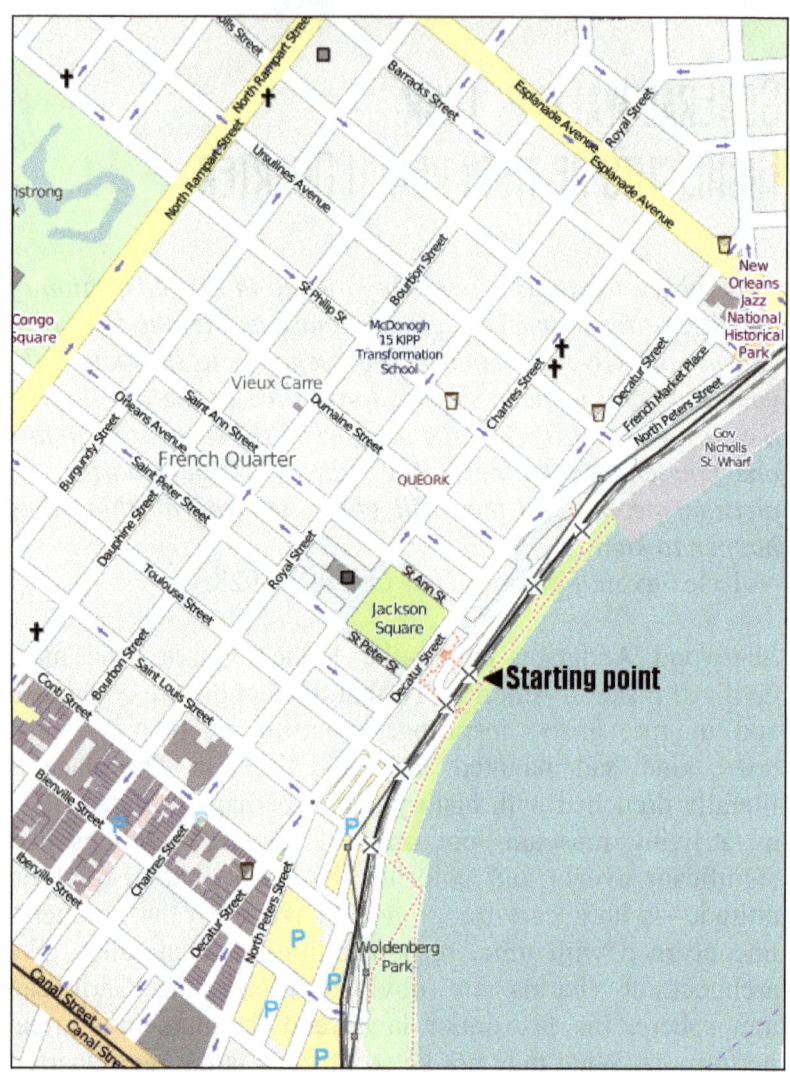

This tour begins on the levee of the Mississippi River at Jackson Square. It covers the major highlights of the Quarter and a few lesser-known yet important points of interest. This tour can take anywhere from a few hours to all day depending on your level of interest at the various stops. It can also be broken up into two or three days. This tour will provide you a general orientation to the French Quarter. Once you have completed it, you will have a much better idea of not only where everything is but also of how you want to spend the remainder of your time in New Orleans.

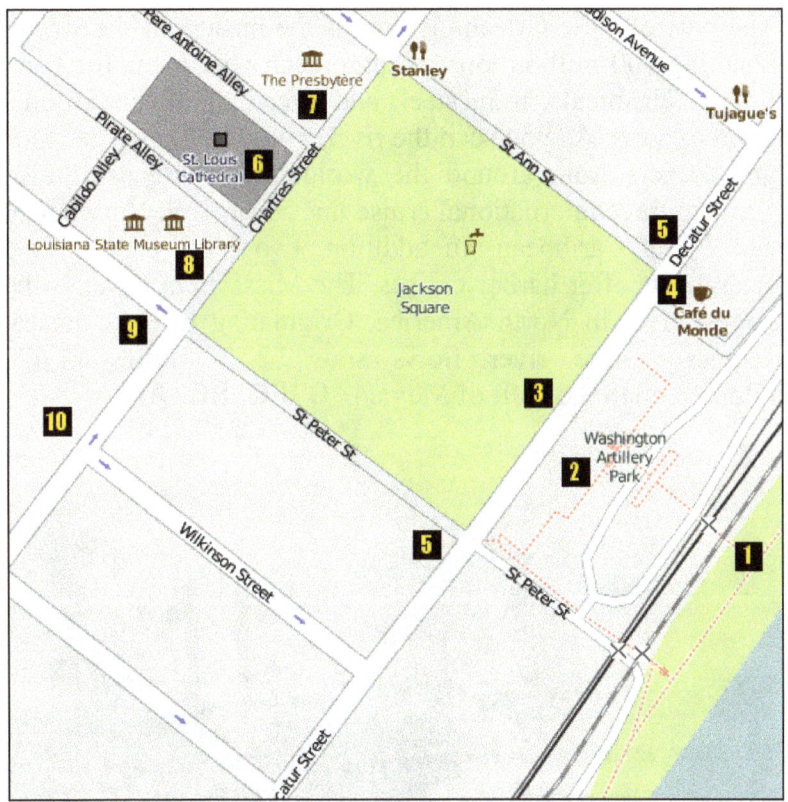

1. 700 Block of Decatur Street—Mississippi River

At the foot of Jackson Square is the Mississippi River, which is the best place to start your tour. As you stand on the levee overlooking the river, you will notice a sharp bend to your left. It is at this point that the river is closest to Lake Pontchartrain, which you probably crossed to come into the city. Bienville chose this site to found New Orleans not only because of its proximity to the lake, but also because this is the highest ground in the area, about eleven feet above sea level. The elevation drops as you move away from the river. The French Quarter did not flood during Hurricane Katrina, although 80% of the city was under water.

The port of New Orleans is one of the busiest in the world, handling 500 million tons of cargo each year including coal, timber, chemicals, iron, steel, and over half of the nation's grain exports. As you scan the river, you will likely see ships and tankers from around the world. New Orleans is also home to three international cruise lines: Carnival, Norwegian, and Royal Caribbean. In addition, two local paddlewheel steamboats offer harbor cruises. The Mississippi River is the largest river in North America. Originating in Lake Itasca, Minnesota, the river flows south 2,530 miles (4,070 kilometers) to the Gulf of Mexico. **G, FC, SC, AA**

Facing away from the river, you will see a small, elevated plaza with two stairwells facing the river. That is stop number two.

2. **700 Block of Decatur Street—Washington Artillery Park**

Directly between the River and Jackson Square is Washington Artillery Park. This is an ideal spot for pictures and for taking in Jackson Square. The Memorial Canon honors those who have defended New Orleans throughout its history since 1718. **G**

3. **700 Block of Decatur Street—Jackson Square**

The Square is named after Andrew Jackson, seventh president of the United States and hero of the Battle of New Orleans. During the War of 1812, Great Britain threatened the city and General Jackson was called upon to defend New Orleans. The battle took place about six miles downriver on January 8, 1815. With the help of the pirate brothers Jean and Pierre Lafitte, Jackson defeated the British and saved New Orleans. The equestrian statue in the center of the square is Jackson offering his hat in salute. It was designed by Clark Mills and erected in 1856. Before it was renamed in his honor, the square was called the *Place d' Armes* and the *Plaza de Armas* by the French and Spanish respectively. Bordering the Square are St. Louis Cathedral, the Cabildo, the Presbytere, and the Pontalba Buildings.

Jackson Square is the heart of the city and always filled with activity. Artists line the Square and the space before the cathedral usually hosts street musicians, fortunetellers, and other street performers. The Square is a wonderful place to picnic, rest, and people watch. **G, FC, SC, R**

Exit the park by the stairwell to the right. The coffee shop at the bottom of the stairs is stop number four.

4. **813 Decatur Street—Café du Monde**

Café du Monde purports to be the oldest continually operating coffee stand in the U. S. The only food item on the menu is beignets—deep fried doughy doughnuts covered in powdered sugar. The coffee is infused with chicory, which serves as an additional stimulant to the caffeine. After you've had your beignets and coffee, walk down the alley at the rear of the building and look for a small window. There, you can see how the beignets are made. Be aware that the wait to get a table can be as long as an hour during weekend mornings or when the city hosts big events. Café du Monde is open 24 hours a day. **G, C**

Cross Decatur Street and walk along St. Ann on the edge of the Square. The red brick building on your right is stop number five.

5. 500 Blocks of St. Peter and St. Ann Streets—The Pontalba Buildings

The two block-long red buildings, which flank the Square, are the Pontalba Buildings. These row houses are named after the Baroness Micaela Almonester de Pontalba, daughter of the philanthropist Don Andreas Almonester y Roxas and date from 1850. Commercial space occupies the first floor while the upper levels are apartments. In the lower Pontalba Building (along St. Ann Street) is the 1850 House, a replica of a typical 1850s New Orleans apartment. The 1850 House is available for viewing Tuesday through Sunday, 10:00 a.m. to 4:30 p.m.

If you look carefully at the ironwork, you will see a cartouche with the letters "A" & "P" representing the family names Almonester and Pontalba. When Micaela was sixteen, she married her cousin, Celestin de Pontalba, who was also from a prominent family. It was not a happy marriage. Micaela was the sole heir to her father's tremendous wealth, and her father-in-law became obsessed with getting his hands on it. Her father in-law tried for years to break up the marriage, and when he finally realized he couldn't, he attempted to kill her by shooting her four times in the chest. After shooting her, he committed suicide, but Micaela survived to commission the building of the apartments named after her and lived to the age of 78. **G, A, SC**

Proceed to the cathedral at the top of the Square.

6. 700 Block of Chartres Street—St. Louis Cathedral

Fronting the Square is the magnificent three-spired St. Louis Cathedral. The original church was constructed in 1727 and served the city until it burned down in 1788. Rebuilding was completed in 1794. By the mid-1800s, major renovations were necessary and the cathedral, as it looks today, was completed in 1850. St. Louis Cathedral was designated a minor basilica in 1964 by Pope Paul VI, and Pope John Paul II visited the cathedral in 1987. The cathedral is named after St. Louis IX, King of France. A number of priests, archbishops, and others are buried under the church. **G, R, A, FC, SC**

Facing the cathedral, proceed to the building on the right.

7. 751 Chartres Street—The Presbytere

The building to the right of the cathedral is the Presbytere or Ecclesiastical House. The name comes from the fact that prior to its construction in the late 1790s, this site was the residence of the Capuchin monks. Construction of the Presbytere, along with the Cabildo and renovations to the cathedral, were paid for by Don Andres Almonester y Roxas, a prominent businessman during the Spanish colonial period. The building was initially used for commercial purposes until 1834. In that year, the Presbytere became a courthouse until 1911 when it was acquired by the Louisiana State Museum. The museum today features rotating exhibits. Open Tuesday through Sunday, 10:00 a.m. to 4:30 p.m. **G, R, FC, SC, A**

Proceed to the identical building to the left of the cathedral.

8. 701 Chartres Street—The Cabildo

The building to the left of the cathedral is the Cabildo, which was built under Spanish colonial rule and completed in 1799. The building is named after the Spanish governing council. The building is where the Louisiana Purchase transfer occurred, a transaction that doubled the size of the United States. Throughout the nineteenth century, the Cabildo functioned as the City Hall, a courthouse, and a prison. In 1908, the Cabildo became a part of the Louisiana State Museum and today features an excellent collection of early Louisiana history. Open Tuesday through Sunday, 10:00 a.m. to 4:30 p.m. **G, A, SC**

Facing the Cabildo, look to your left. The red brick building is stop number nine.

9. 616 St. Peter Street—Le Petit Theatre

On the corner of the Square, at the corner of St. Peter and Chartres Streets, is Le Petit Theatre. In 1916, a group of local theatre lovers began producing plays in the drawing room of one of its members. Audiences grew and the Drawing Room Players began renting space in the lower part of the Pontalba Building before opening Le Petit in 1919. The building you see today dates from 1922 and is a reproduction of Spanish colonial-style architecture. The ironwork is original and dates from 1796. **A, SC, H**

Walk down Chartres Street away from Jackson Square half a block to Wilkinson Street. Stop and look to your right.

10. 619 Chartres Street—The Great Fire of 1788

In 1788, this was the home of Don Vincente Jose Nunez, the Spanish military treasurer. On Good Friday of that year, a candle in his private chapel started a fire that quickly engulfed much of the city. In total, 856 buildings were destroyed. Six years later in 1794, yet another fire destroyed 212 buildings. When the Spanish rebuilt, they instituted building codes and introduced Spanish-Caribbean architectural features: side-to-side buildings with firewalls, brick covered with brightly colored stucco, iron balconies, and courtyards. By the 1800s, the French Quarter began to look like it is today. Ironically, much of the architecture in the French Quarter is actually Spanish and most of it is American. **G, R, SC, A**

Proceed down Chartres Street away from Jackson Square. Cross Toulouse Street and proceed three-quarters of a block. Stop and turn to your left.

11. 514 Chartres Street—The Pharmacy Museum

In 1804, Louisiana became the first state in the nation to require pharmacists to become licensed, and in that year, Louis Dufilho, Jr. became the first licensed pharmacist in the United States. In 1823, he opened an apothecary at this address. Many of the artifacts in the museum were unearthed in the rear courtyard during excavations in the 1980s. Note the brightly colored bottles in the window. During yellow fever outbreaks in the nineteenth century, all the bottles were the same color; this served as a warning signal to locals and insiders since the newspapers didn't print such news for fear of scaring away business. Inside don't miss the antique soda fountain and the voodoo potions. The Pharmacy Museum is open Tuesday through Friday, 10:00 a.m. to 2:00 p.m. and Saturday 10:00 a.m. to 5:00 p.m. **G**

Proceed up Chartres Street away from Jackson Square a quarter block to the corner of St. Louis Street. Stop and look to your left.

12. 500 Chartres Street—The Napoleon House

On the corner of Chartres and St. Louis Streets stands one of the most interesting buildings in the French Quarter, the Napoleon House. The best view of the home is across the street on the opposite corner. From there, you can take in the full grandeur of this beautifully decayed structure and its majestic cupola. The building dates back to the early 1800s and was once the home of the first elected mayor of New Orleans, Nicholas Girod. Legend holds that when the French Emperor Napoleon Bonaparte went into exile, a plot was hatched here in New Orleans to rescue the emperor and bring him here to New Orleans. Mayor Girod graciously offered his home as refuge, but Napoleon died before the daring plan could be completed. Since 1914, the Napoleon House has been a popular restaurant and bar. Its signature cocktail is the Pimm's Cup. **G, A, C**

Cross the street heading toward Canal Street. Stop and look down St. Louis Street away from the river.

13. 621 St. Louis Street—The Old St. Louis Hotel / City Exchange

Across the street is the site of the old St. Louis Hotel, one of the grandest hotels of its time. In the first half of the nineteenth century, a café / bar called the City Exchange stood on this site and boasted an auction area where stocks, produce, goods, real estate, and slaves were exchanged. In 1838, the opulent St. Louis Hotel opened and boasted a magnificent rotunda where the auctions continued. The hotel quickly became an important financial center and hosted elaborate masked balls, events for which the Creoles were very fond. After the fall of New Orleans during the U. S. Civil War in 1862, the hotel was used as a military hospital.

The hotel reopened after the war, but by the dawn of the twentieth century, business had declined and the "Creole Palace" closed for good. The abandoned building began to decay and was destroyed in the hurricane of 1915. The site is now occupied by the Omni Royal Orleans. You can still see a portion of the original St. Louis Hotel brickwork facing the Napoleon House. **G, AA**

Proceed up Chartres toward Canal Street three-quarters of a block. Turn to your left.

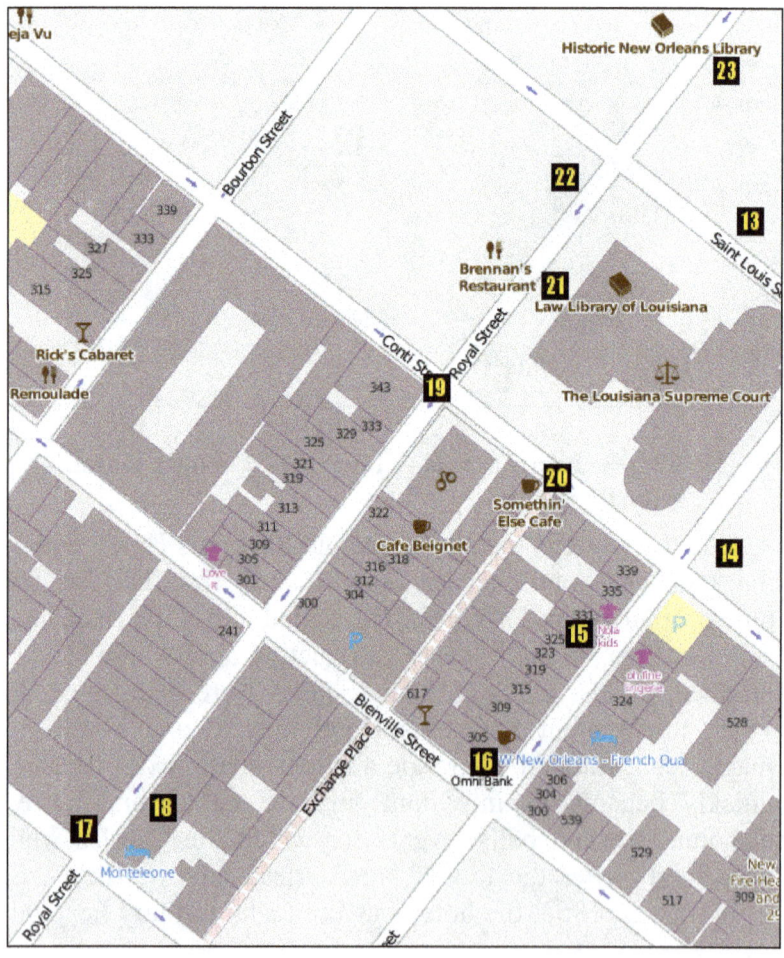

14. 410 Chartres Street—The Williams Research Center

The handsome building at this address is the Williams Research Center of the Historic New Orleans Collection. The Beaux Arts building dates to 1915 and was originally a police station and courthouse. The Research Center contains a library specializing in rare and important holdings. Open to the public 9:30 a.m. to 4:30 p.m., Tuesday through Saturday. **G**

Proceed up Chartres toward Canal one block. Turn to your right.

15. 327 Chartres Street—The Bottom of the Cup Tearoom

Since 1929, the Bottom of the Cup Tearoom has been offering locals and visitors alike authentic psychic readings. It is the oldest psychic reading room in the city and offers a wide variety of teas in addition to tarot, palm, and tea readings. It also features a metaphysical gift shop. **G**

Proceed up Chartres Street toward Canal. Stop at the corner.

16. 301 Chartres Street—1st Charity Hospital

On this corner, which now houses a bank (lakeside, downriver), the First Charity Hospital was founded in 1736. French shipbuilder Jean Louis had died the year before and in his will donated a sum of money for the construction of a hospital to care for the indigent. When the modern incarnation of Charity Hospital closed in 2005 after Hurricane Katrina, it was the second oldest continually operating public hospital in the United States. The hospital was located here from 1736 to 1743. **G**

Turn onto Bienville Street away from the river. Walk one block to Royal Street and turn left. Walk a block and look for the plaque on the wall of Walgreen's pharmacy. **G, FC**

17. Corner of Iberville and Royal Streets—Birthplace of Dixie

Here where a Walgreens now exists once stood the Citizen's State Bank. In the bank's early days, it issued a ten-dollar note with the French word for ten, *dix*, on it. Soon thereafter, the "land of the *dix* became shortened to Dixieland," a moniker which has come to mean the American South. The original bank was on Toulouse Street. **G**

Turn around and walk half a block down Royal away from Canal Street. Look to your right.

18. 214 Royal Street—The Monteleone Hotel

This majestic hotel dates back to 1886 and was a favorite among writers such as Tennessee Williams, Ernest Hemmingway, Eudora Welty, and Truman Capote. The Carousel Bar, so named because the floor revolves slowly around the bar, is a favorite among locals and visitors alike. Like many hotels in New Orleans, the Monteleone is home to several ghosts, including the spirit of a ten-year-old boy who likes to play hide and seek with guests. **G, A, L, H**

Proceed down Royal Street to the corner of Conti Street.

19. Intersection of Royal and Conti Streets

This intersection, because of its proximity to the Exchange at the St. Louis Hotel, was once the center of the city's financial district. The Latrobe Building on the lakeside-downriver corner was erected in 1822 and functioned as the Louisiana State Bank until 1870. The building is named for its designer, Benjamin Henry Latrobe. Latrobe also designed the U.S. Capitol Building in Washington D.C. and is generally considered the father of American architecture. Latrobe died in New Orleans in 1820 of yellow fever. The building on the lakeside-downriver corner is the Rillieux-Waldorn House.

Built in 1800 as the home of Vincent Rillieux, great-grandfather of artist Edgar Degas, the building also housed the Bank of the United States from 1820 to 1836. **G, A**

Proceed along Conti Street toward the river half a block. Look to your right.

20. Exchange Place Alley

This charming alley used to extend four blocks from Canal Street to the grand St. Louis Hotel (now the Omni Orleans). The opulent hotel's rotunda boasted an auction area and bustled with commercial activity. In its nineteenth century heyday, the alley was home to many brokers and businessmen. The alley was also the site of fencing classes. Today, the alley plays host to art galleries, restaurants, and a tobacco chop. **G**

Back track onto Royal Street and walk half a block away from Canal Street.

21. 400 Royal Street—The Louisiana Supreme Court Building

This imposing Beaux Arts structure was erected in 1910 and now serves as home of the Louisiana Supreme Court. The statue in front of the building is Edward Douglas White, Jr., native of Thibodeaux, Louisiana, and ninth Chief Justice of the United States Supreme Court. Architecturally, the building does not fit in with the rest of the buildings in the French Quarter. In the early 1900s, the Quarter was a run-down slum and developers were eager to demolish many buildings to make way for new ones. This entire block was destroyed so the courthouse could be built. This alarmed many people and led to a preservation movement that persists today. **G, A**

Turn around and look across Royal Street.

22. 437 Royal Street—Peychaud's Drugstore

In 1811, Antoine Peychaud opened an apothecary shop at this location. In addition to dispensing medicine, Peychaud also served refreshments. One of the more popular drinks he invented was a curious mixture of bitters, cognac or brandy, and sugar, which he served in an eggcup. This drink was the original Sazerac, still a favorite cocktail among locals. The word for eggcup in French is *cocquetier* and after a few years of Anglicization, the drink became known as a cocktail. Hence, Peychaud is often credited with inventing the cocktail even though the word "cocktail" predates Peychaud. **V**

Proceed down Royal Street one block. Look to your right.

23. 520 Royal Street—The Brulatour Court

This home was built in 1816 for Francois Seignouret, a French wine importer and furniture maker. In 1870, another French wine importer named Brulatour acquired the property.

The building contains one of the most beautiful courtyards in all the French Quarter. **A**

Turn around and look to the right.

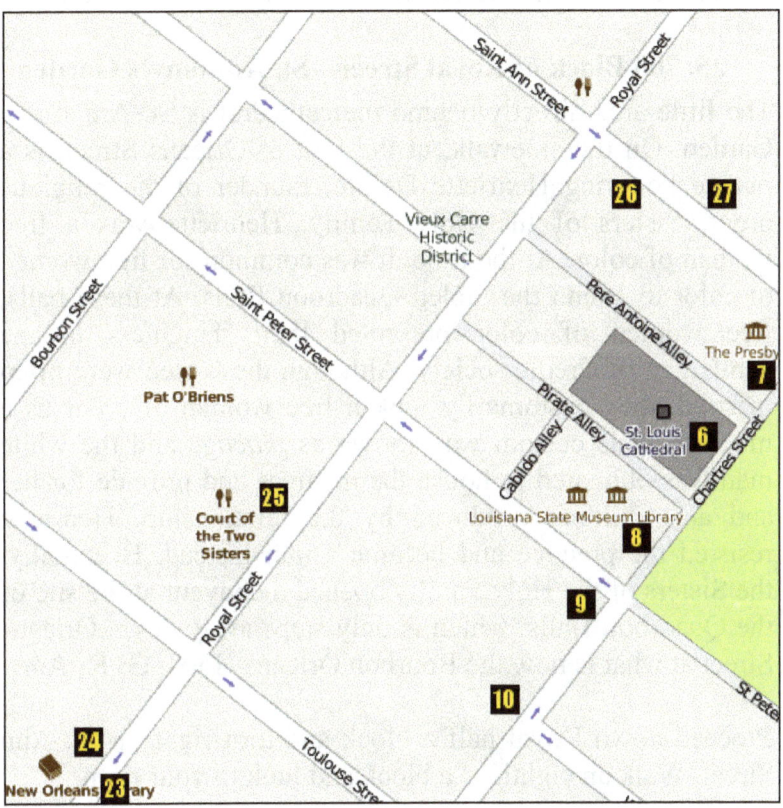

24. 533 Royal Street—The Merieult House / The Historic New Orleans Collection

Jean Francois Merieult, a prosperous merchant, built this house in 1792. The structure was renovated in the 1830s according to the then-popular Greek Revival style. Today, the building houses the Historic New Orleans Collection, which features a museum focusing on the history of New Orleans. General and Mrs. L. Kemper Williams established the collection in 1966. Tours are available Tuesday through Saturday at 10:00 a.m., 11:00 a.m., 2:00 p.m., and 3:00 p.m.; Sundays at 11:00 a.m., 2:00 p.m., and 3:00 p.m. **G, SC, A**

Proceed down Royal Street a block and a half. Look to your right.

25. 700 Block of Royal Street—St. Anthony's Garden

The little area directly behind the cathedral is St. Anthony's Garden. On the sidewalk, at the foot of Orleans Street, is a plaque honoring Henriette Delille, founder of the religious order, Sisters of the Holy Family. Henriette was a free woman of color. At the time, it was common for free women of color to attend the fabled Quadroon Balls. At these balls, free women of color presented their daughters to the gentlemen of Creole society. Although these men were often married, they customarily took a free woman of color as a mistress. This custom was known as *placage* and the white man was obligated to house the mistress and provide for her and any children produced by the relationship. Henriette resisted the practice and became a nun instead. Eventually, the Sisters of the Holy Family opened a convent at the site of the Quadroon Balls, which is only steps away down Orleans Street at what is now the Bourbon Orleans Hotel. **G, R, AA**

Proceed down Royal half a block and turn right on St. Ann Street. Walk an eighth of a block and look to your right.

26. 638 St. Ann Street—The Crescent City Tour Booking Agency

This is an excellent place for information about the city and its attractions. Unlike most visitor centers, this booking agency is not owned by a specific tour company and offers unbiased recommendations. It also happens to be owned by the author of the book you now hold in your hands. Please feel free to pop in with any questions or just to say hello. **G**

Proceed along St. Ann Street a quarter block and look to your left.

27. 625 St. Ann Street—Site of the First Louisiana School

On this site in 1725, Father Raphael de Luxembourg opened the first school in French colonial Louisiana. It is now the Place d'Armes Hotel. **G, FC**

Proceed along St. Ann Street toward the river and turn left on to Chartres Street. Proceed down Chartres Street one block and turn left onto Dumaine Street. Proceed half a block and look to your left.

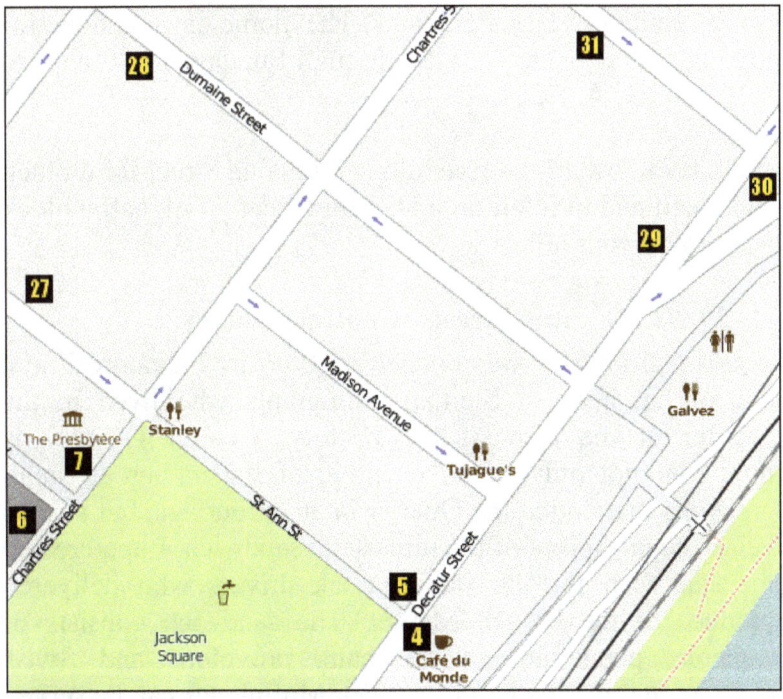

28. 632 Dumaine Street—Madame John's Legacy

This charming house, commonly called Madame John's Legacy, dates back to 1789 and is a fine example of late eighteenth century French colonial design. The structure closely resembles its predecessor, which was built circa 1730 and destroyed in the great fire of 1788. For much of the eighteenth century, Elizabeth Real-Marin, a widow who ran the property as an inn, owned the property. After her death in 1777, Renato Beluche, father of the famous pirate René Beluche, who worked closely with Jean Lafitte, acquired the home. The home then had a long string of owners until it was acquired by the Louisiana State Museum in 1947. There are few homes like this left in the French Quarter, but at one time, this architectural style was the norm. The name is derived from a story by Louisiana author George Washington Cable entitled "Tite Poulette." The home is available for touring and is open Tuesday through Sunday, 10:00 a.m. to 4:30 p.m. **G, A, FC, L**

Walk back toward the river along Dumaine Street for a block and a half and turn left onto Decatur Street. Walk half a block and turn to your left.

29. 923 Decatur Street—Central Grocery

This small grocery was opened in 1906 by Salvatore Lupo, one of hundreds of Sicilian immigrants who lived in the Quarter at the turn of the century. Central Grocery is important not only as an example of the numerous small groceries that dotted the Quarter in an earlier age, but also as being the birthplace of the muffaletta sandwich. Lupo created the sandwich for the Italian truck drivers who delivered produce to the French Market. The sandwich consists of capicola, pepperoni, salami, ham, provolone and Swiss cheeses, and marinated olive salad. Muffalettas can be served hot or cold and are offered in quarters, halves, and wholes. **C**

Proceed down Decatur Street toward the gold statue of a woman on a horse.

30. Corner of Decatur and N. Peters Streets—Joan of Arc Statue

The people of France gifted this statue, a replica of the famous statue designed by Emmanuel Fremiet in 1880, to the City of New Orleans in 1958. It was originally placed at the foot of Canal St. in front of the World Trade Mart but was moved to this location in 1999 to make way for Harrah's Casino. Some locals refer to the statue as Joni on the pony. New Orleans celebrates Joan of Arc's birthday, January 6, each year with a parade in which women dressed in medieval garb ride horses through the French Quarter. Incidentally, January 6 is also the start of the Carnival season. **G**

Turn around, walk half a block and turn right onto St. Phillip Street. Walk a quarter block and turn to your left.

31. 528 St. Phillip Street—Early Home of Ruthie the Duck Girl

In a neighborhood filled with eccentric characters, Ruthie the Duck Girl was one of the most beloved. From her youth, she wandered the streets of the Quarter with a handful of ducks in tow. In later years, she was given to skate through the Quarter wearing roller-skates and sometimes a wedding dress. She was a fixture at many Quarter watering holes, often appearing in the entrance and announcing her presence. This proclamation was followed by a request for a beer and cigarette. Ruthie would then return to the streets posing for photographs (for which she charged money) with locals and tourists alike. Sadly, Ruthie died in 2008. This was her family home when she was young. **G**

Proceed along St. Phillip Street away from the river and turn right onto Chartres Street.

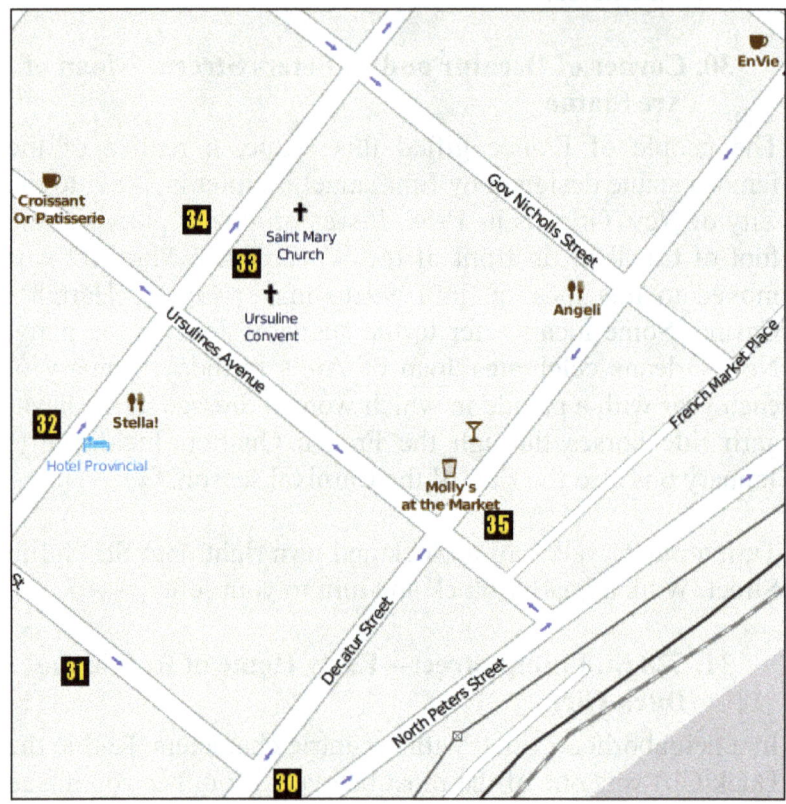

32. 1021 Chartres Street—The De Le Ronde House

Erected around 1807, this was the city home of Pierre Denis de la Ronde, whose plantation downriver was the site of the first skirmish in the Battle of New Orleans. **G**

Proceed down Chartres Street one block and look to your right.

33. 1114 Chartres Street—The Ursuline Convent

Built in 1752, the Ursuline Convent is the oldest building in the Mississippi River Valley and an excellent example of

French colonial architecture. The first Ursuline nuns arrived in New Orleans from Rouen, France, in 1727. The Ursulines administered both a hospital to care for the poor as well as a school for girls. Among the first Ursuline nuns to arrive was Marie-Madeleine Hachard, who is credited with writing one of the first books about Louisiana—a collection of personal letters she sent to her family in France from the convent. Tours of the Convent are available Monday through Saturday, 10:00 a.m. to 4:00 p.m. **G, FC, A, R**

Turn around and look across Chartres Street.

34. 1113 Chartres Street—The Beauregard-Keyes House

This home was built in 1826 and is named for two of its most famous residents—Confederate General Pierre Gustave Toutant Beauregard and writer Frances Parkinson Keyes. Beauregard gave the order to fire the first shot on Fort Sumter in South Carolina, thus beginning the U.S. Civil War. Keyes authored a number of novels, including *Dinner at Antoine's*. The home was also the site of one the city's most dramatic murders in 1908. At that time, an Italian businessman named Pietro Giancona lived here and had a deadly confrontation with the local Mafia, who was trying to extort him. One evening, Pietro invited four Mafioso to his home for dinner to discuss their demands. After they were seated, Pietro and his son opened fire and shot all four, three of whom died immediately. Tours of the home are available Monday through Saturday, 10:00 a.m. to 3:00 p.m. **G, L, A, H**

Proceed along Ursulines Street toward the river. Across Decatur Street is the French Market.

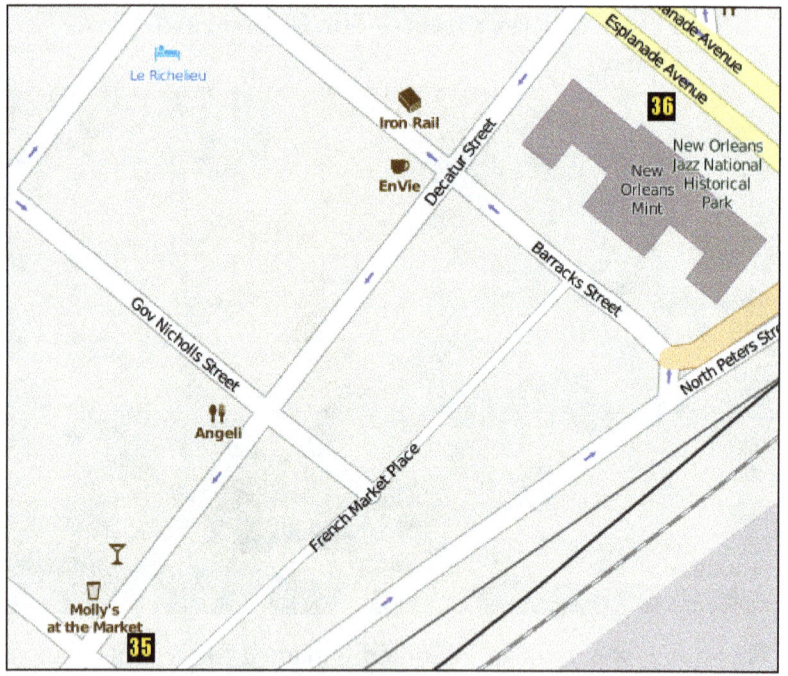

35. The French Market

Opened in 1791, the French Market is the oldest public market in America. The Spanish colonial government, as an attempt to consolidate the city's food vendors, which it was thought would help improve sanitation created the French Market. Prior to its founding, this site was a Native American trading post. For most of its history, the market was the primary place for locals to purchase food. There was a butchers market, a fruit and vegetable market, a fish market, and so forth. Typically, each specialized market was operated by various ethnic groups; for example, Sicilians sold produce, African Americans sold pralines and rice fritters, the Native American Choctaws sold herbs and spices, and so forth. The ethnic diversity of the market vendors has always reflected the cosmopolitan make-up of the city itself. Today, the French Market offers art, cuisine, crafts, and souvenirs. Many of the vendors are willing to haggle over prices. Open daily. **G, SC**

Proceed down Decatur Street two blocks away from Canal Street.

36. 400 Esplanade Avenue.—The Old U.S. Mint

The Old U.S. Mint was built in 1835 and holds the distinction of being the only facility to mint both U.S. and Confederate money. It was here that General Andrew Jackson inspected the troops before marching ten miles downriver to the Battle of New Orleans in 1815. During the Civil War, after New Orleans fell to the Union in 1862, a Confederate sympathizer named William Mumford scaled the wall of the Mint and tore down the American Flag. General Butler, the Union governor, had him arrested and promptly executed. Seventy years before the Mint was constructed, this was also the site of a brutal execution. When France gave Louisiana to Spain, the French revolted and several leading businessmen mounted an insurrection against the first Spanish governor and forced him out of town. The second Spanish governor, an Irish mercenary named O'Reilly, had the leaders of the rebellion arrested and shot to death at this location. The massacre gave rise to the name of Frenchmen Street, which is just across Esplanade Avenue. Since the execution, O'Reilly has been remembered as Bloody O'Reilly in the annals of Louisiana history. The Mint is now used as a museum and is home to the New Orleans Jazz Club Collections of the Louisiana State Museum. It also hosts numerous festivals throughout the year. Open Tuesday through Sunday, 10:30 a.m. to 4:30 p.m. **G, M**

Proceed along Barracks Street three blocks and turn left onto Bourbon Street. Walk three blocks to the corner of Bourbon and St. Phillip Streets.

Treasures of the Vieux Carré

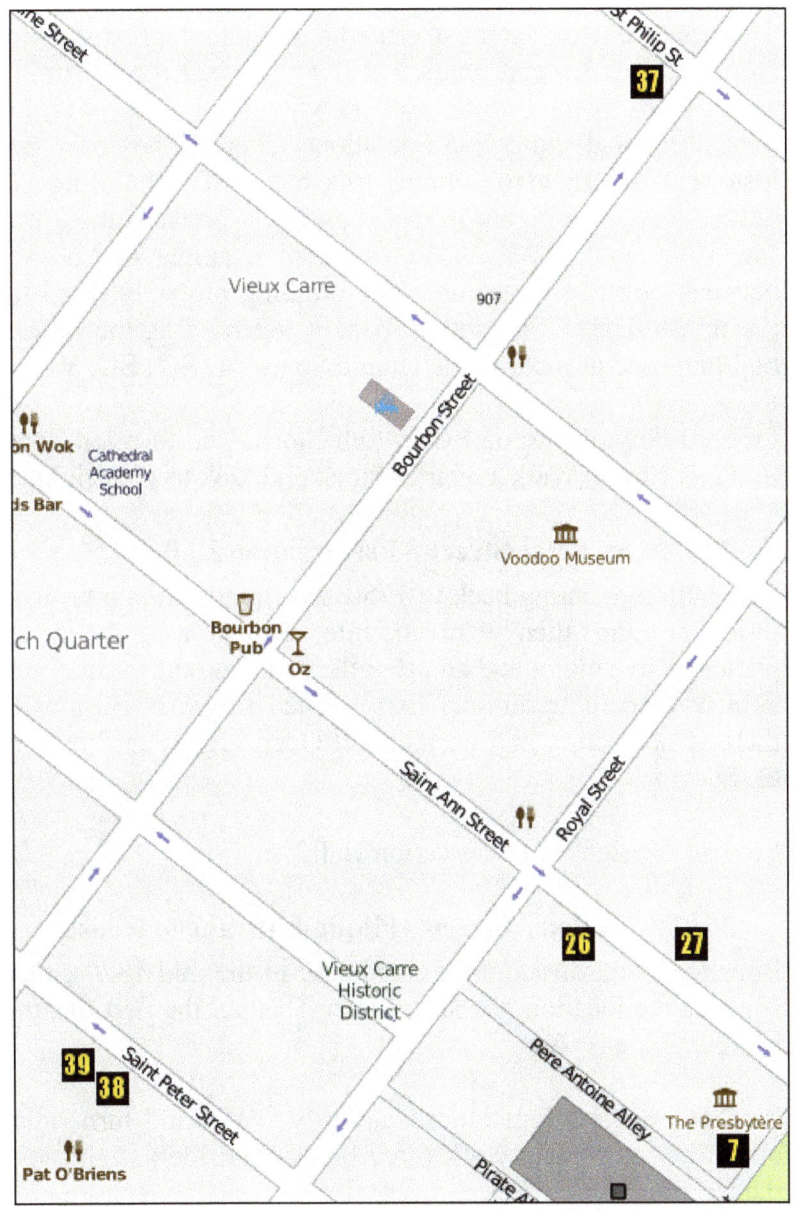

37. 941 Bourbon Street—Lafitte's Blacksmith Shop

This bar is one of the most visited and photographed sites in New Orleans. Legend holds that this was once a blacksmith shop owned by the Lafitte brothers who used it as a cover for their pirate and smuggling operations. There is, however, no historical evidence to support this claim. The building is, nevertheless, significant in that it probably predates the great fire 1788 and serves as an excellent example of "bricks between posts" architecture. The building probably dates to the mid-to-late 1700s and is widely regarded as the oldest building used as a bar in the United States. **A, FC, SC, V**

Proceed down Bourbon Street four blocks and turn left onto St. Peter Street. Walk a quarter block and look to your right.

38. 726 St. Peter Street—Preservation Hall

This building, dating back to 1750, was first used as a private residence and then evolved into a tavern, a hotel, a photography studio, and an art gallery. Its current incarnation as a bastion of traditional jazz opened in 1961. Be aware there is no seating and no alcohol. Open nightly at 8:00pm. **G, M**

Look to the right of Preservation Hall.

39. 730 St. Peter Street—Plique-LaBranche House

Prior to the construction of this home in the mid-1820s, this site was the location of the St. Peter Theatre, the first theatre in New Orleans. **A**

Proceed two and half blocks along St. Peter and turn right onto Decatur Street. Walk three blocks and look slightly to the left.

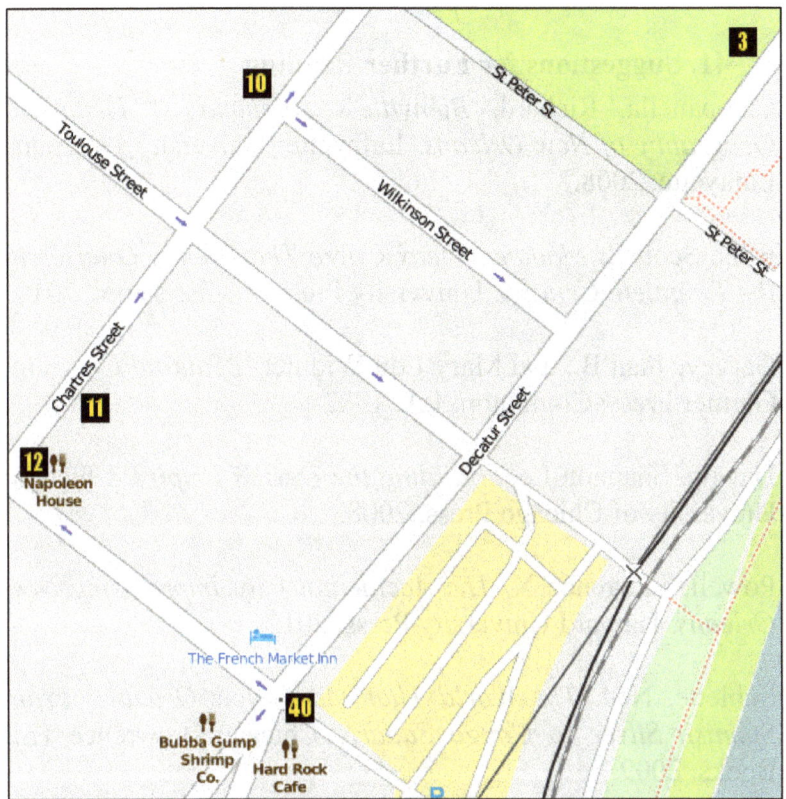

40. Intersection of Conti, Decatur, and N. Peters Streets--Bienville's Statue

This statue of the founder of New Orleans was erected in 1955 by sculptor Angela Gregory. The Native American represents the indigenous people of Louisiana and the clergyman represents France's efforts to Christianize the New World. Interestingly, the date at the base of statue is incorrect; New Orleans was founded in 1718, not 1717. **G, FC**

41. Suggestions for Further Reading

Campanella, Richard. *Bienville's Dilemma: A Historical Geography of New Orleans.* Lafayette: University Louisiana Lafayette, 2008.

Ellis, Scott S. *Madame Vieux Carré The French Quarter in the Twentieth Century.* University Press of Mississippi, 2010.

Garvey, Joan B., and Mary Lou Widmer. *Beautiful Crescent.* Garmer Press: Covington, LA, 1982.

Dawdy, Shannon Lee. *Building the Devil's Empire.* Chicago: University of Chicago Press, 2008.

Powell, Lawrence N. *The Accidental City Improvising New Orleans.* Harvard University Press, 2012.

Sublette, Ned. *The World That Made New Orleans: From Spanish Silver to Congo Square.* Chicago: Lawrence Hill Books, 2009.

African American Heritage Walking Tour

"Anglo-American slavery was designed to erase African American history. But African Americans made their own history, and in New Orleans, history parades down the street."
— Ned Sublette, 2009

New Orleans would not be New Orleans without black people. From the city's earliest years, Africans and their descendants have contributed immeasurably to its architectural, culinary, cultural, musical, and spiritual complexity. And yet, these contributions pale in comparison to their economic impact on the city. During the French colonial period, there were about 6,000 slaves in New Orleans, most of which came from Senegal by way of Santo Domingue in present-day Haiti. Many of these slaves were skilled artisans (especially ironworkers) and farmers (who brought rice and indigo to Louisiana). French King Louis XIV instituted the *Code Noir* in 1685, which governed the treatment of slaves throughout the French Empire. The Black Code was instituted in Louisiana in 1724. Among other things, the *Code Noir* forced slaves to become Roman Catholic, gave them Sundays off, and stipulated that they had to paid for work done on their days off. These stipulations gave rise to voodoo, free people of color, and jazz music. During the Spanish dominion, there was an influx of slaves primarily from Angola but also from other regions. Slaves were treated somewhat better under colonial Spanish rule but not much. In colonial times, slaves were allowed to purchase their freedom but records suggest only a small percentage actually did so. Life for slaves was considerably harsher under American rule. After the Civil War, blacks enjoyed a brief period of political power. For 35 days in 1872 -1873, P.B.S. Pinchback became the first person of African descent to become the governor of a U. S. state. *Plessy v. Ferguson*, the Supreme Court case that established segregation as the law of the land under the principle of "separate but equal," originated in New Orleans when Homer Plessy, a native New Orleanian, tried to board a "whites only" streetcar. The African American experience in New Orleans is distinctive because of the existence the free people of color, a unique class that enjoyed certain freedoms unheard of in other cities. In 1845, Armand Lanusse edited and published *Les Cenelles*, a collection of poems all written by free men of color, which is generally regarded as the most important African American literary work of the Antebellum era. During the Storyville Era (1897-1917), African American musicians drew upon their African musical traditions that had been kept alive at Congo Square and created jazz.

This tour begins at Washington Artillery Park between Jackson Square and the Mississippi River.

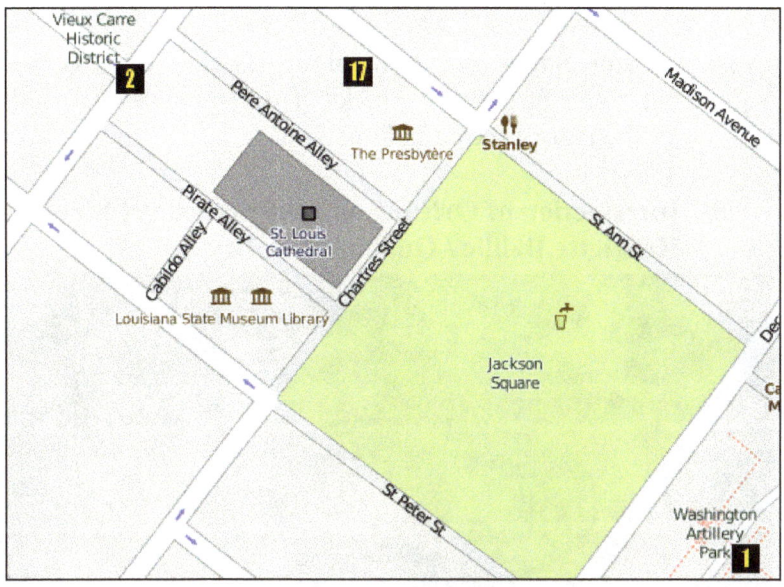

1. Mississippi River at Jackson Square—Slave Ships

The very first slaves in colonial Louisiana were Native Americans. The earliest record of African slaves (prisoners from the Spanish War of Succession) dates to 1710. Slave ships from Africa first arrived in 1719. These ships docked across the river at what is now called Algiers' Point and also in what is present-day Biloxi, Mississippi. The slaves that survived the trans-Atlantic crossing were held there for quarantining until they were ready to be transferred across the river. Before they were sold at auction, slaves were held in slave pens, essentially cages where anywhere from 50 to 150 slaves were crammed in together in filthy conditions. Most of the slave pens were in what is now the Central Business District along Baronne and Gravier Streets. Between 1719 and 1721, over 2,000 African slaves arrived in New Orleans on at least eight boats. Most of these slaves were Bambaras. The Company of the Indies, which had a Royal grant from France to develop the Louisiana colony, administered the early slave trade. **G, AA, FC, SC**

Cross Decatur Street and walk along the left edge of the Square (St. Peter Street) two blocks. Turn right and walk half a block to the rear of the cathedral.

2. **Intersection of Orleans Avenue and Royal Street— Henriette Delille / Quadroon Balls**

On the sidewalk here at the foot Orleans Avenue is a plaque honoring Henriette Delille, founder of the religious order, Sisters of the Holy Family. Delille, "a free person of color," was born in 1813 to a white father and a free black mother. At the time, it was common for white men (usually French or Spanish) to take a free woman of color as a mistress. The white man was contractually obligated to provide for the woman and any offspring the relationship might produce. This practice was called *placage*. If you look down Orleans Avenue to the right, you will see the Bourbon Orleans Hotel. It was at this site that many of the fabled Quadroon Balls were held. At these balls, free women of color would present their daughters (the quadroons or in some cases octoroons) to the gentlemen of Creole society. Henriette Delille refused to attend the balls and chose not to participate in the *placage* system. Rather, she opted for a life of religious devotion and in 1842 founded the Sisters of the Holy Family, an order of nuns who provided education, took in orphans, and cared for the sick. In 2001, a movie about Delille's life, *The Courage to Love*, premiered on the Lifetime cable television network. Henriette Delille is in the formal process of beatification in order to be declared a saint by the Roman Catholic Church. **AA**

Walk up Royal Street toward Canal Street two and half blocks to St Louis Street. Turn left onto St. Louis Street and look to your left.

3. 621 St. Louis Street—Slave Auctions

Here is the site of the old St. Louis Hotel, one of the grandest hotels of its time. In the first half of the nineteenth century, a café / bar called the City Exchange stood on this site and boasted an auction area where stocks, produce, goods, real estate, and slaves were exchanged. In 1838, the opulent St. Louis Hotel opened and boasted a magnificent rotunda where the auctions continued. (The restaurant on the corner of St. Louis and Chartres Streets across from the Napoleon House was also the site of slave exchanges and auctions). The hotel quickly became an important financial center and hosted elaborate masked balls, events for which the Creoles were very fond. Auctions were held in the afternoon. As potential slaves stepped onto the block, their attributes, work skills, and special talents were explained in both French and English. It is widely believed that the St. Louis Hotel was the scene Harriet Beecher Stowe had in mind when she described the auction of Uncle Tom in *Uncle Tom's Cabin*. The Omni Royal Orleans now occupies the site. You can still see a portion of the original St. Louis Hotel brickwork facing the Napoleon House on the corner of St. Louis Street and Chartres Streets. **G, A, AA**

Walk back to Royal and turn left. Walk half a block and turn to your left.

4. 400 Royal Street—Supreme Court Building / *Plessy v. Ferguson*

In 1892, Homer Plessy was arrested for violating the Separate Car Act, an act that mandated the separation of whites and blacks on public streetcars. Plessy's defense team argued, unsuccessfully, the law violated the Thirteenth and Fourteenth Amendments to the U.S. Constitution. The case eventually went all the way to the U. S. Supreme Court, which ruled against Plessy and established the "separate but equal" precedent. Basically, the court ruled that segregation was legal as long as it was equal. This ruling would stand until it was overturned by *Brown v. Board of Education* in 1954. Homer Plessy is buried in St. Louis Cemetery Number One. This imposing Beaux Arts structure was erected in 1910 and now serves as home of the Louisiana Supreme Court. The statue in front of the building is Edward Douglas White, Jr., native of Thibodeaux, Louisiana, and Ninth Chief Justice of the United States Supreme Court. **G, A, H, AA**

Walk toward Canal Street half a block and turn left on Conti Street. Walk one block and turn right onto Chartres Street. Proceed up Chartres Street toward Canal Street two and a half blocks.

5. 123 Chartres Street—Francois Lacroix

In the mid-1800s, Francois Lacroix was one of the wealthiest men in New Orleans and a leader among the free people of color. He was born in Cuba to former slaves who had fled St. Domingue (Haiti) during the slave insurrections there at the turn of the nineteenth century. Lacroix himself went on to own several slaves in New Orleans, a practice not uncommon among the free people of color. In addition to extensive land holdings, he owned a fashionable clothing store at this address along with his business partner, Etienne Cordeviolle. Lacroix was also a philanthropist, donating money and resources to a variety of local charities, including an orphanage, the Sisters of the Holy Family, and others. He died in 1876 and is buried in St. Louis Cemetery Number Two. **AA**

Walk away from Canal Street half a block and turn right onto Iberville Street. Walk one block to Decatur. Stop at Decatur and look toward the river.

6. 197 Iberville Street—Home of Dr. Louis Charles Roudanez

Although it no longer stands, the home of Dr. Louis Charles Roudanez stood near the intersection of Iberville Street and the river. Born of a Frenchman and a free woman of color in 1823, Dr. Roudanez was a pioneering Creole who established the first black-owned daily newspaper in the United States. He grew up in St. James Parish and then went to France where he earned the first of two medical degrees. He moved to New Orleans in the 1850s and began caring for both black and white patients. His wife, Celie Saulay, worked closely with the Sisters of the Holy Family, a black religious order founded by free woman of color, Henriette Delille. Dr. Roudanez joined a group of men to found *L'Union*, the first black-owned newspaper in the South to advocate for the abolition of slavery and the civil rights of people of color. *L'Union* ceased publication in 1864 when a group of white supremacists threatened to burn down the newspaper offices and murder its editor. Shortly thereafter, Dr. Roudanez started another newspaper, *La Tribune de la Nouvelle Orleans*, which was published in both French and English. The *Tribune* was the oldest black-owned daily newspaper in the U.S. The paper's influence grew and it quickly became internationally known with correspondents in France and Mexico. It also published letters from literary luminaries such as Victor Hugo and Alexandre Dumas. In addition, the *Tribune* also published black poets and serialized novels. The paper ceased publication in 1870. Dr. Roudanez died at his home in 1890. **AA, L**

Walk one block toward Canal Street. Turn left on Canal Street and walk half a block. Look to your left

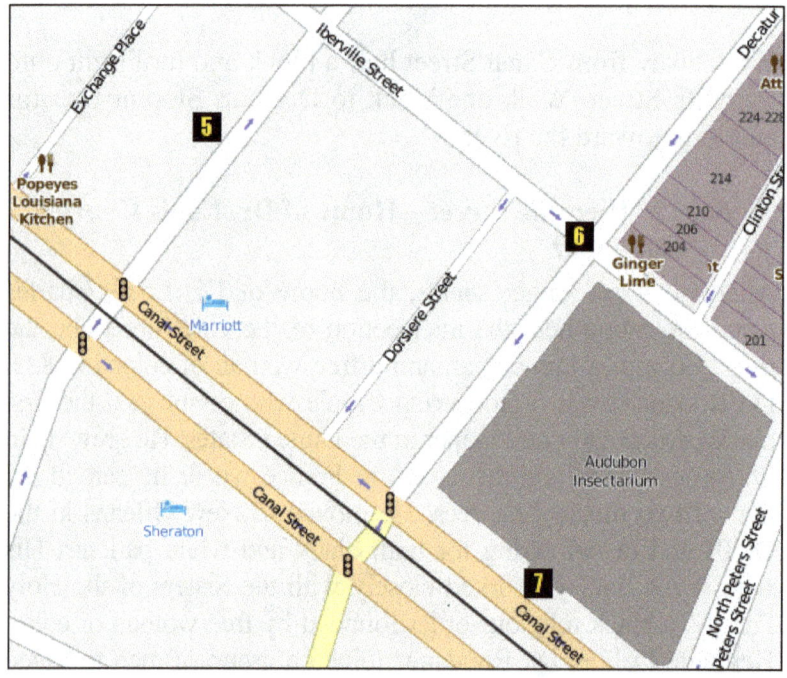

7. 423 Canal Street—Rodolphe Lucien Desdunes

This granite colossus (the old Customs House) was commissioned by the federal government in 1847 and completed in 1881. In the 1840s, New Orleans was in its golden years as a bustling port city and the largest city in the American South. As the number of imports and exports flowing up and down the Mississippi River swelled, plans were drawn for a grand federal building that would process customs and also house other federal offices. This is where the Creole scholar and civil rights activist, Rodolphe Lucien Desdunes, worked for much of his career as a clerk with the U.S. Customs Service. Desdunes was an influential author who in 1911 published *Our People Our History*, a serious of fifty biographical sketches featuring prominent black New Orleanians and their contributions to the civic, business, and cultural life of the city. Prior to the publication of this landmark work, he was the editorial voice of *The Tribune* and served on the committee that convinced Homer Plessy to challenge the Separate Car Act. He died in 1928 and is buried in St. Louis Cemetery Number Two. **AA, L**

Walk four and a half blocks along Canal Street away from the river. Turn right onto Dauphine Street. Walk four blocks and turn left onto St. Louis Street. Walk a block and a half and look to your right.

8. 1025 St. Louis Street—Cheval House

Louison Cheval, who was born a slave in 1747, purchased this cottage in 1785. Her freedom was ultimately purchased, thus elevating her social status to a free person of color. The *Code Noir*, a set of rules governing the treatment of slaves in French colonial Louisiana, stipulated that slaves could purchase their freedom and that of their immediate families. Because of this and other Creole legal precedents, free women of color at one time owned much of the property in the French Quarter. Cheval's grandson, Norbert Rillieux, became an engineer after studying at *L'Ecole Centrale* in Paris and invented the multiple-effect evaporator, a device which played a crucial role in the expansion of the sugar-refining industry. Rillieux died in 1894 and is buried in the Père Lachaise Cemetery in Paris. **AA**

Walk half a block away from the river and turn right onto North Rampart Street. Proceed two and a half blocks to Orleans Avenue. As you walk, observe the neighborhood across North Rampart Street.

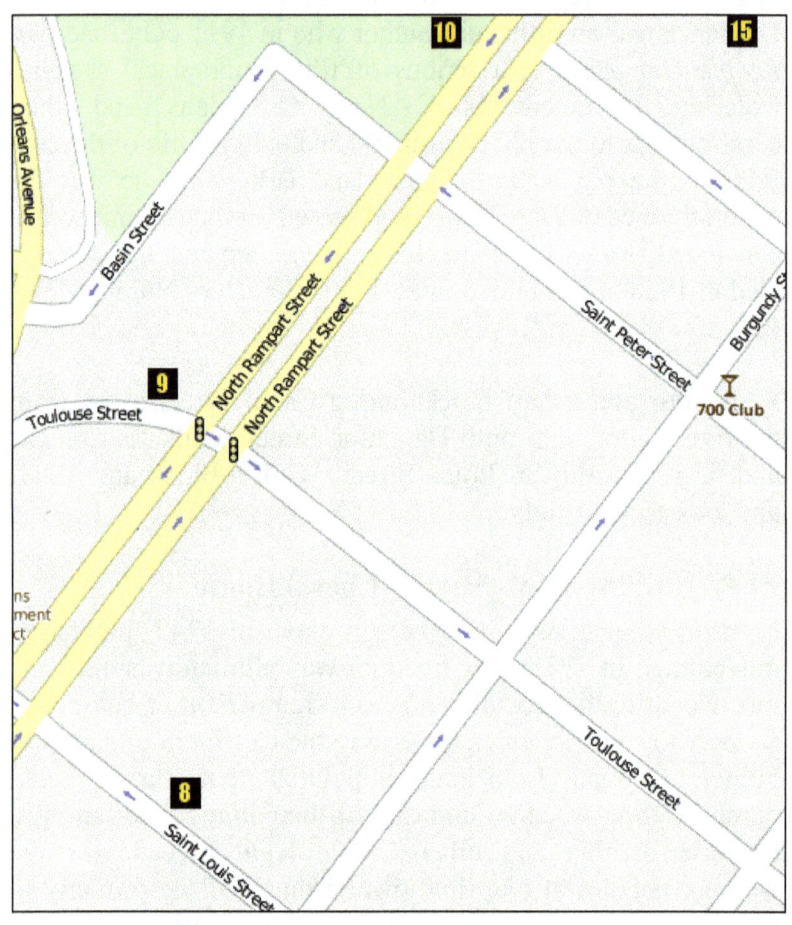

9. Tremé

Tremé is widely considered to be the oldest surviving African American neighborhood in the United States although this belief is not exactly true; the neighborhood has always had a mixed population. Nevertheless, Tremé is incredibly rich in history and culture. The neighborhood is adjacent to the lower French Quarter on the other side of North Rampart Street and is named after Claude Tremé, a hat-maker who immigrated to New Orleans in 1783. In 1722, the site was the location of a brickyard, which serviced the Company of the Indies. In 1810, Claude Tremé sold a portion of the property to the city for residential development. Subsequently, a large number of free people of color and former slaves who managed to buy their freedom began settling in the neighborhood. Tremé has always been a cultural and political hotbed of activity. Homer Plessy, of *Plessy v. Ferguson* legal fame, lived in the neighborhood and is buried at St. Louis Cemetery Number One. The New Orleans African American Museum is also located in the neighborhood. **G, AA**

At Orleans Avenue, cross North Rampart Street and visit the little park on the corner.

10. Intersection of N. Rampart and Orleans Streets—Congo Square

The *Code Noir*, a set of rules governing the treatment of slaves in French colonial Louisiana, stipulated that slaves were not to work on Sundays, or if they did, they had to be paid. On their Sundays off, many of the slaves would gather here at the *Place de Negres*, or as it was commonly called, Congo Square. Here the slaves would play music, sing and dance, and trade goods with each other. These Sunday gatherings became the means by which many slaves kept the culture, especially the music and dance, of their African ancestors alive. Visitors to New Orleans in those days often visited Congo Square. Americans from the North and East were shocked not only that so many slaves (usually 500-700) were allowed to gather without supervision, but also at the music they produced because African music had been outlawed in the American colonies. The preservation of African music through the weekly gatherings at Congo Square became crucial in the development of jazz. For this reason, Congo Square is considered sacred ground, not only by African Americans, but also by jazz enthusiasts. **G, M, AA**

Walk half a block along North Rampart away from Canal Street and turn to your left.

11. Intersection of N. Rampart and St. Ann Streets— Louis Armstrong

The park before you is named after and honors New Orleans' most famous son, Louis "Satchmo" Armstrong. Born the grandson of slaves in 1901 in a poor neighborhood near the present site of the Superdome, Armstrong grew up in poverty during the freewheeling era of Storyville, the red-light district where prostitution was permitted and bordellos and music clubs served as an incubator for jazz during its infancy. After dropping out of school at age eleven, he joined a quartet and began playing music on the streets. Armstrong immersed himself in the musical culture of the city, developed his

natural talent, and in 1919, joined Kid Ory's band, replacing the legendary Joe "King" Oliver who had left New Orleans to pursue his career in Northern markets. Armstrong eventually followed Oliver to Chicago and joined his famous Creole Jazz Band. Later, he went to New York, where his solo career began to skyrocket in no small part due to his distinctive voice and innovative improvisation. Armstrong won two Grammy Awards: the first in 1964 for Male Vocal Performance ("Hello Dolly"), the second for Lifetime Achievement, awarded posthumously in 1972. Louis Armstrong died in 1971. This park contains Congo Square, the Municipal Auditorium, the Mahalia Jackson Theatre for the Performing Arts, and a section of the New Orleans Jazz National Historic Park. Elizabeth Catlett sculpted the statue of Armstrong at the park's entrance. **G, M, AA**

Walk into the park a bit and veer to the right. Then look to your left.

12. 1419 Basin Street—Mahalia Jackson

This Performing Arts Theatre is named after Mahalia Jackson, who is widely considered by many to be the greatest

Gospel singer of the twentieth century. Jackson grew up in the Carrollton section of New Orleans before moving to Chicago at age sixteen. There, she began singing in churches and eventually toured with Thomas Dorsey. This association launched her recording career, and by the 1950s, she was internationally famous, often packing concert halls in Europe. Jackson also championed the civil rights movement, maintaining a close relationship with Dr. Martin Luther King, Jr.; Jackson sang at the Washington Rally just before Dr. King gave his famous "I Have a Dream Speech." Jackson also performed at President Kennedy's inaugural ball. The theatre named in her honor opened in 1973. In the aftermath of Hurricane Katrina in 2005, the theatre sustained fourteen feet of water and remained closed until it reopened in 2009. **AA, M**

Exit the park and walk along North Rampart Street away from Canal Street four blocks to Gov. Nicholls Street. Turn left onto Gov. Nicholls Street and walk four and a quarter blocks. Look to your left.

13. 1418 Gov. Nicholls Street—The New Orleans African American Museum

This museum is dedicated to preserving the history, art, and culture of African Americans in New Orleans. Technically, this museum is not in the French Quarter but is worth the walk a few blocks into Tremé. The New Orleans African American Museum is housed in a beautiful Creole Villa dating back to 1828. Open Wednesday through Saturday, 11:00 a.m. to 4:00 p.m. and by special appointment on off days. Phone 504-566-1136. **AA**

Walk back to North Rampart Street and turn right. Walk three blocks to Dumaine Street. Cross North Rampart Street.

14. 840 N. Rampart Street—Cosimo Matassa's Recording Studio

The laundromat on this corner was the location of Cosimo Matassa's recording studio from 1945-1955. During that time, J&M recorded some of rock-n-roll and R & B's earliest recordings including Fats Domino's "Fat Man," Little Richard's "Tutti Frutti," Ernie K-Doe's "Mother In Law," Lloyd Price's "Lawdy Miss Clawdy," Big Joe Turner's "Shake, Rattle and Roll," and Roy Brown's "Good Rockin' Tonight." Ray Charles, Professor Longhair, James Booker, and many others also recorded here. Matassa recorded 250 songs that made the national charts and twenty-one gold records. In 2012, Cosimo Matassa was inducted into the Rock-N-Roll Hall of Fame. **AA, M**

Walk one block toward Canal Street and turn left onto St. Ann Street. Walk a quarter block and look tour right.

15. 1020 St. Ann Street—Marie Laveau

No figure in New Orleans' history has been mythologized as much as Marie Laveau, the famed Voodoo Queen. The legends around her abound, some claiming she was a mysterious and evil witch who danced with snakes during voodoo rituals, others that she was a saintly spiritual healer who ministered to sick folks. Newspaper accounts in her day refer to her as a powerful voodoo priestess. Whether or not she sold *gris-gris* or granted enchanted favors to the members of Creole society or summoned spirits in order to cast spells seems less important to most people now than what she has come to represent—New Orleans' intriguing history of voodoo. Nevertheless, historical records do tell us a few things about her life. Born in 1801, Marie grew up a free person of color and married Jacques Paris at the age of eighteen years old. After being widowed, she began a relationship with Louis Christopher Dominick Duminy de Glapion. In 1842, Marie Laveau inherited a house on the site before you from her maternal grandmother who had been a slave and who purchased her freedom in 1795. She bore many children (Baptismal records indicate seven). One of her daughters is alleged to have inherited the voodoo mantle from her. Marie Laveau is buried in St. Louis Cemetery Number One. **AA, R**

Walk along St. Ann Street toward the river three and a half blocks to Royal Street. Look to your left.

16. 801 Royal Street—Slave Quarters

If you look carefully throughout the French Quarter, you will often see narrow, multistoried dependencies behind larger homes like the one here at the intersection of St. Ann and Royal Streets. These structures are often called slave quarters because they often housed slaves and / or servants. Alternately, they are sometimes called *garconieres* because when the boys of a household reached a certain age (adolescence), they were given their own room in these dependencies. Today, these spaces are typically used as studio or efficiency apartments. **AA, A**

Walk a quarter block along St. Ann Street toward the river and look to your right.

17. 638 St. Ann Street—The Crescent City Tour Booking Agency

This is an excellent place for information about the city and its attractions. Unlike most visitor centers, this booking agency is not owned by a specific tour company and offers unbiased recommendations. It also happens to be owned by the author of the book you now hold in your hands. Please feel free to pop in with any questions or just to say hello. **G**

18. Suggestions for Further Reading

Blassingame, John W. *Black New Orleans 1860-1880.* Chicago: University of Chicago Press, 2007.

Evans, Freddi Williams. *Congo Square African Roots in New Orleans.* Lafayette, LA: University of Louisiana at Lafayette Press, 2011.

Hall, Gwendolyn Midlo. *Africans in Colonial Louisiana: The Development of Afro-Creole Culture in the Eighteenth Century.* Baton Rouge: Louisiana State University Press, 1992.

Johnson, Walter. *Soul by Soul: Life Inside the Antebellum Market.* Cambridge, MA: Harvard University Press, 1999.

Hirsch, Arnold Richard. *Creole New Orleans: Race and Americanization.* Baton Rouge: Louisiana State University Press, 1992.

Kein, Sybil. *Creole: The History and Legacy of Louisiana's Free People of Color.* Baton Rouge: Louisiana State University Press, 2000.

Nystrom, Justin A. *New Orleans After the Civil War Race, Politics, And a New Birth of Freedom.* Baltimore: John Hopkins University Press, 2010.

Sublette, Ned. *The World That Made New Orleans From Spanish Silver to Congo Square.* Lawrence Hill Books: Chicago, 2009.

Turner, Richard Brent. *Jazz Religion, The Second Line, and Black New Orleans.* Bloomington: Indiana University Press, 2009.

Architectural and Historic Homes Walking Tour

"The glory of the Quarter is its mass of Creole townhouses, with shops below and homes above."
— Sally Reeves

The French Quarter is an architectural smorgasbord serving everything from French and Spanish colonial to Italianate to Greek Revival to Victorian to Beaux Arts to Creole cottages and American townhouses. Much like the ethnography of the city itself, many of the buildings are an amalgamation of these various styles. Because of the great fires of 1788 and 1794, very little remains of the French Colonial Town. Much of what we see today in the French Quarter is actually Spanish and American. The influx of Americans in the first half of the nineteenth century and their development of Uptown New Orleans had a tremendous influence on the existing structures in the Quarter. The legendary Creole-American conflict manifested itself in the city's architecture; for example, Pouilly's St. Louis Exchange Hotel competed with Dakin and Gallier's Hotel St. Charles for the title of Grandest Hotel in the South. The most common building types in the French Quarter are the Creole Cottage, the Raised Cottage, the Row House, the American Townhouse, and the Shotgun House. Creole cottages date from the French colonial period and typically consist of four rooms with no hallways. The Raised Cottage evolved out of a response to New Orleans tropical climate by avoiding ground moisture and facilitating breezes. The Row House is an American architectural form and was commonly built between 1820 and 1850. The American Townhouse was also popular during this period and introduced interior corridors. The second half of the nineteenth century saw the rise of the Shotgun House, narrow rectangular structures with no hallways. By the early 1900s, the French Quarter was essentially a run-down slum and generally considered a shabby part of town. Preservation efforts began in earnest in the 1920s and culminated with the creation of the Vieux Carré Commission in 1936, an entity charged with preserving the architectural heritage of the neighborhood. Notable architects and engineers who have worked in the Quarter include Pierre Le Blond de La Tour, Adrien de Pauger, J. N. B. Pouilly, James Gallier (both Sr. and Jr.), and Benjamin Latrobe.

This tour begins on Canal Street across from Harrah's Casino.

1. 423 Canal Street—The Customs House

This granite colossus was commissioned by the federal government in 1847 and completed in 1881. In the 1840s, New Orleans was in its golden years as a bustling port city and the largest city in the American South. As the number of imports and exports flowing up and down the Mississippi River swelled, plans were drawn for a grand federal building that would process customs and also house other federal offices. Over the thirty-four-year period it took to complete, eight different architects worked on the project, each one modifying his predecessor's design. The result is an impressive combination of Greek- and Egyptian-Revival style. Each side of the first floor has a series of empty niches. The original architect, Alexander Thompson Wood, intended to place statues in these niches but later architects abandoned the plan. The Customs House is now home to the Audubon Institute's Insectarium. **A**

Walk three and a half blocks along Canal Street away from the river to Bourbon Street. Turn right and walk two blocks. Look to your right.

2. 240 Bourbon Street—The Old Absinthe House

Occasionally, you will find in the French Quarter a building with an unusually high balcony such as the Old Absinthe House. This normally indicates an entresol house, that is to say a building with a mezzanine or intermediate level between the first and second floors, which was / is used for storage. The entresol style was popular among the Creoles living in the Quarter in the years after the Louisiana Purchase in 1803 and typically featured arched doorways / windows on the ground floor, and an iron adorned balcony high on the façade. Other famous examples of the entresol townhouse include the buildings at 441 Royal Street (at the corner of St. Louis) and 534 Royal Street. **A, V**

Walk down Bourbon two blocks away from Canal Street and turn left on St. Louis Street. Walk a quarter block and look to your left.

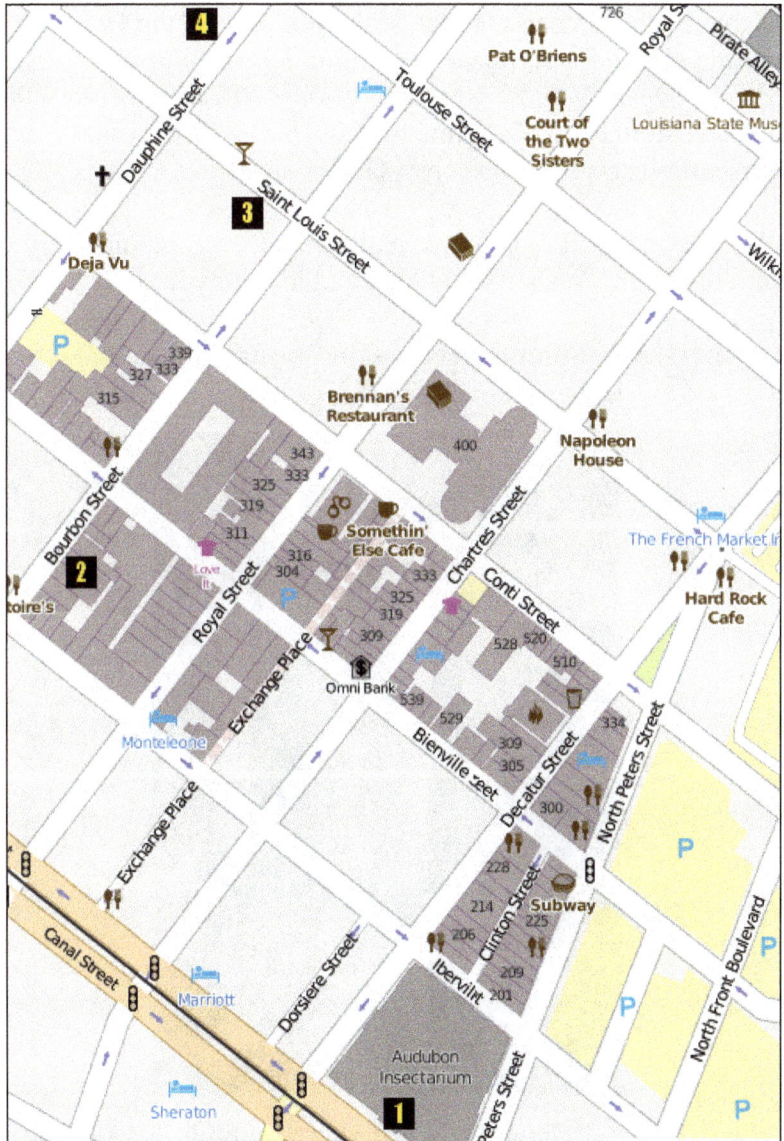

3. 820 St. Louis Street—The Hermann-Grima House

This home was built in 1831 and is an excellent example of American architecture of the period. The home features the only remaining fully functional outdoor kitchen and horse stable in the French Quarter. Take the tour of the Hermann-Grima House for an inside peek of mid-1800s French Quarter living. Open Monday through Friday, 10:00 a.m. to 3:00 p.m.; Saturday, 12:00 p.m. to 4:00 p.m.; (Wednesdays are typically reserved for groups). **G, A**

Walk along St. Louis Street half a block to Dauphine Street and turn right. Walk half a block and look to your left.

4. 523 Dauphine Street—The Xiques House

This enigmatic Greek Revival home was built in 1852 for a local importer named Angel Xiques. From 1871 to 1877, it was the home of the Spanish Consulate. In later years, it functioned as a gambling house, cigar factory, bottle storage facility, and rooming house. The Greek Revival design has been attributed to architect J. N. B. De Pouilly. **A**

Walk along Dauphine Street half a block and turn right on Toulouse Street. Walk one block and turn left on Bourbon Street. Walk half a block and turn to your left.

5. 623 Bourbon Street—Lindy Boggs Home

This lovely townhouse dates to 1795 and from 1970 to 2010 was the home of Lindy Boggs, the first woman elected to Congress from Louisiana and former Ambassador to the Vatican. She was elected to the House of Representatives after her husband, House Majority Leader Hale Boggs, was killed in a plane crash in Alaska in 1973. In the nineteenth century, the first floor was a blacksmith shop. **G**

Walk half a block away from Canal Street and turn right on St. Peter Street. Walk one block toward Royal Street and look across the street.

6. 700 Royal Street—The LaBranche House

Built in the 1830s, this beautiful collection of townhomes is one of the most photographed buildings in New Orleans because of its rounded cast iron grillwork, which features acorn and oak leaf designs. The buildings were constructed for a sugar planter named Jean Baptiste LaBranche. LaBranche was actually a German immigrant whose last name was Zweig. When he arrived in New Orleans, the immigration official who processed him spoke only French and did not understand the German name "Zweig." Zweig then went out and picked up a branch from a tree and returned with it. Pointing to it he said, "zweig, zweig." The French-speaking official then said, "Ah! La Branche." **A**

Walk along St. Peter Street one block toward the river. Turn left on Chartres Street.

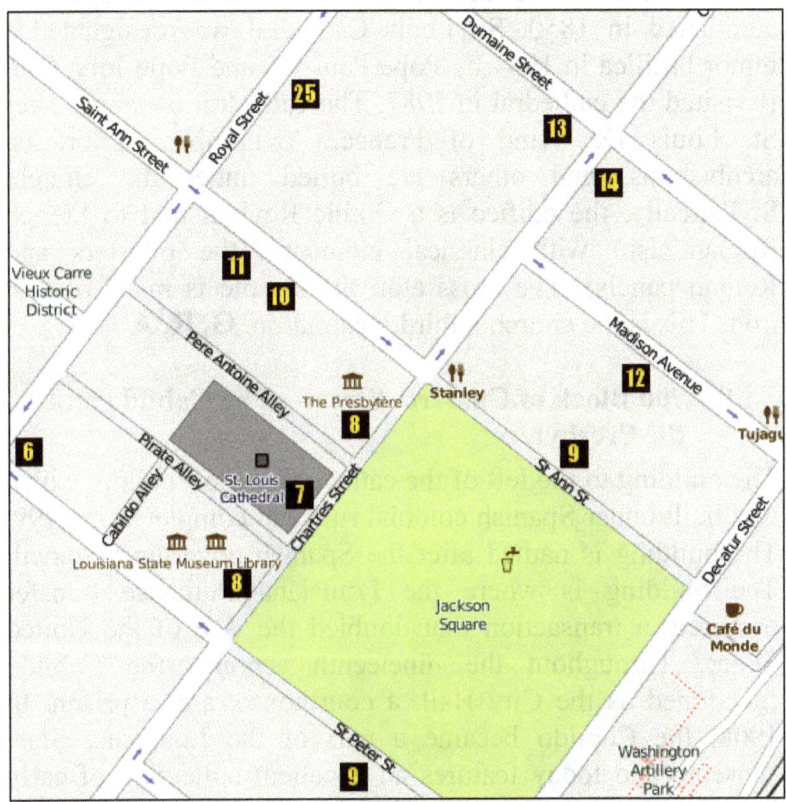

7. 700 Block of Chartres Street—St. Louis Cathedral

The famed French architect Jacques Nicolas Bussiere de Pouilly arrived in New Orleans in 1833 and quickly made a name for him by designing the grand St. Louis Exchange Hotel. He soon became the architect of choice among the city's wealthiest citizens and by the 1840s was the most sought after architect in the city. His crowning achievement came in 1849 when the Catholic Diocese hired him to build a new church to replace the aging colonial structure at Jackson Square. The original church was dedicated in 1727 and served the city until it burned down in 1788. Rebuilding was completed in 1794. By the mid-1800s, major renovations were necessary and the cathedral as it looks today was completed in 1850. St. Louis Cathedral was designated a minor basilica in 1964 by Pope Paul VI, and Pope John Paul II visited the cathedral in 1987. The cathedral is named after St. Louis IX, King of France. A number of priests, archbishops, and others are buried under the church. Stylistically, the edifice is a Gothic Revival nod to French Romanticism with classical elements (the pilasters and Roman panels). The cross atop the steeple is made of cast iron. This is the church's third incarnation. **G, R, A**

8. 700 Block of Chartres Street—The Cabildo and the Presbytere

The building to the left of the cathedral is the Cabildo, which was built under Spanish colonial rule and completed in 1799. The building is named after the Spanish governing council. The building is where the Louisiana Purchase transfer occurred, a transaction that doubled the size of the United States. Throughout the nineteenth century, the Cabildo functioned as the City Hall, a courthouse, and a prison. In 1908, the Cabildo became a part of the Louisiana State Museum and today features an excellent collection of early Louisiana history. Open Tuesday through Sunday, 10:00 a.m. to 4:30 p.m. **G, SC**

The building to the right of the cathedral is the Presbytere or Ecclesiastical House. The name comes from the fact that prior to its construction in the late 1790s, this site was the residence of the Capuchin monks. Construction of the Presbytere, along with the Cabildo and renovations to the cathedral, were paid for by Don Andreas Almonester y Roxas, a prominent businessman during the Spanish colonial period. The building was initially used for commercial purposes until 1834. In that year, the Presbytere became a courthouse until 1911 when it was acquired by the Louisiana State Museum. The museum today features rotating exhibits. Open Tuesday through Sunday, 10:00 a.m. to 4:30 p.m. **G, FC, SC, A**

Built between 1795 and 1813, these two buildings are essentially Spanish colonial architecture with a heavy Baroque influence. The balustrades are Renaissance inspired and the French-style Mansard roofs were added later to make the roof lines symmetrical with the Pontalba Buildings, which flank the Square.

9. 500 Blocks of St. Peter and St. Ann Streets—The Pontalba Buildings

The two block-long red row houses that flank the Square are the Pontalba Buildings. These buildings are named after the Baroness Micaela Almonester de Pontalba, daughter of the philanthropist Don Andreas Almonester y Roxas and date to 1850. Commercial space occupies the first floor while the upper levels are apartments. In the lower Pontalba Building (along St. Ann Street) is the 1850 House, a replica of a typical 1850s New Orleans apartment. The 1850 House is available for viewing Tuesday through Sunday, 10:00 a.m. to 4:30 p.m.

If you look carefully at the ironwork, you will see a cartouche with the letters "A" & "P," representing the family names Almonester and Pontalba. When Micaela was sixteen, she married her cousin, Celestin de Pontalba, who was also from a prominent family. It was not a happy marriage. Her father-in-law was obsessed with the substantial fortune she inherited from her father and unrelentingly tried to gain access to it. The struggle eventually came to a head when Micaela's father-in-law attempted to kill her by shooting her four times in the chest. After shooting her, he committed suicide, but Micaela survived to commission the building of the apartments named after her and lived to the age of 78. Henry Howard was the architect but Micaela contributed to the design of the buildings herself with the Palais Royal and the Place des Vosges of Paris in mind. Architecturally, the buildings are a Creole take on a Parisian influenced Greek Revival style. **G, A**

Walk along St. Ann Street a half block away from the river.

10. 630 St. Ann Street—Elizabeth Werlein Home

Elizabeth Werlein was the founder and first leader of the Louisiana League of Women Voters and a French Quarter preservationist. Werlein advocated tirelessly for the preservation of the Quarter, so much so that in the 1930s, Mayor Maestri dubbed her the "Mayor of the French Quarter." In 1936, Werlein successfully persuaded the Louisiana Legislature to create the Vieux Carré Commission, which to this day is charged with preserving the historical and architectural integrity of the French Quarter. **G, A**

Walk a quarter block along St. Ann Street away from the river. Look to your left.

11. 638 St. Ann Street—The Crescent City Tour Booking Agency

This is an excellent place for information about the city and its attractions. Unlike most visitor centers, this booking agency is not owned by a specific tour company and offers unbiased recommendations. It also happens to be owned by the author of the book you now hold in your hands. Please feel free to pop in with any questions or just to say hello. **G**

Walk back toward the Square and turn left onto Chartres Street. Walk half a block and turn right onto Madison Street. Walk half a block and turn to your right.

12. 536 Madison Street—Lyle Saxon's Home

Here is the home of Lyle Saxon, writer and French Quarter preservationist. In the 1920s and 1930s, Lyle Saxon, a successful writer, began restoring dilapidated homes in the French Quarter and promoting the area to other writers and artists as a haven of artistic inspiration. Saxon galvanized the preservation and restoration of the French Quarter and, more than anyone, ensured the Quarter's survival as one of America's most historic neighborhoods. In the 1930s, Saxon was the Louisiana Director of the Federal Writers Project, a program within FDR's New Deal. Books by Saxon include: *Fabulous New Orleans*, *New Orleans City Guide*, *Gumbo Ya-Ya*, and *The Friends of Joe Gilmore*. **L, A, Q**

Walk back to Chartres Street and turn right. Walk half a block and turn left onto Dumaine Street. Walk half a block and look to your left.

13. 632 Dumaine Street—Madame John's Legacy

This charming house dates back to 1789 and is a fine

example of late eighteenth century French colonial design. The structure closely resembles its predecessor, which was built circa 1730 and destroyed in the great fire of 1788. For much of the eighteenth century, Elizabeth Real-Marin, a widow who ran the property as an inn, owned the property. After her death in 1777, Renato Beluche, father of the famous pirate René Beluche who worked closely with Jean Lafitte, acquired the home. The home then had a long string of owners until it was acquired by the Louisiana State Museum in 1947. There are few homes like this left in the French Quarter, but at one time, this architectural style was the norm. The name derives from a story by Louisiana author George Washington Cable entitled "Tite Poulette." Madame John's Legacy is available for touring and is open Tuesday through Sunday, 10:00 a.m. to 4:30 p.m. **G, A, L, FC, SC**

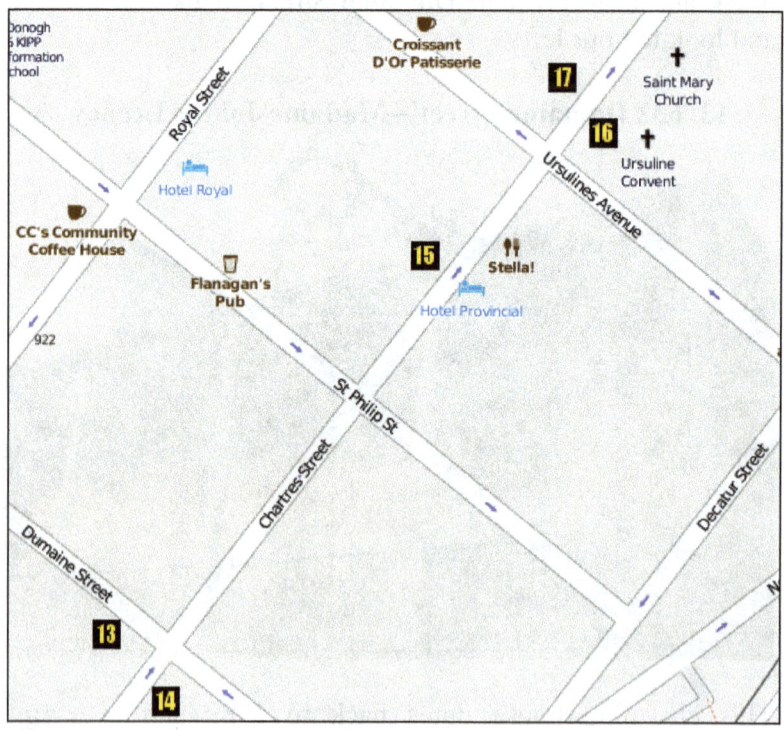

Walk back to Chartres Street and look across the street to your right.

14. 838 Chartres Street—Cucullu Row

These six row houses known as Cucullu Row were built in 1828 and endure as the oldest intact row in the French Quarter. In 1730, this site was the location of Pierre Baron's astronomical observatory, one of the oldest observatories in America. **A, G**

Walk down Chartres Street two blocks and look to your left.

15. 1021 Chartres Street—The De Le Ronde House

Erected around 1807, this was the city home of Pierre Denis de la Ronde, whose plantation downriver was the site of the first skirmish in the Battle of New Orleans. **G, A**

Walk down Chartres Street half a block to the corner of Ursulines Street. Look to your right.

16. 1100 Chartres Street—The Ursuline Convent

This building is the oldest surviving structure in the Mississippi River Valley and an excellent example of French colonial architecture. The Ursuline nuns first arrived in New Orleans in 1727, but this building was not completed until 1752. Throughout its history, the convent has served as an orphanage, a hospital, a school, a Presbytere, and, for a brief period, the seat of the Louisiana Legislature. St. Mary's Church, which is part of the complex opposite the Beauregard-Keyes House, dates to 1845. The Ursuline Convent is available for touring Monday through Saturday, 10:00 a.m. to 4:00 p.m. **A, R, G**

Turn around and look across the street.

17. 1113 Chartres Street—The Beauregard-Keyes House

This raised center hall house was built in 1826 for an auctioneer named Joseph Le Carpentier. Designed by renowned architect Francois Correjolles, the home blends elements of Greek Revivalism with a Tuscan portico. Peek inside the opening in the brick wall next to the home for a glimpse at the fantastic garden. The house is named for two of its most famous residents—Confederate General Pierre Gustave Toutant Beauregard and writer Frances Parkinson Keyes. Beauregard gave the order to fire the first shot on Fort Sumter in South Carolina, thus beginning the U.S. Civil War. Keyes authored a number of novels, including *Dinner at Antoine's*. General Beauregard's ghost is said to haunt the home, sometimes appearing in full Confederate uniform dancing with a woman, presumably his wife who died while the general was off fighting the Civil War. Gunfire has also been heard in the house but some speculate that these shots are not the echoes of warfare but rather the reenactment of a grisly murder that occurred in the house in 1908. At that time, an Italian businessman named Pietro Giancona lived there and had a deadly confrontation with the local Mafia, who was trying to extort him. One evening, Pietro invited four Mafioso to his home for dinner and to discuss their demands. After they were seated, Pietro and his son opened fire and shot all four, three of whom died immediately. The house is also believed to be haunted by novelist Frances Parkinson Keyes, who died here in 1971, as well as by her dog, Lucky, who died a few weeks after Keyes. Tour guides have also reported a ghost cat named Caroline that rubs their legs during guided tours. Tours of the home are available Monday through Saturday, 10:00 a.m. to 3:00 p.m. **H, L, G, V**

Walk along Chartres Street two blocks away from Canal Street to the corner of Esplanade Avenue.

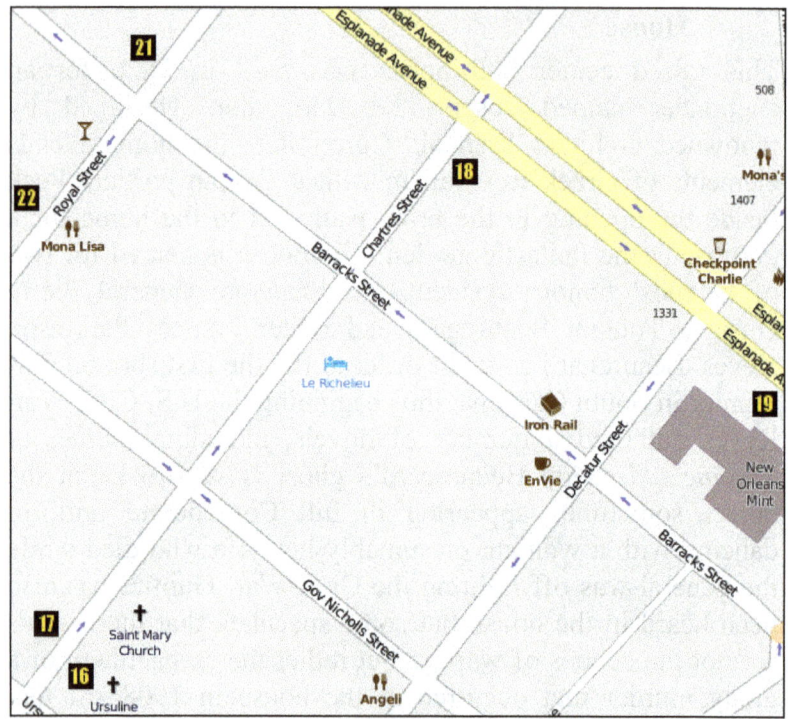

18. 1321 Chartres Street—The Denis House

This home at the corner of Chartres Street and Esplanade Avenue was erected in 1834 for a local attorney named Henry Raphael Denis. During the World's Cotton Exposition in 1884, Exposition Commissioner Dr. Jokichi Takamine, A Japanese chemist, lived here. Dr. Takamine is credited with discovering the hormone adrenalin in 1900 and is widely considered to be a pioneer of the biotechnology industry. **G, A**

Walk one block along Esplanade Avenue toward the river. Look to your right.

19. 400 Esplanade Avenue—The Old U.S. Mint

The Old U.S. Mint was built in 1835 and holds the distinction of being the only facility to mint both U.S. and Confederate money. It was here that General Andrew Jackson inspected the troops before marching ten miles downriver to the Battle of New Orleans in 1815. During the Civil War, after New Orleans fell to the Union, a Confederate sympathizer named William Mumford scaled the wall of the Mint and tore down the American Flag. General Butler, the Union governor, had him arrested and promptly executed. The Mint is now used as a museum and is home to the New Orleans Jazz Club Collections of the Louisiana State Museum. One of the prized artifacts in the museum is Louis Armstrong's first cornet. The Old U.S. Mint also hosts numerous festivals throughout the year. Open Tuesday through Sunday, 10:30 a.m. to 4:30 p.m. **G, CW, M**

Walk four blocks along Esplanade Avenue away from the river. Turn left onto Dauphine Street. Walk two blocks and look to your left.

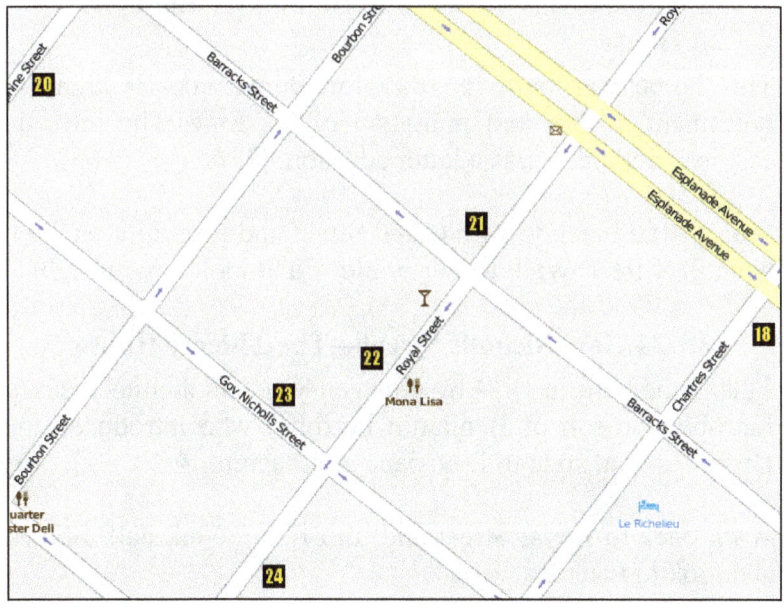

20. 1220 Dauphine Street—Maison Hospitaliere

This home was established in 1893 by *La Société des Dames Hospitalières* to care for downtrodden women. Today, it functions as a nursing home. **G, R**

Walk half a block away from Canal Street and turn right on Barracks Street. Walk two blocks to Royal Street and turn left. Walk a quarter block and look to your left.

21. 1315 Royal Street—The Gauche House

John Gauche, a local importer and merchant, built this beautiful Italianate Villa in 1856. Italianate architecture features low-pitched or flat roofs, projecting eaves, dentals, cornice structures, and angled bay windows. **G, A**

Walk up Royal Street one block toward Canal Street and look to your right.

22. 1217 Royal Street—The Dominique Bouligny House

This home was built in 1831 for Dominique Bouligny, a prominent planter and politician of his time. The intricate cast iron verandah was a latter addition. **G, A**

Walk half a block toward Canal Street and turn right on Gov. Nicholls Street. Walk a quarter block and look to your right.

23. 721 Gov. Nicholls Street—The Thierry House

This home built in 1814 by nineteen-year-old architect Henry Latrobe (the son of Benjamin Latrobe) who introduced the Greek Revival style to Louisiana architecture. **A**

Walk back to Royal Street and turn right. Walk half a block and look to your left.

24. 1132 Royal Street—The Gallier House

Famed architect James Gallier, Jr. designed and lived in this house from 1860-1897. Gallier, along with his father, designed some of the most noteworthy buildings in New Orleans, including the old City Hall and the French Opera House. Gallier is buried in St. Louis Cemetery Three. Museum is open Monday, Thursday, Friday 10:00 a.m. to 2:00 p.m.; Tuesday, Thursday by appointment; Saturday 10:00 a.m. to 3:00 p.m. **A, G**

Walk three blocks up Royal Street toward Canal Street and look to your left.

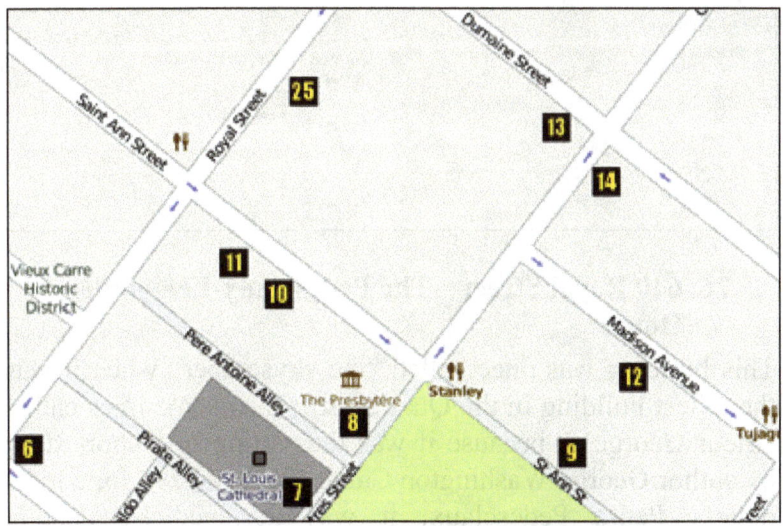

25. 824 Royal Street—Thomas Poree House

This home dates to 1789 and was once the home to Thomas Poree, uncle of the Creole historian Charles Gayarre. Gayarre was the grandson of Etienne de Bore', who discovered the process for granulating sugar. Gayarre was a prominent politician and historian. As a child, Gayarre stood on the home's balcony and cheered General Andrew Jackson as he marched downriver to fight the British at the Battle of New Orleans in 1814. **G**

Walk up Royal Street toward Canal Street two blocks to the corner of St. Peter Street. Look to your left.

26. 640 Royal Street—The Pedesclaux-Lemonnier House

This building was once called "the skyscraper" when it was the tallest building in the Quarter. It is also sometimes called "Sieur George's" because it was the setting of a short story by author George Washington Cable. Built in 1795 for a local notary, Pedro Pedesclaux, it was designed by notable architect and engineer Barthelemy Lafon. Lafon also subdivided the Faubourg Marigny, the neighborhood adjacent to the French Quarter downriver, and gave Greek names to the streets of the lower Garden District. **A, L**

27. Suggestions for Further Reading

American Institute of Architects, New Orleans Chapter. *A Guide to New Orleans Architecture*. 1974.

Delehanty, Randolph. *New Orleans: Elegance and Decadence.* San Francisco, Chronicle Books, 2003.

Gross, Steve, *et al. Creole Houses: Traditional Homes of Old Louisiana.*

Heard, Malcolm, and Scott Bernhard. *French Quarter Manual: An Architectural Guide to New Orleans Vieux Carré.* New Orleans: Tulane School of Architecture, 1997.

McCaffety, Kerri. *The Majesty of the French Quarter.* Gretna, LA: Pelican Publishing, 1999.

Sully, Susan. *New Orleans Style: Past and Present.* Rizzoli, 2007.

Toledano, Roulhac. *A Pattern Book of New Orleans Architecture.* Gretna, LA: Pelican Publishing, 2010.

Vogt, Lloyd. *Historic Buildings of the French Quarter.* Gretna, LA: Pelican, 2002.

Culinary Walking Tour

"In New Orleans, gluttony is a way of life."
— Morton J. Horowitz

According to legend, the first civil uprising in colonial North America occurred in New Orleans in the 1720s and had nothing to do with slaves or Native Americans or taxes. Rather, it had to do with food. The story goes that the French women living in the Quarter took to the streets banging their pots and pans in protest and frustration over not knowing how to cook the locally available food properly. Bienville himself, the founder of New Orleans and governor of the Louisiana colony, had to personally broker a deal with the women of a local Native American tribe to teach the French women about local ingredients. This legend may or may not be true but it is appropriate for New Orleans has been obsessed with food ever since. The arrival and assimilation of various ethnic groups throughout the city's history contributed greatly to New Orleans' wonderfully rich and complex culinary heritage. Among these are included French, Native American, Senegalese, Gambian, Angolan, Spanish, German, Irish, Cajuns, Italian, Cuban, Haitian, Vietnamese, and Mexican. Gumbo, Oysters Rockefeller, Bananas Foster, the Po-Boy and the Muffaletta were all invented here. Throughout the twentieth century, the menus at upscale restaurants were, for the most part, interchangeable. That began to change in 1976 when Paul Prudhomme took over the kitchen at Commander's Palace. In addition to introducing Cajun staples to New Orleans, Prudhomme preached a culinary gospel focused on local ingredients and in the process ushered in the era of celebrity chefs.

This tour begins on Iberville Street just off Bourbon Street.

Iberville Street is the first street past Canal Street in the French Quarter.

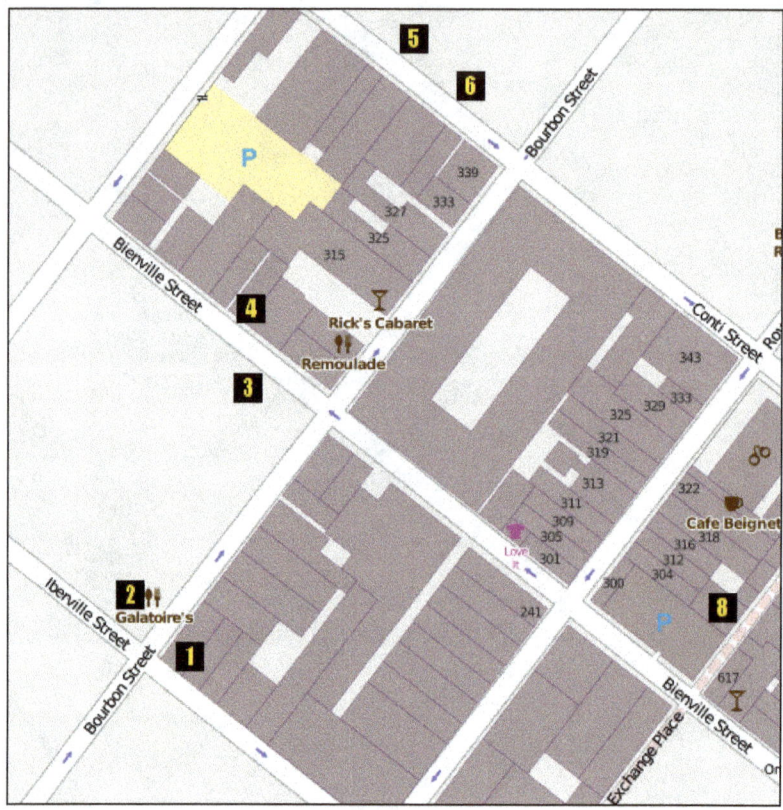

1. 739 Iberville Street—Felix's

Many dishes come to mind when one thinks of New Orleans, but perhaps, chief among them is oysters, and the oysters don't get any better than they do at Felix's. Today, there are a number of places to get oysters in New Orleans, but for many decades, there were only two major galaxies in the French Quarter oyster universe—Felix's and its neighbor across the street, the Acme Oyster House. Because of their proximity to Bourbon Street, both Felix's and Acme tend to be touristy, but Felix's has managed to retain some of its local ambience and following. Felix's menu offers all the standard local dishes (po-boys, jambalaya, red beans and rice, etc.) but the thing to order here is raw oysters. For those who remember it, the legendary restaurant, La Louisiane, was located nearby at 725 Iberville St. **C**

Proceed to Bourbon Street and turn right. Stop and turn to your left.

2. 209 Bourbon Street—Galatoire's

No restaurant in the city better exemplifies New Orleans' "upper-crust" than Galatoire's. It is *the* place to see and be seen, especially on Fridays. Because Friday lunch at Galatoire's is such a venerable tradition, and because of the main dining room's no reservations policy, regulars will actually pay homeless people to stake out a place in line for them on Thursday nights. Opened in 1905 by Jean Galatoire (who came from Pardies, France—a small village on the edge of the Pyrenees), Galatoire's embodies New Orleans love of tradition and love of socializing. The menu and the décor have not changed in over 100 years and when the restaurant announced it was no longer using hand cracked ice but an ice machine instead, the regular crowd went ballistic. Lunches are long social affairs that often turn into dinner, and table hopping is common. Reservations are now accepted for the upstairs dining room; the main dining room remains first come, first serve. Jackets are required for dinner and Sunday brunch. If you have a seersucker suit, this is the place to wear it. **C**

Continue down Bourbon Street away from Canal Street. At the first intersection you come to, turn left on Bienville Street. Walk a quarter block, stop, and turn to your left.

3. 808 Bienville Street—GW Fins

Although it's only been open since 2001, GW Fins has established itself as one of the finest seafood restaurants in the United States. Co-owner / Chef Tenney Flynn insists on using only the freshest and best seafood available. Chef Flynn's high standards and rigorous selection process are legendary, much to the chagrin of seafood suppliers from around the world. As a result, the menu at GW Fins changes daily. In addition to the high quality of the seafood, the cooking techniques here are straightforward and designed to enhance the natural flavors of the seafood. The wine list is impressive and offers over 70 wines by the glass. The dress code is business casual. Reservations are strongly recommended. **C**

Turn around and look across the street slightly to your left.

4. 813 Bienville Street—Arnaud's

In 1918, a colorful French wine salesman, who fancied himself a count, opened Arnaud's. Before long, the restaurant became one of the finest in the city and soon began to win national accolades. Count Arnaud believed a fine meal was one of life's greatest pleasures and that philosophy is still alive at Arnaud's. Unfortunately, a year after the restaurant opened, the United States outlawed the possession, sale, and consumption of alcohol. A luxurious meal without wine or a cordial afterward was unthinkable to the count, and Arnaud's, like most restaurants in New Orleans, bypassed the law by serving alcohol in coffee cups or in secret rooms. The law did eventually catch up with the count, and he was briefly jailed while the restaurant was padlocked. A sympathetic jury quickly released him and the good times began to roll once again at Arnaud's. In time, the count's larger-than-life daughter—the indomitable Germaine Wells—took stewardship of Arnaud's and spread its fame around the world. Germaine embodied New Orleans' *joie de vivre* and ultimately ruled over twenty-two Carnival Balls, a record likely to remain unbeaten. Upstairs, above the French 75 Bar, is a small museum (free to the public) of the Carnival Ball gowns Germaine wore as she reigned over various Carnival krewes. **C, H**

Proceed away from Bourbon Street and turn right on Dauphine Street. Walk one block and turn right on Conti Street. Proceed half a block and stop. Turn to your left.

5. 819 Conti St.—Broussard's

Since 1920, Broussard's has offered the quintessential New Orleans' fine dining experience—classic French cuisine with a strong Creole influence in an elegant atmosphere. Founder Joe Broussard had a passionate disposition and a legendary temper. It was not uncommon for him to throw dishes across the kitchen that didn't meet his high standards. He also had a fixation with Napoleon Bonaparte, which may explain his imperious personality. In the restaurant's early years, whenever a guest ordered a Brandy Napoleon, a bell would ring and waiters would gather around a statue of the emperor and sing *La Marseillaise*. The spacious courtyard at Broussard's has been called the most beautiful in the all the French Quarter. **C**

Walk a quarter block along Conti Street toward the river and look to your left.

6. 811 Conti Street—Killer PoBoys

In the back room of the Erin Rose, an excellent neighborhood Irish Pub, is a makeshift kitchen where Chefs Cam Boudreaux and his wife April serve some of the most innovative po-boys anywhere in New Orleans. The ingredients are all local but the influence is global: Moroccan spiced lamb, Guinness braised beef, Vietnamese style bread, etc. Po-boys are a staple in New Orleans and they've been around a long time. Killer PoBoys represents a fresh and modern interpretation of a New Orleans' classic. Nothing is fried and vegetarian options are available. Dress code: very casual. **C**

Cross Bourbon Street and proceed down Conti Street one block. Turn left on Royal Street and proceed a quarter block. Look to your left for a pink-colored building.

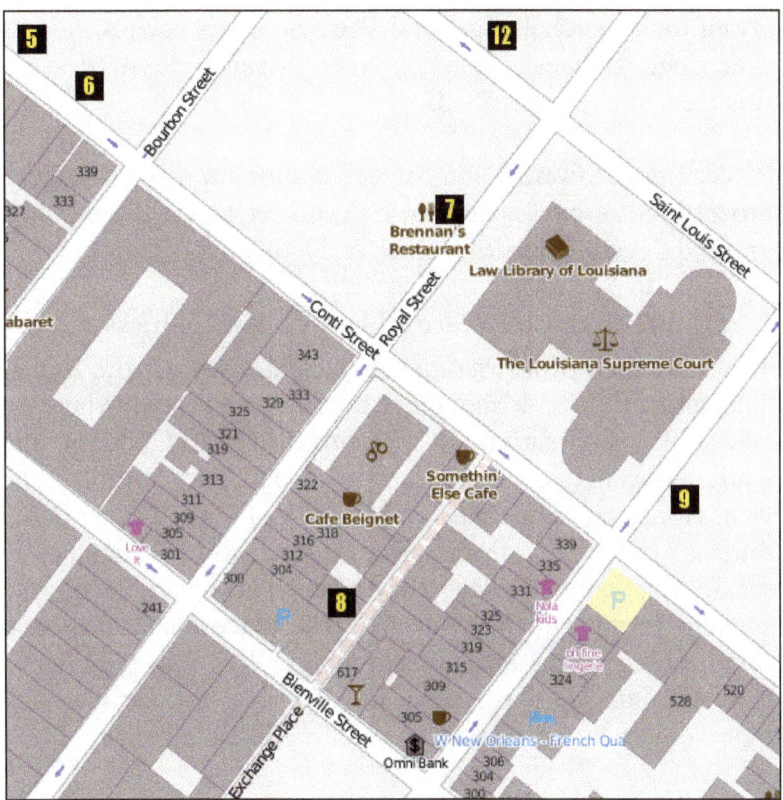

7. 417 Royal Street—Brennan's

One of the crown jewels in New Orleans' culinary crown, Brennan's opened in 1946 and has forever changed New Orleans dining. Before opening Brennan's, founder Owen Brennan owned the Old Absinthe House on Bourbon St. There, each night, he would chat with his friend, the legendary Count Arnaud, founder of Arnaud's restaurant. Owen delighted in telling the count of the numerous complaints he heard from bar patrons who dined at Arnaud's, which is only steps away from the Old Absinthe House. One night, Count Arnaud became fed up and challenged Owen to open his own restaurant if he thought he could do better. The count also added that the Irish knew nothing about food. Owen took the challenge, and Brennan's has been a success ever since. Bananas Foster, a New Orleans' classic dessert, was created at Brennan's. **C**

Proceed back toward Conti Street and turn left on Conti Street. Proceed half a block and turn right on Exchange Place Alley. Proceed three-quarters of a block and look to your right.

8. 307 Exchange Place Alley—Green Goddess

This little gem of a restaurant is tucked away off the beaten path and offers one the most eclectic menus anywhere in New Orleans. Creativity is the norm at Green Goddess, and while many of the dishes may seem odd, they are all done well. Honoring New Orleans' history as a port city, the menu reflects influences from around the world. The exotic sensibility that permeates the menu is also evident in the cocktail menu and the wine list. The place consists of two small dining rooms and outside tables. When the weather is nice, eat outside. If you have to eat inside, ask for the back room, otherwise you'll end up smelling like the kitchen. **C**

Proceed back toward Conti Street and turn right. Proceed half a block and turn left on Chartres Street. Walk a quarter block and turn to your right.

9. 416 Chartres Street—K-Paul's

Contrary to popular belief, the terms Cajun and Creole are not synonymous. The Cajuns, or Acadians, were French Canadian exiles who settled the rural areas south and west of New Orleans. The Creoles, on the other hand, were descendants of the French and Spanish colonists who were born here. The

Cajuns tended to be more rustic and agrarian, deriving their living from farming, fishing, and trapping while the Creoles tended to be more urbane, developing a cultured and sophisticated society. These differences are reflected in the two group's cuisines. Chef Paul Prudhomme hails from Opelousas, a small city in the heart of Cajun country. He is generally credited with bringing Cajun cuisine to New Orleans in the 1970s when he took over the kitchen at Commander's Palace. Not long after his tenure at Commander's Palace, Chef Prudhomme opened his signature restaurant, K-Paul's. During the day, K-Paul's offers a deli-style lunch. In the evening, dinner is a bit more upscale. The dishes here are full flavored and represent the very soul of Cajun cooking. **C**

Proceed along Chartres Street away from Canal to the next corner. Stop.

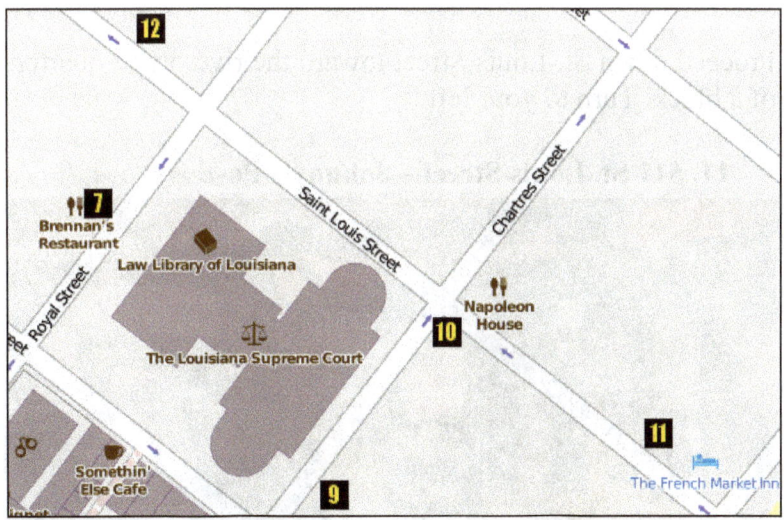

10. 500 Chartres Street—The Napoleon House

Here at the corner of St. Louis and Chartres is one of the most decrepitly beautiful buildings in all the French Quarter—the Napoleon House. Built around the time of the Louisiana Purchase in 1803, this home was owned by New

Orleans Mayor Nicholas Girod. When Napoleon Bonaparte was forced into exile, Girod offered the home to the emperor. Several businessmen in the city even devised a plot to sail for Europe in order to rescue Napoleon and bring him to New Orleans, but he died before the plan was realized. The name, however, stuck. Although the place opened as a bar in 1914, they've only been serving food for the last forty years or so. In its early decades, the Napoleon House was a popular gathering place for locals, including writers and artists. Today, the Napoleon House serves one of the best muffulettas in town along with other sandwiches and salads. The signature drink here is the Pimm's Cup, a gin-based cocktail made with muddled cucumber and lemon and soda. This is a great place to have an inexpensive lunch in a genuine French Quarter setting. On the downside, service tends to be less than great. **C**

Proceed down St. Louis Street toward the river three-quarters of a block. Turn to your left.

11. 511 St. Louis Street—Johnny's Po-Boys

Opened in 1950, Johnny's is the oldest family owned po-boy

shop in New Orleans. New Orleanians have very strong opinions about their po-boys, and if you ask ten different locals who has the best po-boys in town, you'll probably get ten different answers. But it's a safe bet that Johnny's will rank near the top of just about everybody's list. Here, you can find all the classic New Orleans' po-boys: shrimp, oyster, catfish, roast beef, etc. Each is done very well and the prices here are more than reasonable. The term po-boy itself dates back to 1929. In that year, there was a railroad worker's strike. Bennie and Clovis Martin, two brothers who operated a coffee and sandwich stand in the French Market, sympathized with the striking workers, having both been streetcar conductors years earlier. To show their support of the strike, they offered free sandwiches to striking workers. Whenever one approached for a free meal, they would say, "Look, here comes another poor boy." C

Proceed back up St. Louis Street past Chartres Street toward Royal Street. Cross Royal and proceed a quarter block. Turn to your right.

12. 713 St. Louis Street—Antoine's

Antoine's is the oldest family-run restaurant in America and the oldest restaurant in New Orleans (1840). It is a bastion of classic French cuisine with a strong Creole influence. But more than that, it is a symbol of old New Orleans Society. During its long reign as the *Grand Dame* of fine dining, Antoine's has become enmeshed within the cultural tapestry of the city. Presidents, popes, and countless celebrities have dined here, most of whose pictures adorn the main dining room. Many of the dining rooms in Antoine's are named and themed after the city's oldest Carnival krewes, including the Rex Room, which contains memorabilia such as scepters and crowns of former kings and queens of Carnival. Yet, another point of interest is the wine cellar, which boasts a capacity of 25,000 bottles when fully stocked. Founder Antoine

Alciatore's son Jules took the helm after his father died and was the creator of Oysters Rockefeller, one of the restaurant's several signature dishes. The venerable restaurant inspired Frances Parkinson Keyes' novel, *Dinner at Antoine's*. If you eat here (and even if you don't), it's well worth a good tip to ask for a tour of the cavernous facility. Reservations strongly required. Dress code is business casual. **C**

Walk along St. Louis Street away from the river a block and a half to Dauphine Street. Turn left and walk a quarter block. Look to your left.

13. 430 Dauphine Street—Bayona

Housed in a 200-year-old Creole cottage, Bayona is charming, elegant, understated, innovative—and the food is delicious. Owner / Chef Susan Spicer (is there any better name for a chef?) has won numerous awards from various culinary institutions and is an active community supporter, lending her name and talents to several local charities. If the weather is nice, ask to dine in the idyllic courtyard. Reservations strongly suggested. Dress code is business casual. **C**

Walk down Dauphine Street away from Canal Street one block to the corner of Dauphine and Toulouse Streets.

14. 827 Toulouse Street—Vacherie

Housed in the Hotel St. Marie and named after a small town along the Mississippi River in the heart of plantation country, Vacherie is a delightful venue offering a restaurant, bar, and café. Chef Jarred Zeringue grew up in Vacherie and his menu is inspired by the rustic, Cajun environs of his youth. The atmosphere, food, and prices are good. This is a great place for breakfast. For lighter fare or for a cup of good local Joe, try the café. The bar features skilled bartenders and an excellent wine list in addition to small plates that far surpass most bar food. Reservations for the formal dining room are suggested but not required. Dress code is casual. **C**

Walk along Toulouse Street toward the river a block and a half and look to your left.

15. 719 Toulouse Street—Little Vic's

This authentic rosticceria is owned by Vic Caracci, whose grandparents immigrated to New Orleans from Sicily. This casual eatery offers pitoni, arancini, pizza, and classic gelato, all made in house and from recipes used by Vic's grandparents back in the old country. The courtyard is stunning and is especially romantic at night. An interesting side note: novelist / journalist Roark Bradford acquired this home in 1928 and lived here through the 1930s and 1940s.

During that time, the home served as a meeting place for the city's literati, including William Faulkner and Sherwood Anderson. Little Vic's is open for breakfast, lunch, and dinner. Prices are among the lowest you will find in the French Quarter. The dress code is casual.

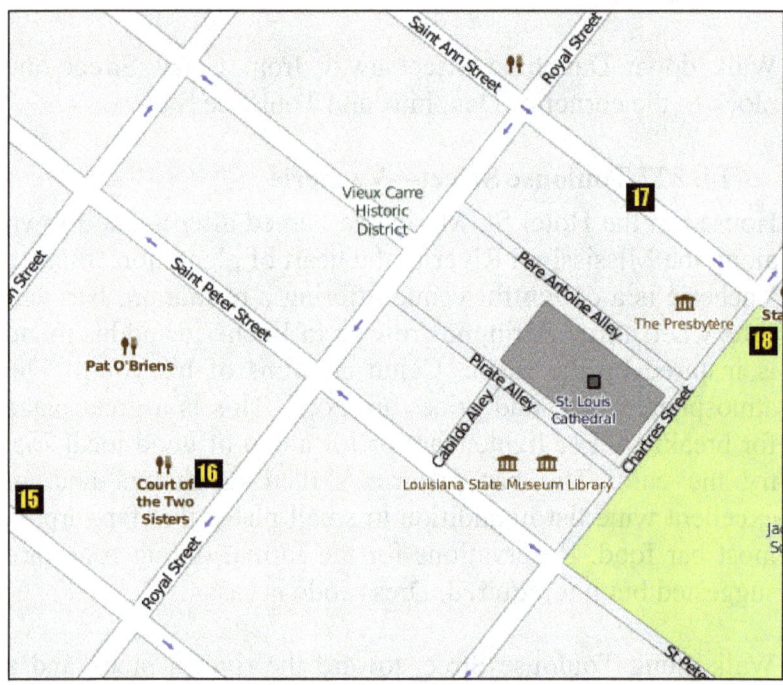

Walk to the corner and turn right on Royal Street. Walk half a block and look to your left.

16. 613 Royal Street—The Court of the Two Sisters

This site was once home of Sieur Etienne de Perier, French colonial governor of Louisiana from 1726-1733. Later, two sisters, Emma and Bertha Camors, opened a *rabais*—a shop that offered the women of Creole society gowns, lace, and other luxuries imported from Paris. The sisters died in 1944 and are buried in St. Louis Cemetery Number Three. Joe Fein opened the restaurant in the 1960s and today offers a daily jazz buffet. The place is touristy but it's not as bad as some locals claim. The big attraction at the Court of the Two Sisters is the courtyard, which is one of the largest in the city. The dress code is casual, though at night people tend to dress a little less casual. **C**

Walk down Royal Street away from Canal Street two blocks and turn right on St. Ann Street. Walk a quarter block and look to your right.

17. 638 St. Ann Street—The Crescent City Tour Booking Agency

This is an excellent place for information about the city and its attractions. Unlike most visitor centers, this booking agency is not owned by a specific tour company and offers unbiased recommendations. It also happens to be owned by the author of the book you now hold in your hands. Please feel free to pop in with any questions or just to say hello. **G**

Walk along St. Ann Street toward the river to the next corner. Look to your left.

18. 801 Chartres Street—Muriel's

On the corner of St. Ann and Chartres Streets, on the edge of Jackson Square, is Muriel's Restaurant. Muriel's offers fresh local ingredients prepared with classic Creole cooking techniques. The food here is very good and the prices are reasonable, especially considering the restaurant's prime location. This Victorian Italianate building dates to the early 1890s and was originally a pasta factory. According to legend, an earlier structure on this site was constructed after the great fire of 1788 by Pierre Antoine Lepardi Jourdan as his dream home. According to local lore, he and his family enjoyed the home for several years until he wagered—and lost—the house in a poker game in 1814. The thought of moving out of his home was too much to bear and Pierre committed suicide in the upstairs slave quarter. His ghost is still widely believed to reside in the building. Restaurant personnel as well as patrons have reported paranormal phenomenon for years. The room where he killed himself is now the Séance Lounge and the staff always leaves an empty table eternally reserved for Monsieur Jourdan. Reservations strongly suggested. Dress code is business casual. **C, H**

Walk one block along St. Ann Street toward the river along the edge of Jackson Square.

19. 800 Decatur Street—Café du Monde

Café du Monde purports to be the oldest continually operating coffee stand in the U. S. The only food item on the menu is beignets—deep fried doughnuts covered in powdered sugar. The coffee is infused with chicory, which serves as an additional stimulant to the caffeine. Be aware that the wait to get a table can be as long as an hour during weekend mornings or when the city hosts big events. Don't miss the small window on the backside of the building facing the river. There, you can see the dough being rolled, cut, and tossed in the vat of hot grease. Café du Monde is open 24 hours a day. Dress code is casual. **G, C**

Walk down Decatur Street away from Canal Street half a block. Look to your left.

20. 823 Decatur Street—Tujague's

Tujague's is the second oldest restaurant in New Orleans and a local institution. In 1856, Guillaume Tujague, an immigrant from Bordeaux, France, and a butcher at the French Market, opened the restaurant with his wife, Marie Abadie. Catering to the dockworkers and market vendors across the street, the place was an instant hit. The legendary Madame Begue (the city's first celebrity chef) also had a restaurant next door, which became subsumed into Tujague's in 1914. Throughout its long history, the menu has been a set six-course affair: Shrimp Remoulade, Soup du Jour, Beef Brisket, Entrée du Jour, Bread Pudding, and Coffee. In recent years, other entrees have been made available. Tujague's is open 365 days a year and is an excellent dining option on major holidays. The bar next door is also worth visiting and boasts other food options. The atmosphere at Tujagues is casual and decidedly "old-school." Having a meal here will give you a feel for what Creole dining was like in a grander age. Dress code is casual. **C**

Walk down Decatur Street away from Canal Street one block and look to your left.

21. 923 Decatur Street—Central Grocery

This small grocery was opened in 1906 by Salvatore Lupo, one of thousands of Sicilian immigrants who lived in the Quarter at the turn of the century. Central Grocery is important not only as an example of the numerous small groceries that dotted the Quarter in an earlier age, but also as being the birthplace of the muffaletta sandwich. Lupo created the sandwich for the Italian truck driver who delivered produce to the French Market. The sandwich consists of capicola, pepperoni, salami, ham, provolone and Swiss cheeses, and marinated olive salad. Muffalettas can be served hot or cold and are offered in quarters, halves, and wholes. C

Walk a block and a half down Decatur Street away from Canal Street and look to your left.

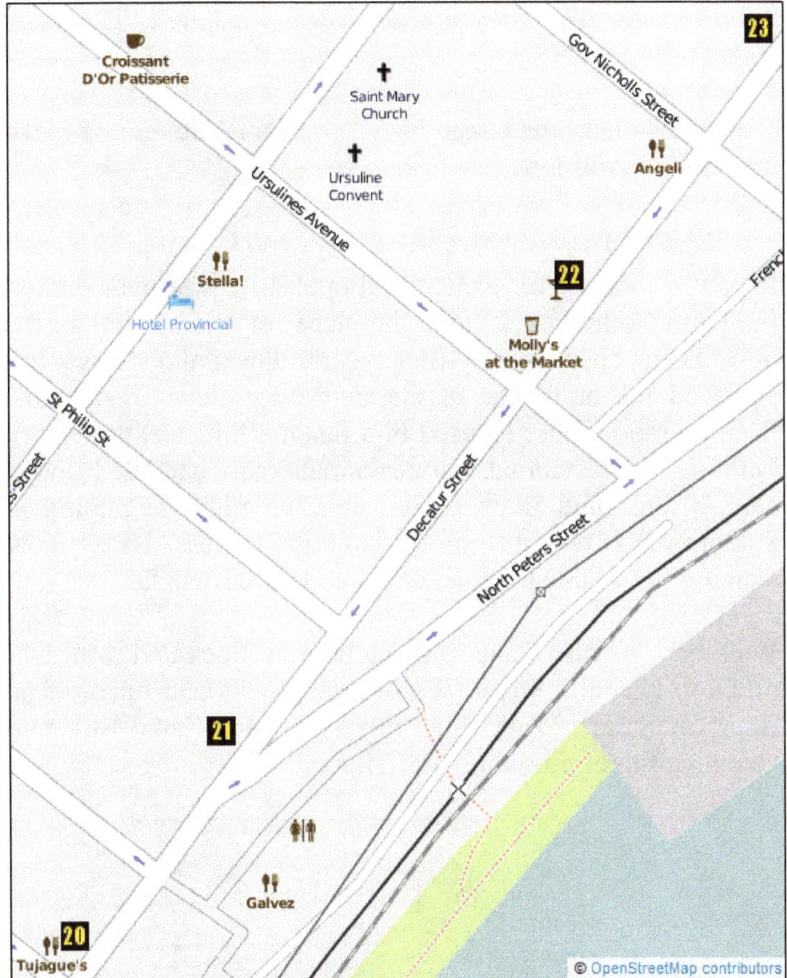

22. 1109 Decatur Street—Coop's Place

Although it's only been open thirty years, Coop's Place has earned a cult following of die-hard loyal locals and frequent visitors. The portions are generous, the prices are cheap, and the food is outstanding. The space is small and almost always crowded. They don't take reservations and there is often a line snaking out the door. The food is worth the wait. If you eat here, try the Smoked Duck Quesadillas and the Chicken Tchopitoulas. The fried chicken is also inspired. The dress code is casual. **C**

Walk down Decatur Street away from Canal Street one block and look to your left.

23. 1204 Decatur Street—Palm Court

If you're looking for some traditional, live jazz over dinner, the Palm Court Jazz Café is the place for you. Although it's only been open twenty-four years, the Palm Court has achieved the ambience of classic New Orleans restaurants from a grander age. Housed in a restored nineteenth century building, the restaurant features a mahogany bar, tiled floors, ceiling fans, and live jazz music each night beginning at 8:00pm. It's not uncommon to find owner Nina Buck dancing from table to table. Dress code is casual. **C**

Walk back toward Canal Street a quarter block and turn right on Gov. Nicholls Street. Walk three blocks and turn left on Bourbon Street. Walk three blocks toward Canal Street to Dumaine Street. Look to your left.

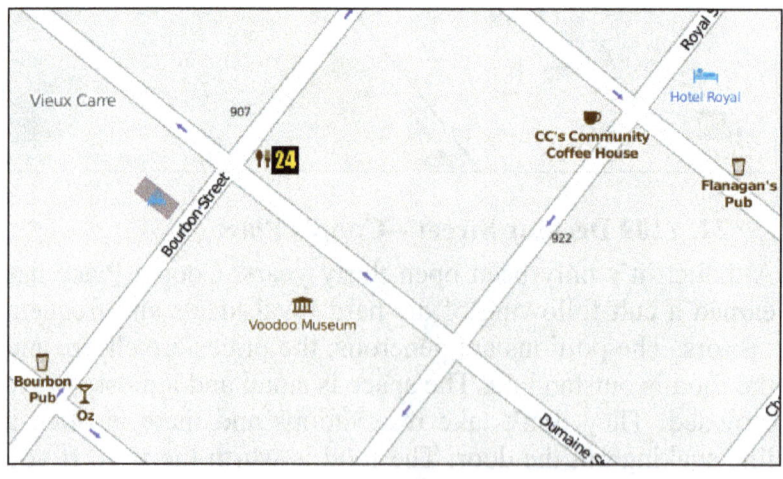

24. 900 Bourbon Street—Clover Grill

This classic diner is a longtime staple of Bourbon Street and the quintessential "greasy spoon." It's open twenty-four hours a day, 365 days a year, and is a perennial favorite among late-night revelers looking for cheap, not-so-healthy food to soak up the alcohol coursing through their veins. The staff is sassy and the vibe is energetic. A jukebox in the corner of this small space belts out everything from the Pet Shop Boys to Ethel Merman. The crowd is an even mix of local and tourist, straight and gay. The hamburgers are grilled under old hubcaps and the omelets are the fluffiest you'll ever find. The restaurant's motto: "We love to fry and it shows." Irreverent, quirky, and eclectic, the Clover Grill is pure New Orleans. The dress code is non-existent and during Mardi Gras and Southern Decadence, clothing, it seems, is optional. **C**

Walk along Dumaine Street away from the river one block to Dauphine Street. Look across the street to your left.

25. 900 Dumaine Street—Eat

Opened after Hurricane Katrina, Eat is a throwback to the vintage neighborhood cafes that used to permeate the French Quarter. The food here represents a key aspect of the New Orleans culinary scene: simple food done creatively well with a dash of sophistication. Local art hangs on the walls as light fills the small space. This contributes to a crisp, clean atmosphere. Eat is a wonderful place to escape the crowds at more well-known restaurants, although there is usually a waiting list for Sunday brunch. Reservations are accepted only for dinner. The dress code is casual. **C**

Walk down Dauphine Street away from Canal Street five blocks to the corner of Esplanade Avenue. Turn right and look to your right.

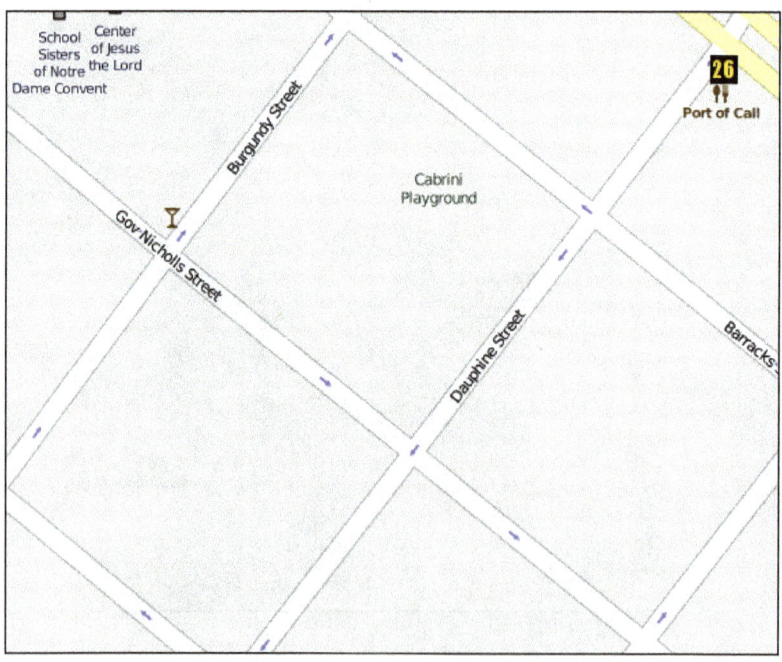

26. 838 Esplanade Avenue—Port of Call

Port of Call opened in 1963 and has since gained an extremely loyal cult-like following. This is essentially a bar that serves very good hamburgers. The menu is small—just hamburgers, a few cuts of steak, baked potatoes and salad—but the prices are more than reasonable and the atmosphere is vintage New Orleans. The place is very popular among locals and visitors alike and a wait to get in is not uncommon. Dress code is casual. **C**

27. Suggestions for Further Reading

Bienvenu, Marcelle., *et al. Stir the Pot: The History of Cajun Cuisine.* New York: Hippocrene Books, 2005.

Collin, Richard H. *The New Orleans Underground Gourmet.* New York: Simon and Schuster, 1970.

Fitzmorris, Tom. *Hungry Town.* New York: Stewart, Tabori, and Chang, 2010.

Roahen, Sara. *Gumbo Tales: Finding My Place at the New Orleans Table.* New York: W.W. Norton and Co., 2008.

Tucker, Susan, and S. Frederick Starr. *New Orleans Cuisine: Fourteen Signature Dishes and Their Histories.* University Press of Mississippi, 2009.

Gay Interest Walking Tour

"Apparently the French Quarter of New Orleans has an atmosphere which appeals to these people (homosexuals), *who are an undesirable element in our community."*
— Police Superintendent Provosty Dayries, 1958

Indeed it does. New Orleans has always been home to a thriving GLBTQ community. Drag performances on Mardi Gras date to 1729. Baron Ludwig Von Reizenstein, a German living in New Orleans in the 1850s, references the gay subculture of New Orleans at that time. A few years earlier, Walt Whitman spent some time in New Orleans working for a newspaper and writing homoerotic poetry about his experiences in the city. Male prostitutes for gay men abounded during the Storyville Era (1897-1917) and continue to work a handful of bars in the upper Quarter. Two prominent gay men of the first half of the twentieth century were Tony Jackson, an important early jazz pianist, and Lyle Saxon, a writer and French Quarter preservationist. Café Lafitte in Exile opened in 1933 and is the oldest gay bar in the city. Gay Carnival began in 1958 when the Krewe of Yuga presented their first ball, which was a satirical spoof on the older, main-line krewes. Several other gay krewes followed, although many would suffer declining membership during the AIDS crisis in the 1980s. Perhaps the most seminal moment in the history of gay New Orleans was the Upstairs Lounge fire in 1973. A disgruntled hustler who had been thrown out of the bar set in on fire and killed thirty-two people. This tragedy engendered several attempts at political activism but these were short-lived. Southern Decadence, held annually over the Labor Day weekend, was born in 1972 and eventually grew into one of the city's top five tourist

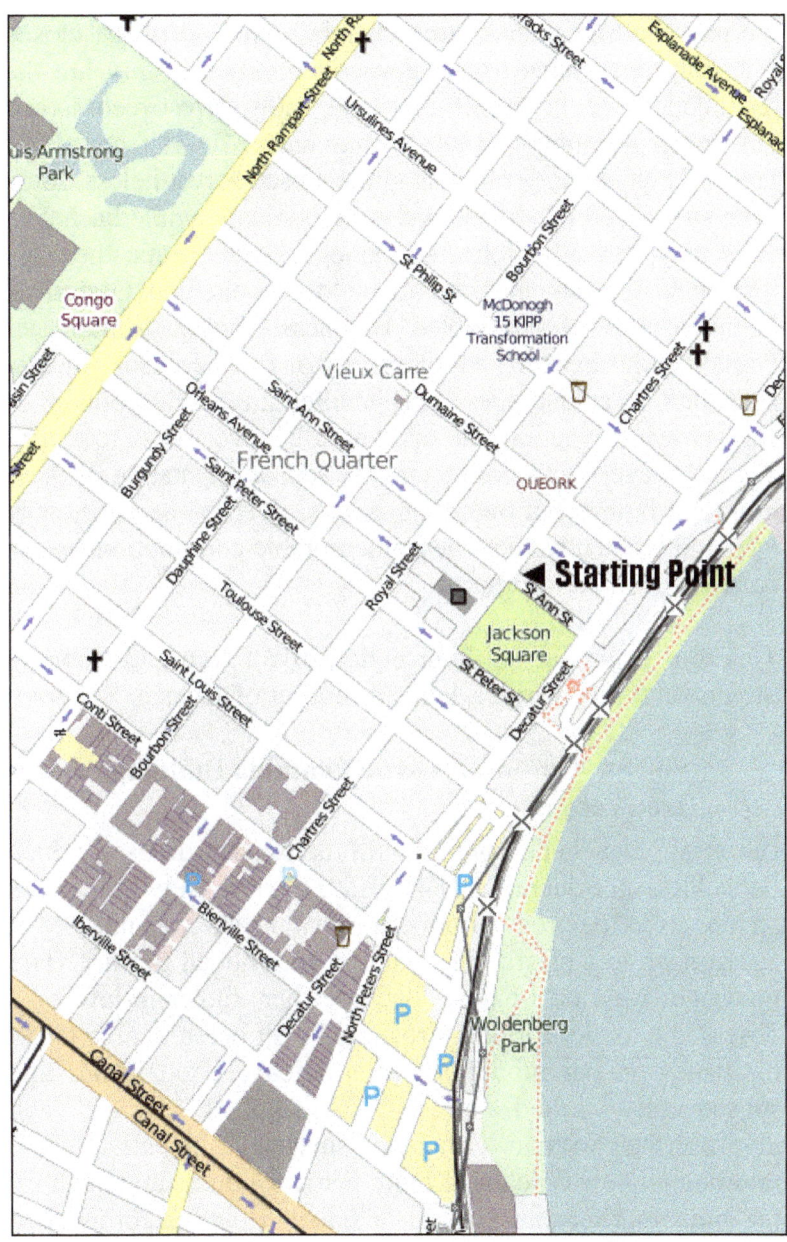

events of the year. The circuit party during Halloween also attracts thousands of gay tourists. From a historical perspective, the gay community has only recently come out of the closet. The only testaments to the gay community's history are the recollections of those still alive and, sadly, arrest records and newspaper accounts of raids on gay bars. Much, if not all, of the city's gay history remains in the closet. Nevertheless, some have speculated that some of the city's most eligible bachelors were gay, notably John McDonogh, who bequeathed his fortune to the city in order to build schools, and Gaston de Pontalba, son of the fabled Baroness Micaela Almonester Pontalba who built the row houses that flank Jackson Square. And then, of course, there is Bienville himself, the founder of New Orleans, who, despite his long life, never chose to marry. We may never know for certain the sexual orientation of these historical figures but one thing is sure; over the centuries, gay men and women have made immeasurable contributions to the cultural life of New Orleans.

This tour begins at the intersection of St. Ann and Chartres Streets on the downriver, lakeside corner of Jackson Square

1. 500 St. Ann Street—The Pontalba Building Ironwork

Baroness Micaela de Pontalb built the two row houses, which flank Jackson Square, in 1849-1850. Born in New Orleans as an heiress to the great Almonester fortune, she was married at age sixteen to Celestin de Pontalba and moved to Paris. Her marriage was not happy because her father-in-law was obsessed with her fortune. Frustrated over being unable to get his hands on her money, he shot Michaela four times and subsequently killed himself. Always a strong and domineering woman, Micaela survived the attack and returned to New Orleans to build her row houses and beautify the Square. Her son, Gaston, a sensitive and accomplished artist who historians conclude was probably gay, designed the AP monogram in the cast iron cartouche and probably designed the rest of the intricate lacework. The ironwork, which adorns the Pontalba galleries, set a trend and made elaborate cast iron balconies and galleries a common feature in the architecture of the French Quarter. **Q, A**

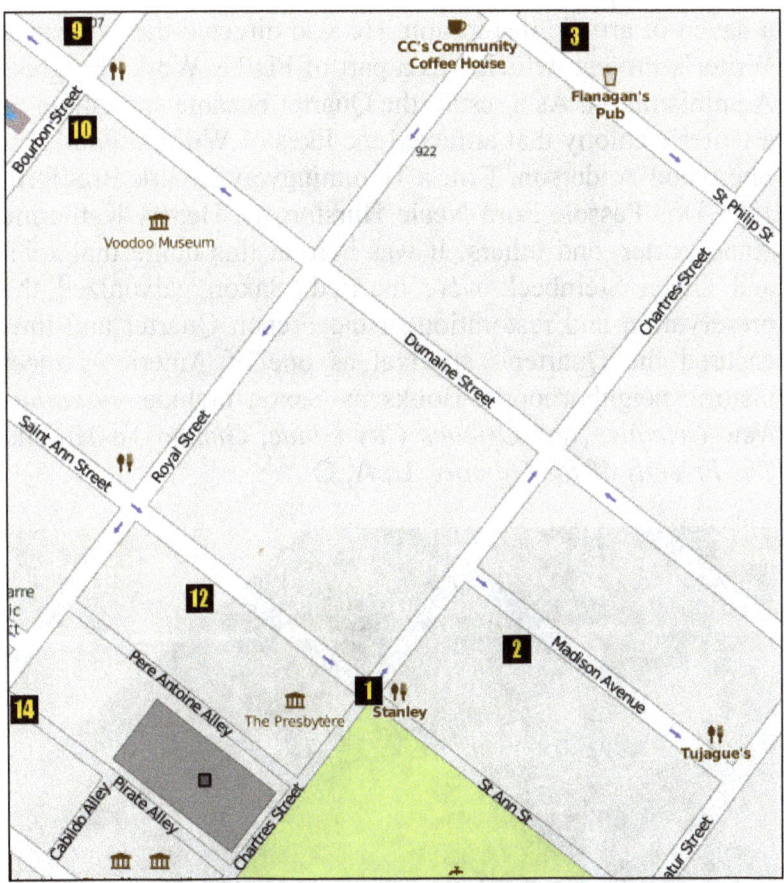

Walk half a block away from Canal Street and turn right onto Madison Street. Walk a quarter block and look to your right.

2. 536 Madison Street—Lyle Saxon's Home

Here is the home of Lyle Saxon, writer, French Quarter preservationist, and perhaps the most influential gay New Orleanian of the last century. By the early 1900s, the French

Quarter had deteriorated into a slum neighborhood consisting mostly of Sicilian immigrants. In the 1920s and 1930s, Lyle Saxon began restoring dilapidated homes in the French Quarter and promoting the area to other writers and artists as a haven of artistic inspiration. He also directed the Louisiana Writer's Project, which was a part of FDR's Works Progress Administration. As a result, the Quarter became something of a writer's colony that attracted the likes of William Faulkner, Sherwood Anderson, Ernest Hemmingway, Roark Bradford, John Dos Passos, Zora Neale Hurston, O. Henry, Katherine Anne Porter, and others. It was here at this home that John and Gwen Steinbeck were married. Saxon galvanized the preservation and restoration of the French Quarter and thus ensured the Quarter's survival as one of America's most historic neighborhoods. Books by Saxon include: *Fabulous New Orleans*, *New Orleans City Guide*, *Gumbo Ya-Ya*, and *The Friends of Joe Gilmore*. **L, A, Q**

Walk to Chartres Street and turn right. Walk a block and a half and turn left on St. Phillip Street. Walk down the block to the corner of Royal and St. Phillip Streets.

3. 721 St. Philip Street—McDonogh 15 School for the Creative Arts

This school is named after the nineteenth century philanthropist John McDonogh. Originally from Baltimore, McDonogh moved to New Orleans to earn a fortune in the shipping business. Upon his death, he bequeathed his fortune to New Orleans and Baltimore on the condition they build schools for poor children. For this reason, many schools in New Orleans bear his name. He also willed land holdings to the city, which eventually became a part of City Park. McDonogh never married and remained a lifelong bachelor and recluse. This has led some contemporary historians to speculate he may have been gay. **Q, G**

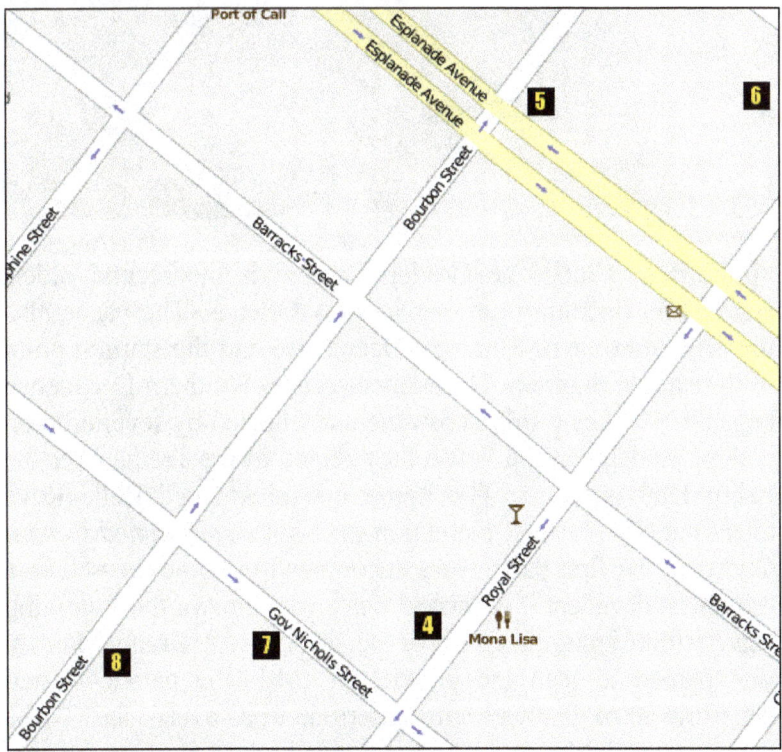

Walk three blocks down Royal Street away from Canal Street and look to your left.

4. 1239 Royal Street—The Golden Lantern / Southern Decadence

Founded in 1966, The Golden Lantern is the second oldest continually operating gay bar in New Orleans. The bar is also the official home of Southern Decadence and the starting point of the annual Southern Decadence parade. Southern Decadence began in 1972 as a small costume party hosted by several bored college students at the house they rented in the Tremé over the Labor Day weekend. The home was nicknamed Belle Reve after Blanche DuBois' plantation in *A Streetcar Named Desire*. Guests at the first party were encouraged to come dressed as a "southern decadent." A second party was thrown the following year, which inaugurated a parade. In 1974, a Grand Marshal was named to lead the parade. In 1981, the parade started departing from The Golden Lantern and has ever since. To be named Grand Marshal is one of the highest honors the gay community can bestow upon an individual. Southern

Decadence has grown in popularity over the last four decades and now draws over 120,000 people to New Orleans each Labor Day weekend. Since 1996, when records began to be kept, the festival's economic impact upon the city is estimated at 1.1 billion dollars. **Q, V**

Walk one block away from Canal Street and turn left on Esplanade Avenue. Walk one block to Bourbon Street and stop. Look across Esplanade Avenue at the house on the corner.

5. 741 Esplanade Avenue—Storyville and Tony Jackson

In the late 1800s, this was the home of City Alderman Sidney Story. It was Story who proposed the creation of a red-light district to confine prostitution to one area. Storyville lasted from 1897 to 1917 and was located not far from here behind the French Quarter closer to Canal Street. Storyville featured opulent mansion bordellos as well as shabby rooms, which could be rented for 50 cents. Some of the bordellos were owned by lesbians and some even offered live lesbian sex acts. The larger bordellos featured live music and the district as a whole served as an incubator for an infant form of jazz. Despite the heterosexual atmosphere of Storyville, Tony Jackson, who lived openly as a gay man, was one of the district's most popular musicians. Jackson's piano-playing style was dynamic and mesmerizing. One of his signature moves was to do a high stepping "cake-walk" while pounding the keys. He also dressed to the nines, usually wearing an ascot tie and a diamond pin. Jackson's impeccable sartorial style set the standard for other performers. In addition to being an amazing pianist, he also composed and sang. His repertoire included ragtime, early jazz, pop, opera, blues, and some classics. His musical genius, incredible versatility, electric style and theatrical performances earned him the praise of his fellow musicians. Jelly Roll Morton called Jackson "the outstanding favorite" musician of New Orleans and jazz great Clarence Williams said, "We all copied

Tony." Similar testimonials also came from Johnny St. Cyr, Bunk Johnson, and Baby Dodds, all significant figures in the early development of New Orleans jazz. **Q, M, V**

The neighborhood across Esplanade Avenue is the subject of the next entry.

6. The Marigny

The Faubourg Marigny is the neighborhood adjacent to the French Quarter (downriver) and is the closest thing to a "gayborhood" in New Orleans. The gay gentrification of the Marigny took place in the 1970s and 1980s. In addition to a high number of gay residents, the neighborhood is also replete with gay-owned businesses, including bars, restaurants, bed & breakfasts, and Faubourg Marigny Arts and Books—the South's oldest gay- and lesbian-themed bookstore. The area is named after Bernard de Marigny, whose family once owned a plantation on the site. Marigny was a colorful politician who spent his long life in public service. The Marigny is also home to Frenchmen Street, one of the hottest live music venues in the city. **Q, G, A, V**

Walk up Bourbon Street toward Canal Street and turn left on Gov. Nicholls. Walk a half block and look to your right.

7. 716 Gov. Nicholls Street—Clay Shaw

The property here was restored by Clay Shaw, one of the most notable gay men in New Orleans history. Shaw's preservation efforts in the French Quarter (recognized here by the historical marker before you) have been overshadowed by the fact he was the only man ever charged and brought to trial in the John F. Kennedy assassination. Jim Garrison, the District Attorney who charged Shaw, is widely believed to have been a closeted gay man. Although he was found not guilty of conspiring to assassinate the president, having been the only person ever charged in the assassination has largely eclipsed Shaw's positive legacy as a war hero, successful businessman, French Quarter preservationist, and accomplished playwright. Like Lyle Saxon, Shaw also had a lifelong interest in literature and co-authored (with Herman S. Cottman) four plays: *Submerged* (1929), *A Message from Khufu* (1931), *The Cuckoo's Nest* (1936), and *Stokers* (1938).

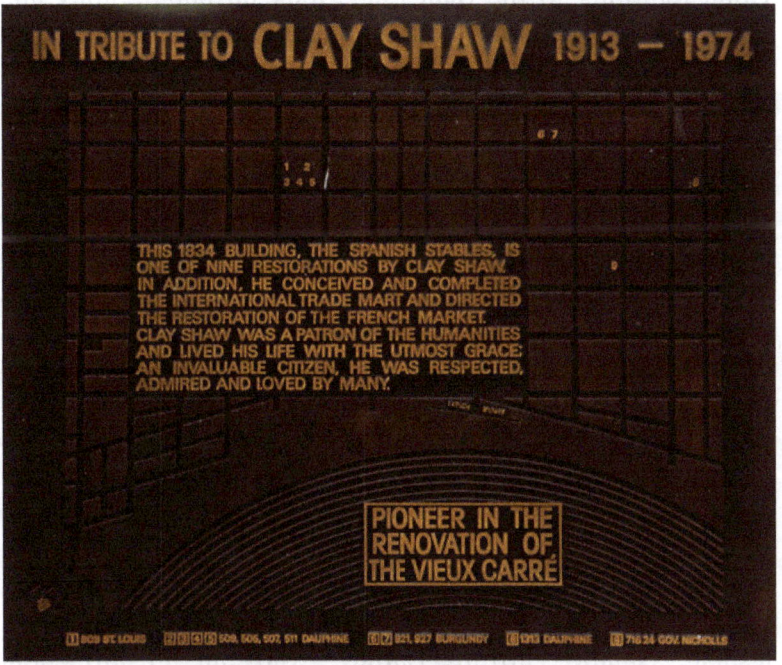

In an excellent literary analysis of Shaw's dramatic works, scholar Michael Snyder notes that all four plays contain strong undercurrents of homoeroticism and often feature "sweaty, muscular men closed together in tight spaces." Shaw's plays have been performed at little theatres across the nation, especially *Submerged*, which was for decades a favorite among high school drama clubs not only because of its quality but also perhaps because Shaw and Cottman wrote it while classmates at Warren Easton High School. **Q, G, L**

Walk back to Bourbon Street and turn left. Walk half a block and look to your left.

8. 1132 Bourbon St.—Frances Benjamin Johnston House

Born in the Victorian era during the Civil War, Johnston grew up in Washington, DC, before studying art in Paris. Upon returning to the States, she took up photography and blazed a trail in that (then) young field for other lesbian photographers such as Clara Sipprell, Alice Austin, and later, Annie Leibovitz. Johnston quickly became one of the country's first female photojournalists before opening her own studio to focus on portraiture. In addition to focusing on female nudes, something quite extraordinary for the time, she also began photographing celebrities, politicians, and members of Washington society. She photographed five U.S. presidents and Theodore Roosevelt named her the first official White House photographer. She then turned her lens to gardens and estates before embarking on a remarkable project to document Southern architecture pictorially. She also documented the lives of factory workers and African American students in the South, most notably the Tuskegee Institute in Alabama. The images in your head when you think of Mark Twain or Susan B. Anthony are likely hers, literally. She also took a memorable photograph of famed lesbian, Natalie Clifford Barney, who ran an influential literary salon in Paris for nearly 60 years. Johnston first photographed New Orleans in 1938, and like any photographer would, she fell in love with the city. Always a strong-willed, independent woman, with a disdain for staid traditions and conventional morality, the bohemian vibe of the Quarter appealed to her, and in 1940, she rented an apartment at 812 Dauphine Street where she lived five years before renting another apartment at 929 Dumaine Street. Shortly thereafter, she purchased a home at 1132 Bourbon Street. Johnston renovated the place and rented out the second and third floors as well as the slave quarters, while retaining the first floor as her residence and studio / darkroom. She called the place "Arkady." In 1951, Johnston purchased a second home at 1438 Euterpe Street but remained living in the Quarter. Johnston spent her time in the Quarter working, drinking, smoking, and socializing with friends. **G, Q**

Walk up Bourbon Street toward Canal Street two and half blocks. Stop at Dumaine Street and look to your right.

9. 901 Bourbon St.—Café Lafitte in Exile

Café Lafitte in Exile is the oldest gay bar in New Orleans and arguably the oldest continually operating gay bar in North America. Founded in 1933, the bar was originally located down the street where Lafitte's Blacksmith Shop now is. Back then, gay bars as we know them now did not exist as homosexuality was illegal, but the owners of Café Lafitte were open-minded and welcomed their gay clientele. The bar was as gay friendly as the times would permit. In 1953, the building came under a new owner who did not want gay people in the bar. The bar owners signed a lease on a new place and called it Café Lafitte in Exile, the "In Exile" referring to the regular patron's status as being "in exile" from their former bar home. According to legend, on the night the bar opened, several regulars from the old bar went there to have one drink and then picked up their barstools and marched down the street to the new bar. Tennessee Williams was a regular at this bar when he lived in New Orleans. By the 1960s, the bar had a notorious reputation as a cruise bar; that is, a place for gay men to have anonymous sex. Because of this notoriety, the U.S. Navy sent a letter to the bar declaring it off limits to personnel of the U.S. Armed Forces. The letter is on permanent and proud display on the wall just inside the front door. **Q, V, L**

Walk up Bourbon Street toward Canal Street half a block and look to your left.

10. 828 Bourbon Street—The Ambush Mansion

The home at 828 Bourbon Street was built by Jean Florent Durel after his purchase of the property in 1831. In 1987, *Ambush Magazine* set up shop on the first floor. Publishers Rip & Marsha Naquin-Delain, made the second and third floors their private residence. The couple opens the Ambush Mansion once a year for their famous King Cake Queen Coronation, a lavish soiree, before the King Cake Queen leads the "official" Gay Mardi Gras Bead Toss from the most famous Bourbon Street balcony. Over Labor Day weekend, the Ambush Mansion Balcony is the setting for the "official" Southern Decadence Bead Toss led by reigning Southern Decadence Grand Marshals following their parade on Sunday tossing thousands of throws to the crowds below. The rest of the year, the South's oldest surviving GLBT publication is produced here. **Q, V, A**

Walk half a block up Bourbon Street toward Canal Street. Stop at the corner of St. Ann Street.

11. Bourbon and St. Ann Streets—The Bourbon Street Awards and Gay Carnival

This intersection is the site of a popular feature of gay Carnival in New Orleans: the Bourbon Street Awards, which is a contest featuring elaborate Carnival costumes. In 1964, the owner of the Clover Grill wanted to drum up business for his diner and inaugurated a Mardi Gras costume contest. This event evolved into the extravaganza it is today. Over the years, the Bourbon Street Awards has garnered the attention of the international media. The modern incarnation of gay Carnival began in 1958 when Doug Jones and a group of his friends formed the Krewe of Yuga (KY) as a spoof of the mainstream krewes. The first four KY "balls" were held in private homes until the growth of the krewe and its ball's popularity necessitated a larger meeting space. One of the members worked at a school in Metairie and suggested they use the school cafeteria as the location of their fifth ball masque. On the night of the ball, the Metairie suburbanites became somewhat alarmed when they noticed dozens of gay men streaming into the school. The Jefferson Parish Sheriff's office was notified and just as the ball got underway, the police arrived and raided the event. Fearing arrest and the subsequent public outing that accompanied such raids, several men ran out of the building and hid in the woods behind the school. Of the mayhem, Armeinius historian Albert Carey writes, "One story has the Queen hiding in these bushes as the troopers came through with their flashlights. Sparkling in the high beams of light, his rhinestone tiara gave him away." After the raid, Miss Dixie, legendary owner of Dixie's Bar of Music, hired an attorney for all those arrested and paid many of the jailed men's bail. The next day's newspaper published the names of nearly 100 men arrested in the raid. The Krewe of Yuga folded as a result of the ensuing scandal. Other gay krewes were formed in subsequent years. Today, there are six gay Carnival Krewes in New Orleans. **Q, V**

Walk along St. Ann Street one block toward the river. Cross Royal Street and look to your right.

12. 638 St. Ann Street—The Crescent City Tour Booking Agency

This is an excellent place for information about the city and its attractions. Unlike most visitor centers, this booking agency is not owned by a specific tour company and offers unbiased recommendations. It also happens to be owned by the author of the book you now hold in your hands. Please feel free to pop in with any questions or just to say hello. **G**

Walk a quarter block away from the river to Royal Street and turn left. Walk three-quarters of a block and look to your right.

13. 711 Royal St.—Truman Capote

New Orleans native and best-selling author Truman Capote lived here in 1945 while he was writing *Other Voices, Other Rooms*—a coming of age story about a young man coming to terms with his homosexuality. Many of Capote's works are American literary classics including *Breakfast at Tiffany's* and *In Cold Blood*. Capote spent the first four years of his life in New Orleans before moving to Alabama and later New York. After establishing himself as an author, Capote returned to New Orleans often and was a regular at Café Lafitte in Exile whenever he was in town. **Q, L**

Walk into the alley next to the garden behind the church.

14. Pirate's Alley—The Murder of Fernando Rios

In 1958, Fernando Rios was savagely attacked and murdered by three homophobes in this alley. It was September and the fall semester at colleges and universities was underway. At that time, a common recreational activity among fraternity brothers at college campuses across the nation was to "roll a queer." This homophobic ritual essentially consisted of two to five fraternity brothers going to the "gay" section of town, or a gay bar if the town had one, and beating up someone they perceived to be gay. In New Orleans, that meant the French Quarter and Café Lafitte in Exile, the oldest gay bar in the city. And so, one night, three fraternity brothers from Tulane University (John Farrell, Alberto A. Calvo, and David P. Drennan) decided to "roll a queer." The three homophobes went to the Quarter in search of a victim. Farrell went to Café Lafitte in Exile about 1:30 in the morning and settled on Fernando Rios, a twenty-six-year-old tour guide visiting from Mexico. The two sat next to each other in the bar and chatted for a while before they decided to leave together. As Rios and Farrell were walking back to Rios' hotel, they entered Pirate's Alley, where Calvo and Drennan were lying in wait. The three undergrads then attacked Rios, beating him repeatedly in the head and kicking him in the stomach several times. After the attack, the three gay bashers returned to campus bragging about the assault and showing off Rios' wallet, which they had stolen. Rios, barely conscious and unable to move, was not discovered until the next morning. His face bloody and swollen, he was rushed to Charity Hospital where he died. During a routine autopsy, the city coroner discovered Rios had an unusually thin cranium and this revelation played a key factor in the subsequent murder trial. Farrell, Calvo, and Drennan were arrested and went to trial on murder charges on January 21, 1959. The defendants admitted to the beating but argued he died because of his "eggshell cranium," not because of their attack. Tortured logic aside, this defense made perfect sense to a homophobic, all male, all white jury in 1959 and the three students were easily acquitted by the jury after deliberating a mere two hours and fifteen minutes. **Q**

Walk along the alley toward the river and turn right into the intersecting alley. Walk half a block to St. Peter Street. Stop and look across the street to your right.

15. 632 St. Peter St.—Tennessee Williams

Preeminent American playwright Tennessee Williams lived here when he wrote his masterpiece, *A Streetcar Named Desire*. From his writing room on the third floor, Williams could hear the Desire streetcar as it rumbled down Royal Street. Williams also lived at 722 Toulouse, 710 Orleans, and 1014 Dumaine. He was a regular at several gay bars, especially Café Lafitte in Exile, and he loved to dine at Marti's—a favorite eatery among gay Quarterites in the 1970s. In the French Quarter, Williams found a certain freedom that eluded him elsewhere. Upon first arriving in New Orleans, he wrote in his journal that the "town is wide open" and "Here, surely, is the place I was made for." He would eventually call New Orleans his "spiritual home." Such a libertine environment allowed Williams' genius to flourish. **L, Q**

Walk along St Peter Street away from the river for a block and a half. Stop at Bourbon Street and look across the street.

16. 701 Bourbon St.—Dixie's Bar of Music

Dixie's Bar of Music moved to this location in 1949 from its previous location on St. Charles Avenue and quickly became one of the trendiest bars on Bourbon Street. Dixie Fasnacht, whose last name means Mardi Gras in German, was something of a minor legend in the history of jazz. An accomplished clarinetist, she traveled in the 1930s with several all-girl bands including *The Harmony Maids, The Smart Set, Sophisticate of Swing,* and *The Southland Rhythm Girls.* Although she didn't advertise it as such, Dixie's Bar of Music was essentially a gay bar. In the 1950s and 1960s, it was a common police practice to raid gay bars and arrest gay patrons. Miss Dixie could always be counted on to pay bail for the release of her customers. **M, V, Q**

Walk up Bourbon Street five blocks and turn left on Iberville Street. Walk two blocks toward the river and look to your right at the corner of Iberville and Chartres Streets.

17. 141 Chartres St.—The Upstairs Lounge Fire

At the corner of Chartres and Iberville Streets is a bar called Jimani's. In 1973, the second floor of the building housed a gay bar called the Upstairs Lounge. On Sunday evening, June 24, 1973, the deadliest crime against gays and lesbians in the history of the United States occurred here. On that night, an arsonist set the gay bar on fire, killing thirty-two people and injuring still more. Many people, then and now, mistakenly believe the fire was a hate crime motivated by homophobia.

It wasn't. Rather, the crime was motivated by anger and revenge. On that fateful evening, an unruly hustler, Rodger Dale Nunez, was thrown out of the bar for badgering and fighting with a regular customer, Mike Scarborough. Scarborough was in the bathroom when Nunez, who was in the next stall, started harassing him through the glory hole. Scarborough complained to the bartender. As he was being escorted out of the bar, Nunez threatened to "burn you all out." About thirty minutes later, a fire broke out on the stairwell. Then, the buzzer in the bar rang, which usually meant a cab had arrived. Luther Boggs, a regular at the lounge, opened the door to the stairwell to be greeted by roaring flames. As the fire spread, panic ensued. Bartender Buddy Rasmussen led about twenty people through a rear fire exit, which was not clearly marked. Many dashed for the windows, but the windows had burglar bars. A few were skinny enough to squeeze through, but the others were doomed. This event triggered the gay rights movement in New Orleans. The victims of the fire are listed on a sidewalk plaque in front of the stairwell. **Q**

Walk along Iberville Street two blocks to the Mississippi River.

18. Mississippi River at Iberville Street—Walt Whitman

One of the earliest known gay men to live in New Orleans was the great American poet Walt Whitman. Whitman arrived in the city in 1848 to work as a reporter for the *Crescent*, one of the city's several daily newspapers at the time. Although he lived only three months in New Orleans, the city profoundly influenced Whitman and his poetry. In his leisure time, Whitman was fond of perusing the French Market before cruising the riverfront where he delighted in meeting stevedores and longshoremen. The gay graybeard absorbed all the sensory imagery the city had to offer and later immortalized those images in much of his masterpiece, *Leaves of Grass*. The poem "I Saw in Louisiana a Live Oak" is a meditation on romantic male companionship and "Once I Pass'd Through a Populous City" is a poetic tribute to a male lover Whitman met in New Orleans (though the word "man" was changed to "woman" for publication). **Q, L**

19. Suggestions for Further Reading

Perez, Frank, and Jeffrey Palmquist. *In Exile: The History and Lore Surrounding New Orleans Gay Culture and Its Oldest Gay Bar.* LL-Publications. 2012.

Ghosts and Spirits Walking Tour

"Ghosts and pirates are as thick as the morning fog . . . The dead pass casually by."
— Andrei Codrescu

New Orleans is widely believed to be the most haunted city in America. This claim is easy to believe for anyone familiar with the city's history. From its inception, New Orleans has been plagued by constant floods, yellow fever and cholera epidemics, two massive fires, and a consistently high murder rate. From 1817 to 1905, over 41,000 people died from yellow fever. The 1853 outbreak was particularly deadly, claiming roughly 9,000 lives. In addition, the city has always been home to ne'er-do-wells, convicts, prostitutes, pirates, transients, and generally lost souls. Many paranormal researchers believe souls who struggled with addiction in life or who died unexpectedly have trouble passing over and remain earthbound. If that's true and if ghosts do indeed exist, it's probably safe to assume that nearly every building in the French Quarter is haunted. This presents a problem for not only ghost hunters but also for tour guides. What to include? At present, there are no less than ten different tour companies offering ghost tours in the French Quarter, some more focused on accuracy than others. The existence of ghosts and hauntings are nearly impossible to prove but the events that may have given rise to them are not. The scenes of death in the stops listed here have all been documented as actual historical events (with one notable exception). Some of the city's more fabled ghost stories are not included here because there is no historical evidence to support the alleged events that led to the supposed hauntings. These include the Sultan's Massacre, which never occurred. That myth developed out of a story about a date tree.

The date tree existed but it was not even located on the site where some tour guides discuss the fictitious Sultan. Another popular tale that has no basis in fact concerns a girl named Julie who supposedly died on a cold night sleeping naked on a roof to prove her love to her aristocratic Creole lover. If you take five guided ghost tours, you will notice she died on five different roofs. And then there is the false tale of the two Mafia murder trial witnesses who were gunned down in court and now haunt the Supreme Court building. No such trial ever occurred, and even if it did, the Supreme Court building never housed criminal trials. One of the most enduring haunted myths in the city revolves around Vampires and the Casket Girls. The story goes that France sent over young, suitable women for the male colonists to marry. Somehow, the Casket Girls smuggled vampires from Europe into New Orleans where they are kept locked up on the third floor of the Ursuline Convent on Chartres Street. Despite all the ghost legends, the old adage really is true: truth is stranger than fiction, especially in New Orleans. In the 1990s, the International Society for Paranormal Research conducted a six-year study of New Orleans and concluded that New Orleans is indeed haunted.

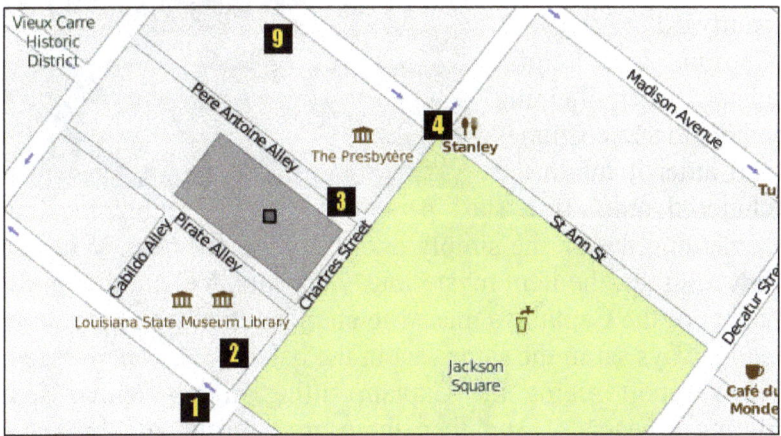

This tour starts at the corner of St. Peter and Chartres Streets on the upriver, lakeside corner of Jackson Square.

1. 616 St. Peter Street—Le Petit Theatre

On the corner of the Square, at the corner of St. Peter and Chartres Streets is Le Petit Theatre. In 1916, a group of local theatre lovers began producing plays in the drawing room of one of its members. Audiences grew and the Drawing Room

Players began renting space in the lower Pontalba Building before opening Le Petit in 1919. Like many theatres, Le Petit plays host to many ghosts. In the late 1920s, an actress named Caroline was walking with her director on the balcony when she tripped, stumbled, and fell to her death in the courtyard below. Caroline is a helpful ghost, often helping others locate costumes and other items in the cluttered attic. If a staff person is having trouble locating something, he or she simply asks Caroline for help. Within a few minutes, the item mysteriously appears. Yet another ghost is that of the Captain, a man who attended the theatre regularly and always sat in the same seat in the balcony. Actors in recent years report seeing the Captain sitting in his regular spot during rehearsals. And then there are a group of children's ghosts who reportedly frolic throughout the theatre much to the chagrin of staffers. **A, SC, H**

Look across St. Peter Street.

2. 701 Chartres Street—The Cabildo

The building to the left of the cathedral is the Cabildo, which was built under Spanish colonial rule and completed in 1799. The building is named after the Spanish governing council.

The building is where the Louisiana Purchase transfer was signed, a transaction that doubled the size of the United States. Throughout the nineteenth century, the Cabildo functioned as the City Hall, a courthouse, and a prison. The Cabildo is believed to be haunted by a number of ghosts, the most common of which is a British soldier who was imprisoned and hung here as a spy during the War of 1812. His apparition, that of a man wearing a tattered soldier's uniform, typically appears in the early morning, a phenomenon that leads some ghost hunters to speculate he was executed at sunrise. Other paranormal activity include shoulder taps by people who are not there, chairs rocking with no one sitting in them, and a sense among the living that someone is rushing past them. In 1908, the Cabildo became a part of the Louisiana State Museum and today features an excellent collection of early Louisiana history and an exhibit on Louisiana's contributions to rock-n-roll music. Open Tuesday through Sunday, 10:00 a.m. to 4:30 p.m. **G, SC, H**

Walk toward the cathedral and look into the alley between the church and the Cabildo.

3. 700 Block of Chartres Street—Pirate's Alley and Père Antoine's Alley—Father Dagobert

In 1766, the first governor of Spanish colonial Louisiana, Don Antonio de Ulloa, arrived in New Orleans and was greeted by fierce opposition by French loyalists who were none too happy about their king, Louis XV, ceding Louisiana to his cousin Charles III of Spain in the Treaty of Fontainebleau. Several prominent citizens conspired to reclaim French rule and de Ulloa was forced to flee the city for Cuba. The Spanish Crown was not pleased with the insurrection and dispatched a rough and tough Irish mercenary to reclaim Louisiana. Don Alejandro O'Reilly arrived in New Orleans on the night of August 16, 1769, with a flotilla from the Spanish fleet. O' Reilly took control of the city and promptly executed several leaders of the insurrection. Instead of burying the bodies, O'Reilly left the corpses exposed to rot in the sun as a warning to other French sympathizers (some say he left the bodies in front of the cathedral; other reports suggest they were left on the levee across Jackson Square). Father Dagobert, a Capuchin monk, was horrified at this act of cruelty and secretly gathered the deceased's family members for a nocturnal mass and proper burial. During the ceremony, Father Dagobert sang "Kyrie Eleison." According to ghost hunters and more than a few tourists, on rainy evenings, Father Dagobert can still be heard singing in the alleys that line the cathedral, his voice echoing between the church and the Cabildo and Presbytere as he reenacts his solemn act of defiance against "Bloody O'Reilly." **H, G, SC**

Walk to the corner of the Square where Chartres and St. Ann Streets intersect.

4. 801 Chartres Street—Muriel's Restaurant / Pierre Jourdan's Ghost

On the corner of St. Ann and Chartres Streets, on the edge of Jackson Square, is Muriel's Restaurant. This Victorian Italinate building dates to the early 1890s but, according to legend, an earlier structure was constructed after the great fire of 1788 by Pierre Antoine Lepardi Jourdan as his dream home. He and his family enjoyed the home for several years until, according to local lore, he wagered—and lost—the house in a poker game in 1814. The thought of moving out of his home was too much to bear and Pierre committed suicide in the upstairs slave quarter. The story is probably an urban myth for notarial records indicate Jourdan sold the home to Julien Poydras in 1824. Nevertheless, Jourdan's ghost is widely believed to reside in the building still. Restaurant personnel as well as patrons have reported paranormal phenomenon for years. The room where he supposedly killed himself is now the Séance Lounge and the staff always leaves an empty table eternally reserved for Monsieur Jourdan. **C, H**

Walk down Chartres Street away from Canal Street three and a quarter blocks. Look to your left.

5. 1113 Chartres Street—The Beauregard-Keyes House

This home was built in 1826 and is named for two of its most famous residents—Confederate General Pierre Gustave Toutant Beauregard and writer Frances Parkinson Keyes. Beauregard gave the order to fire the first shot on Fort Sumter in South Carolina, thus beginning the U.S. Civil War. Keyes authored a number of books, including *Dinner at Antoine's*. General Beauregard's ghost is said to haunt the home, sometimes appearing in full Confederate uniform dancing with a woman, presumably his wife who died while the general was off fighting the Civil War. Gunfire has also been heard in the house but some speculate that these shots are not the echoes of warfare but rather the reenactment of a grisly murder that occurred in the house in 1908. At that time, an Italian businessman named Pietro Giancona lived there and had a deadly confrontation with the local Mafia, who was trying to extort him. One evening, Pietro invited four Mafioso to his home for dinner and to discuss their demands. After they were seated, Pietro and his son opened fire and shot all four, three of whom died immediately. The house is also believed to be haunted by novelist Frances Parkinson Keyes, who died here in 1971, as well as by her dog, Lucky, who died a few weeks after Keyes. Tour guides have also reported a ghost cat named Caroline that rubs their legs during guided tours. Tours of the home are available Monday through Saturday, 10:00 a.m. to 3:00 p.m. **H, L, G, V**

Walk one block away from Canal Street to Gov. Nicholls Street and turn left. Walk one block to the corner of Royal Street and look to your left.

6. 1140 Royal Street—The LaLaurie Mansion

On the corner of Royal and Gov. Nicholls Streets is supposedly the most haunted site in all New Orleans—the

LaLaurie Mansion. The home you see now was built in 1837 after a fire destroyed the former structure. According to legend, Madame LaLaurie was a cruel mistress and once chased a slave girl with a whip until the poor girl fell off the balcony to her death. Because of this and other alleged horrors Madame LaLaurie inflicted upon her slaves, a slave woman in charge of the kitchen decided she would rather die than serve the sadistic family any longer and set fire to the house. The myth holds that when the local citizenry responded, they discovered a number of slaves shackled in their quarters with chains. A scandal ensued and the LaLauries fled the city for France as a mob ransacked the mansion. Over decades of fanciful storytelling based on the yellow journalism of the time, a myth has developed that the LaLauries had a torture chamber where they conducted medical experiments on their slaves. Hence, the widespread belief that the spirits of the tortured slaves haunt the house. **G, A, H**

Walk up Royal Street two blocks and turn right on St. Phillip Street. Walk one block to Bourbon and look across the street to your right.

7. 1003 Bourbon Street—Lafitte Guest House

This hotel is just one of dozens in New Orleans that purports to be haunted. The lot, which was once owned by the famed pirate brothers, Jean and Pierre Lafitte (or perhaps Pierre's girlfriend) was also the site of a hospital. The spirit of a little girl named Marie who died of yellow fever in 1853 is widely believed to be trapped in a mirror at the end of a hallway on the second floor. Marie is believed to be the daughter of the home's owners in the 1850s, Paul Joseph Gleises and his wife, Marie Odalie Ducayet. Marie sometimes appears in the mirror as following behind guests but is never there when the guests turn around to see her. She is also reported to appear to other children her age, usually lost and crying. **H**

Walk along St. Phillip Street toward the river one block and turn right on Royal Street. Walk three-quarters of a block and look to your right.

8. 919 Royal Street—The Andrew Jackson Hotel

In the eighteenth century, a boarding school for boys stood on this site. In 1794, the school burned down, killing several children in the process. The ghosts of the dead boys still roam the grounds and the hallways of the hotel often causing guests to complain about noise and raucous behavior—even when no children are registered at the hotel. Before the age of digital cameras, a couple staying at the hotel went to bed with two exposures left on their film camera. When they returned home and had the film developed, the last two pictures were of them sleeping in their hotel room. The ghost of Andrew Jackson is also said to haunt this site. After the boarding school fire, a courthouse was constructed here and Andrew Jackson himself was a defendant here in 1815 when he was charged with contempt of court and obstruction of justice. **H**

Walk along Royal Street toward Canal Street one block to St. Ann Street and turn left. Look to your right.

9. 638 St. Ann Street—The Crescent City Tour Booking Agency

This is an excellent place for information about the city and its attractions. Unlike most visitor centers, this booking agency is not owned by a specific tour company and offers unbiased recommendations. It also happens to be owned by the author of the book you now hold in your hands. Please feel free to pop in with any questions or just to say hello. **G**

Walk up Royal Street toward Canal Street two blocks and turn left on Toulouse Street. Walk a block and a half and look to your right.

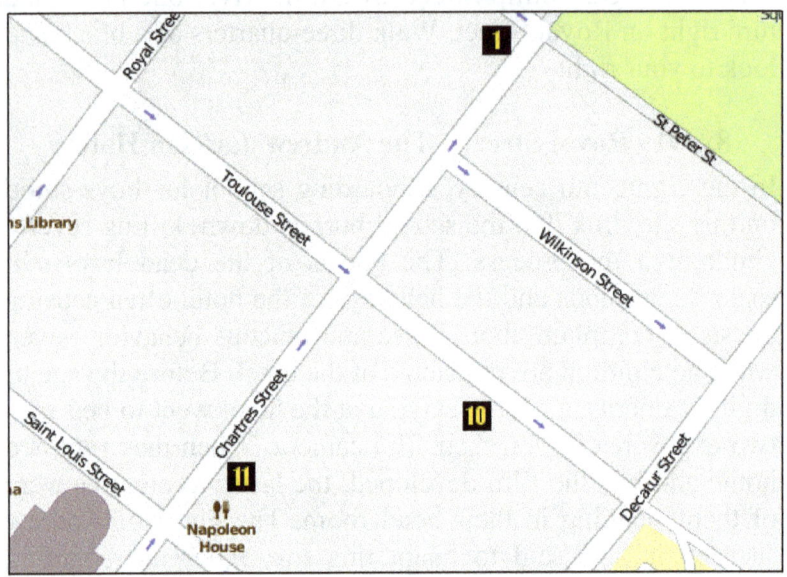

10. 508 Toulouse Street—Haunted Love Triangle

In 1806, Mary Wheaton Sevre and her third husband, Joseph Baptandiere, lived in this building on the second floor and operated a store on the first floor. Around 1810, Joseph began an affair with Angelique DuBois, a beautiful girl who worked in the store. Before long, Angelique demanded that Joseph leave his wife for her but he refused. One day, during a heated argument in which Angelique threatened to tell Mary of the affair, Joseph pushed her out of the third floor window. Angelique's neck snapped and she died instantly when she hit the ground. Legend holds that a boy, who was seen by Joseph just after the crime, witnessed the murder. Fearing prison, Joseph secured a rope and hung himself in his despair. Mary continued to live in the home as a widow until her death in 1817. The spirits of Joseph, Angelique, and Mary are said to haunt the building and are considered to be three of the most persistent ghosts in the city because they refused to leave the premises despite being "cleansed." In the years before Hurricane Katrina, this spot was the location of O' Flaherty's Irish Pub, which featured live Celtic music. When Mary's ghost began showing up for the concerts, the pub was flooded with paranormal researchers and ghost tour groups. The ghost seekers became such a nuisance, the bar's owner Danny O' Flaherty actually hired a parapsychologist to perform a cleansing ritual to rid the property of the three souls. O Flaherty announced the ghosts were gone, but not long after, the three wayward spirits turned up again. **H**

Walk half a block away from the river and turn left onto Chartres Street. Walk three-quarters of a block and look to your left.

11. 514 Chartres Street—The Pharmacy Museum and Dr. Dupas

In 1804, Louisiana became the first state in the nation to require pharmacists to become licensed, and in that year, Louis Dufilho, Jr. became the first licensed pharmacist in the United States. In 1823, he opened an apothecary at this address. Around 1855, Dr. J. Dupas acquired the building and used the second floor as an office for his medical practice. According to legend, Dr. Dupas began conducting medical experiments on his patients, especially pregnant slaves. Several patients reportedly disappeared. Many people report experiencing a sense of grieving when visiting the museum. It is not uncommon for pregnant women to feel nauseous at the site. Dr. Dupas' spirit is believed to haunt the building along with many of his deceased patients. The museum is open Tuesday through Friday, 10:00 a.m. to 2:00 p.m. and Saturday 10:00 a.m. to 5:00 p.m. **H, G**

Walk up Chartres Street two blocks and turn right on Bienville Street. Walk two and half blocks and look to your right.

12. 813 Bienville Street—Count Arnaud and Germaine Wells

In 1918, a colorful French wine salesman, who fancied himself a count, opened Arnaud's. Before long, the restaurant became one of the finest in the city and soon began to win national accolades. Count Arnaud believed a fine meal was one of life's greatest pleasures and that philosophy is still alive at Arnaud's. When the count died, stewardship of Arnaud's was passed down to his flamboyant daughter, Germaine—one of New Orleans' most celebrated characters. Germaine was an impressive figure with volcanic appetites. She loved strong drink and strong men almost as much as good food. She reined over 22 Carnival Balls (still the record to beat) and she began an Easter Day parade to show off her collection of outlandish hats, a tradition that continues today. Upstairs, there is a small exhibit of her various Carnival Ball gowns. Diners and staff often detect her spirit near the women's restroom. Count Arnaud, however, prefers to haunt the main dining room. Several years ago, a local woman was hosting a meal for a few of her friends. One of these ladies had brought along a guest from out of town, a man who had never been to New Orleans. Unbeknownst to the group, this gentleman was a psychic, and in the middle of the meal, he puzzled his host by asking who were the two men standing in the corner. The host responded that she saw no one in the corner. "Look," the man insisted, "one is wearing a chef's jacket and the other is wearing a very old suit." By now, the entire table was looking and finally concluded the man was mad for they saw no one standing in the corner. They quickly brushed his insistence aside and returned to their conversation. After the meal, the group went upstairs to tour the little museum of Germaine's Carnival Ball gowns. In one of the display cases was a picture that caught the psychic's eye. "That's them!" The man exclaimed, "Those are the men I saw in the dining room." The ladies studied the picture and dread befell their faces. It was a picture of Count Arnaud in his chef's coat standing next to his brother, who was clad in a suit. Both had been dead for decades. **H, C**

Walk along Bienville Street toward the river one and a half blocks and turn right on Royal Street. Walk half a block and look to your left.

13. 214 Royal Street—Hotel Monteleone

Antonio Monteleone, a Sicilian immigrant, opened this stately hotel in 1886. The hotel has a long and distinguished history and is widely considered to be one of the most haunted hotels in the United States. In 2003, the International Society for Paranormal Research conducted an investigation of the Monteleone and contacted over a dozen departed spirits, including former employees and several children, who regularly roam the hotel. The fourteenth floor is a popular hotspot of paranormal activity. Many guests over the years have reported seeing the ghost of a three-year-old boy in their rooms. Researchers believe the boy is Maurice Begere, who came to New Orleans with his parents to attend the opera at the old French Opera House. The boy's father died in an accident during the trip and his mother passed away less than a year later. Many believe little Maurice wanders the hotel in search of his parents. **H**

14. Suggestions for Further Reading

Dwyer, Jeff. *Ghost Hunter's Guide to New Orleans.* Gretna, LA: Pelican Publishing, 2007.

Klein, Victor C. *New Orleans Ghosts.* Metairie, LA: Lycanthrope Press, 1998.

Montz, Larry, and Daena Smoller. *The Ghosts of New Orleans.* Atglen, PA: Whitford Press, 2000.

Taylor, Troy. *Haunted New Orleans: History and Hauntings of the Crescent City.* Charleston, SC: History Press, 2010.

Hollywood South Walking Tour

"The most interesting place I've gone on location is New Orleans."
— Taryn Manning

New Orleans' intriguing mystique, diverse architecture, exotic setting, and abundant history have proved irresistible to filmmakers for decades. The beautiful complexity of New Orleans has inspired artists in every field from music to painting to literature, and filmmakers are no exception. The city's dreamy romanticism, its exotic environment, the pervasiveness of eccentricity, the mythology of the Antebellum South and a legacy of supernatural arts and phenomenon have all combined to make New Orleans a natural setting for the movies. Classic films such as *Tarzan of the Apes, Jezebel, Panic in the Streets, A Streetcar Named Desire, King Creole, The Cincinnati Kid, Suddenly Last Summer, The Buccaneer, Easy Rider, Pretty Baby,* and *The Big Easy* among others were all set in New Orleans. But until recent years, many of the films set in New Orleans were not actually shot in New Orleans. That began to change in 2002 when the Louisiana Legislature began offering massive tax credits to producers and studios willing to shoot their films in Louisiana. More specifically, if a production company spends at least $300,000 and hires at least 90% locals to work on the crew, it receives a 30% tax credit. Since then, New Orleans has come to be dubbed "Hollywood South." As of this writing, New Orleans is the third largest hub for film and television production, behind Los Angeles and New York. In 2011 alone, the film industry pumped half a billion dollars into the local economy. On average, about forty-five films

TEN SELF-GUIDED WALKING TOURS OF THE FRENCH QUARTER

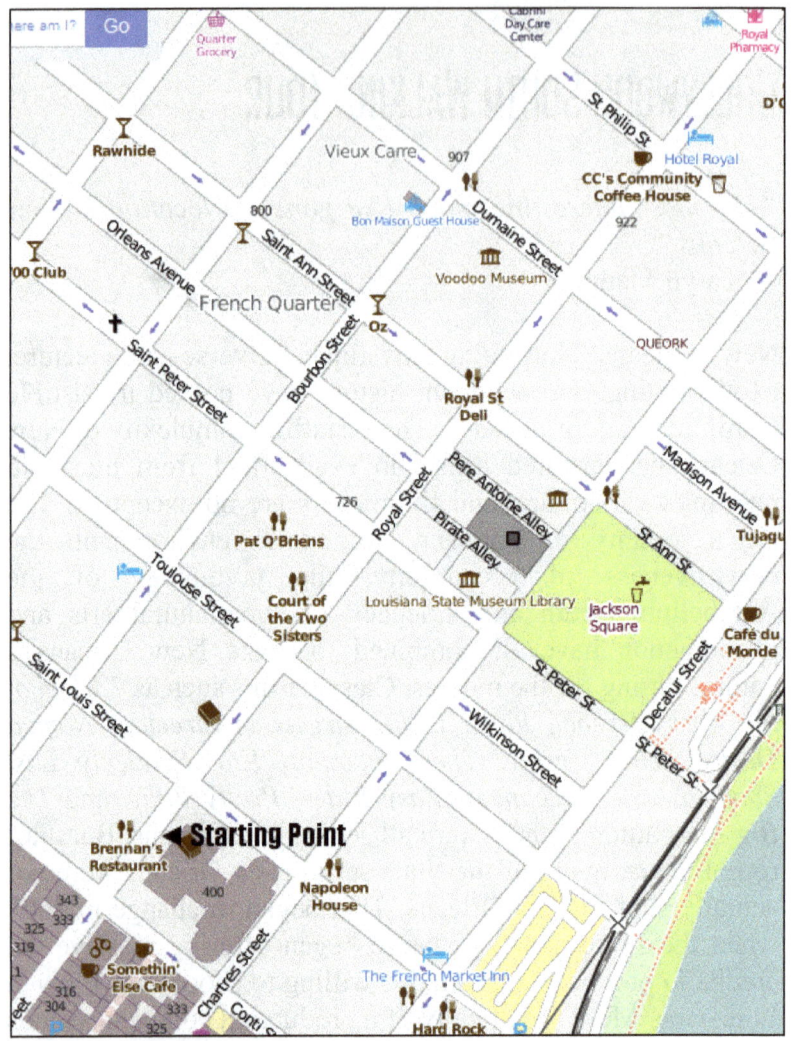

are made each year in Louisiana, about half of which are shot in New Orleans. Several celebrities have homes in the city, including Brad Pitt and Angelina Jolie, Sandra Bullock, and John Goodman.

This tour begins at the Louisiana Supreme Court Building.

TREASURES OF THE VIEUX CARRÉ

1. 400 Royal St.—*JFK*

Oliver Stone's 1991 *JFK* chronicle's New Orleans District Attorney Jim Garrison's investigation of the Kennedy assassination and the prosecution of local New Orleans businessman Clay Shaw. The film was shot on location at various sites throughout New Orleans. The outside courthouse scenes were shot here at the Louisiana Supreme Court Building. In the film, Garrison watches the news coverage of the assassination at the Napoleon House, which is across the street from the courthouse on the corner of St. Louis and Chartres Streets. The scene where Garrison's wife and kids wait for him on Easter Sunday as he interrogates Clay Shaw is just around the corner on St Louis Street at the legendary Antoine's restaurant. Lee Harvey Oswald actually lived in New Orleans for a while, residing around the opposite corner on Exchange Place Alley. The scene in which Oswald distributes pro-Castro leaflets was shot on Canal Street. Shaw was ultimately acquitted of conspiring to assassinate the president, but the damage to his reputation was irreparable. Many New Orleanians did not appreciate Stone's unflattering depiction of Shaw, a man many locals considered an admirable civic and business leader. This imposing Beaux Arts structure was erected in 1910 and now serves as home of the Louisiana Supreme Court. The statue in front of the building is Edward Douglas White, Jr., native of Thibodeaux, Louisiana, and ninth Chief Justice of the United States Supreme Court. The building has been used in a number of other films set in New Orleans. **F, G**

Walk toward Canal Street to the corner of Royal and Conti Streets and look across the street.

2. 334 Royal Street—*The Big Easy*

This 1986 classic from director Daniel Petrie, Jr. stars Dennis Quaid and Ellen Barkin and focuses on corruption in the New Orleans Police Department. Quaid plays Remy McSwain, a detective in the homicide division who falls for an attractive attorney, played by Barkin, investigating police corruption. Detective McSwain was stationed here at the 8th District Police Station. In the 1820s, the building was the home of the Bank of Louisiana. One of the film's more memorable scenes in which a dead body is found in a public fountain was filmed at the Piazza d'Italia just outside the French Quarter in the Central Business District. **F**

Walk along Conti Street one block toward the river and turn left on Chartres Street. Walk one block to the corner of Chartres and St. Louis Streets.

3. 500 Chartres St.—*Runaway Jury*

Gary Fleder's 2003 *Runaway Jury* is an adaptation of the John Grisham bestseller and centers on Nicholas Easter's attempt to manipulate a jury in order to sell the verdict. The Napoleon House, here on the corner of St. Louis and Chartres Streets was the location of the post-verdict scene where Rankin Fitch retreats for a drink before being confronted by Easter and his girlfriend, Marlee, who reveal the scheme to Fitch and effectively retire him. Built around the time of the

Louisiana Purchase in 1803, this home was owned by New Orleans Mayor Nicholas Girod. When Napoleon Bonaparte was forced into exile, Girod offered the home to the emperor. Several businessmen in the city even devised a plot to sail for Europe in order to rescue Napoleon and bring him to New Orleans, but he died before the plan was realized. The name, however, stuck. Although the place opened as a bar in 1914, they've only been serving food for the last forty years or so. In its early decades, the Napoleon House was a popular gathering place for locals, including writers and artists. Today, the Napoleon House serves one of the best muffulettas in town along with other sandwiches and salads. The signature drink here is the Pimm's Cup. Two blocks away, on the corner of Jackson Square where Chartres Street intersects St. Peter Street, is Café Pontalba, location of the humorous scene where Easter and his fellow jurors dine with the judge. **F**

Walk half a block along St Louis Street away from the river and look to your right.

4. 621 St. Louis Street—*Jezebel*

Perhaps no movie has depicted the opulence and grandeur of nineteenth century Creole society more than William Wyler's 1938 *Jezebel*. The luxury and affluence of the Creole aristocracy was depicted in the scenes featuring the interior of the St. Louis Hotel, which once stood on this site. The Omni Royal Orleans now occupies the site. You can still see a portion of the original St. Louis Hotel brickwork facing the Napoleon House on the corner of St. Louis and Chartres Streets. **F, A**

Walk along St. Louis Street two blocks and look to your left.

5. 820 St. Louis St.—*Double Jeopardy*

Bruce Beresford's 1999 crime thriller *Double Jeopardy* stars Ashley Judd, Tommy Lee Jones, and Bruce Greenwood. Judd plays Libby, a woman framed for murdering her husband. While in prison, she learns her husband is actually alive and well in New Orleans where he owns a hotel. The Hermann-Grima House was used as the site of the hotel. This home was built in 1831 and is an excellent example of American architecture of the period. The home features the only remaining fully functional outdoor kitchen and horse stable in the French Quarter. Take the tour of this home for an inside peek of mid-1800s French Quarter living. Open Monday through Friday, 10:00 a.m. to 3:00 p.m.; Saturday, 12:00 p.m. to 4:00 p.m.; (Wednesdays are typically reserved for groups). One of the more memorable scenes in the film was shot in the Garden District at Lafayette Cemetery Number One. In that scene, Libby becomes trapped in a casket in one of the tombs. F

Walk along St. Louis Street toward the river a block and a half and turn left on Royal Street. Walk two and half blocks down Royal Street away from Canal Street and look to your right.

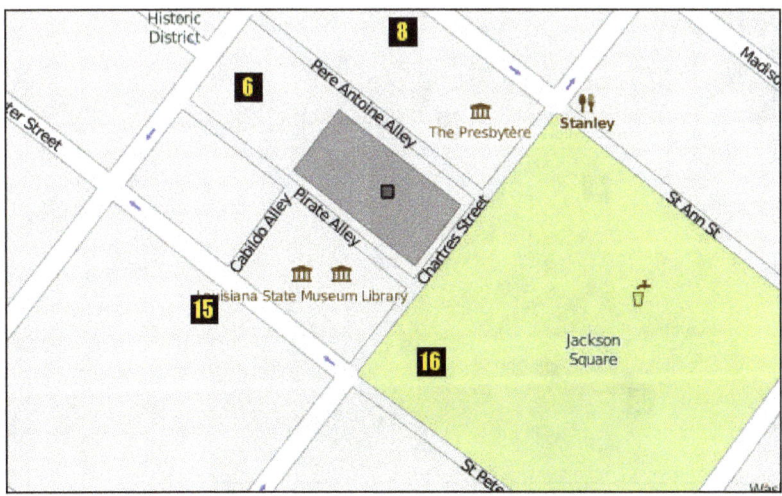

6. 700 Block of Royal St.—*The Pelican Brief*

The little garden behind St. Louis Cathedral is where the funeral scene in *The Pelican Brief* was filmed. Alan J. Pakula's film version of the John Grisham bestseller starred Julia Roberts, Denzel Washington, and Sam Shepard. In the movie, Roberts' character, Darby Shaw, develops a theory of who assassinated two U.S. Supreme Court justices. In the course of the action, Shaw's boyfriend and law professor, played by Shepard, is murdered in a car explosion and his funeral takes place here in St. Anthony's garden. Other scenes were shot on Bourbon Street, at Antoine's restaurant, the Warehouse District, and the Riverwalk Plaza. St. Anthony's Garden is a calm oasis in the midst of the hustle and bustle of the French Quarter. **F**

Walk along Orleans Avenue away from the river half a block and look to your right.

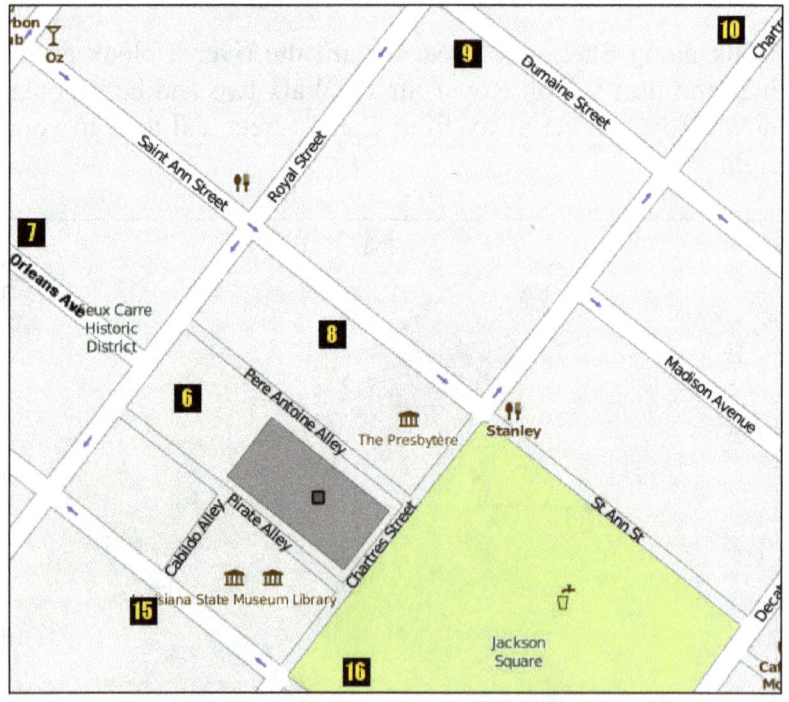

7. 717 Orleans Avenue—*The Feast of All Saints*

Peter Medak's 2001 made-for-television movie, *The Feast of All Saints*, is an adaptation of New Orleans' native Anne Rice's novel. Starring Robert Richard, Peter Gallagher, Gloria Reuben, and Jennifer Beals, the film is a fascinating exploration of the social dynamics of the famed free people of color. The hotel on your right was the site of many Quadroon Balls, where young free women of color were presented to free white men. Many of these girls became kept women in an arrangement that was known as *placage*. **F**

Walk back to Royal Street and turn left. Walk one block to St. Ann Street and turn right and then look to your right.

8. 638 St. Ann Street—The Crescent City Tour Booking Agency

This is an excellent place for information about the city and its attractions. Unlike most visitor centers, this booking agency is not owned by a specific tour company and offers unbiased recommendations. It also happens to be owned by the author of the book you now hold in your hands. Please feel free to pop in with any questions or just to say hello. **G**

Walk down Royal Street away from Canal Street one block to Dumaine Street and turn right. Walk a quarter block and look to your right.

9. 632 Dumaine St.—*Interview with the Vampire*

Neil Jordan's 1994 adaptation of the best-selling novel by native New Orleanian Anne Rice features Brad Pitt, Tom Cruise, Kirsten Dunst, Antonio Banderas, and Christian Slater. In the film, Louis de Point du Lac recounts for a reporter his 200-year tenure as a vampire. Much of the film is set in New Orleans and several scenes were shot in the city. The scene in which coffins are being loaded onto a carriage took place here at Madame John's Legacy. This charming house dates back to 1789 and is a fine example of late eighteenth century Creole residential design. There are few homes like this left in the French Quarter, but at one time, this architectural style was the norm. The name is derived from a story by Louisiana author George Washington Cable. Anne Rice was living in the Garden District neighborhood in uptown New Orleans when she wrote *Interview with the Vampire*. **F, G, A**

Walk along Dumaine Street toward the river three-quarters of a block and turn left on Chartres Street. Walk half a block and look to your left.

10. 931 Chartres Street—*Walk on the Wild Side*

Jane Fonda, Laurence Harvey, Capucine, Anne Baxter, and Barbara Stanwyck starred in this 1962 classic film directed by Edward Dmytryk. *Walk On the Wild Side* is set in the 1930s, and this home was used as a brothel known as the Doll House. The plot involves Harvey's character's attempt to rescue Hallie, played by Capucine, from the bordello. He eventually rents a second-floor apartment for her above the Faulkner House in Pirate's Alley. **F**

Walk along Chartres Street away from Canal Street two and half blocks and turn right on Gov. Nicholls Street. Walk half a block and look to your left.

11. 521 Gov. Nicholls—Brad Pitt and Angelina Jolie's Home

Brad Pitt and Angelina Jolie bought this six-bedroom home in 2007 for 3.5 million dollars. Also in that year, Brad Pitt established the Make It Right Foundation, a charity devoted to rebuilding homes in the lower Ninth Ward. This neighborhood was virtually destroyed by the floodwaters of Hurricane Katrina. **F, G**

Walk along Gov. Nicholls Street toward the river half a block and turn left on Decatur Street. Walk two blocks to Esplanade Avenue and look across the street.

12. 547 Esplanade Avenue—*Cat People*

Several scenes in Paul Schrader's 1982 remake of the classic 1942 film *Cat People* were shot here at this handsome Italianate Mansion. In this horror-fantasy movie, Irene Gallier, played by Nastassja Kinski, experiences a sexual awakening that transforms her into a black leopard. The Victorian building, known locally as the Lanaux Mansion, was built in 1879 and now functions as a bed and breakfast.
F, A

Walk along Esplanade Avenue away from the river two blocks and turn left onto Royal Street. Walk three and a half blocks and look to your left.

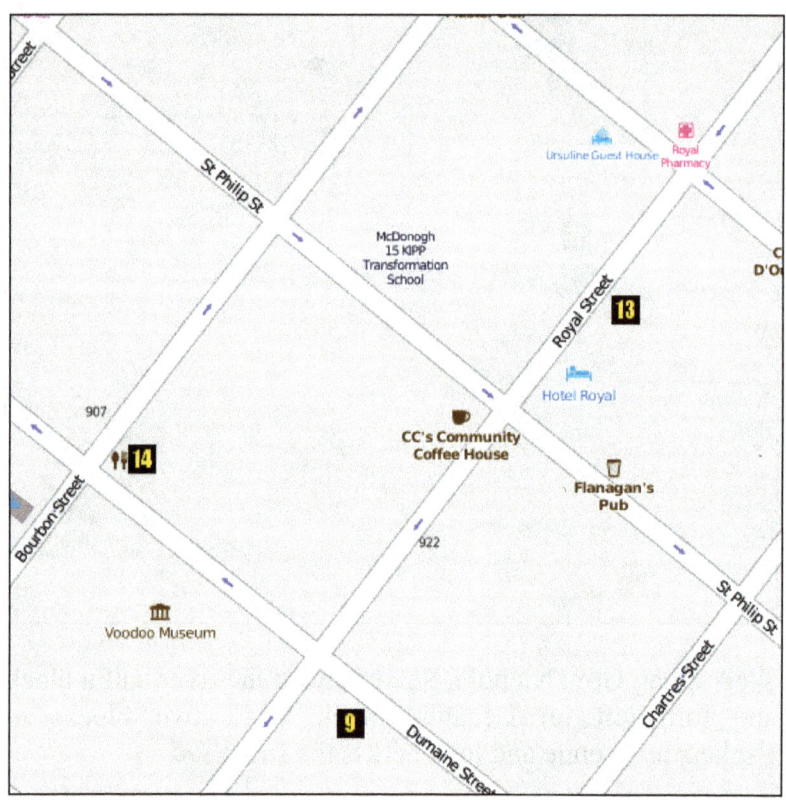

13. 1018 Royal Street—*King Creole*
The gallery at this address is where Elvis Presley sings along with a street vendor in Michael Curtiz' 1958 *King Creole*. In addition to Elvis Presley, the film also starred Carolyn Jones and Walter Matthau and features Elvis as a young ne'r-do-well named Danny who gets a gig singing in a Bourbon Street nightclub. The school at the corner of Royal and St. Phillip Streets was also used in the film as the site of Danny's high school. **F**

Walk up Royal Street toward Canal Street a block and a half and turn right on Dumaine Street. Walk one block and look at the diner on your right.

14. 900 Bourbon St.—*The Curious Case of Benjamin Button*

Based on a short story by F. Scott Fitzgerald, David Fincher's 2008 fantasy *The Curious Case of Benjamin Button* stars Brad Pitt as Benjamin Button and Kate Blanchet as his love interest. In the film, Button ages backward. The memorable diner scene in which Button sees his former lover on television being interviewed after swimming across the English Channel was shot here at the Clover Grill. This classic diner is a longtime staple of Bourbon Street and the quintessential "greasy spoon." It's open twenty-four hours a day, 365 days a year and is a perennial favorite among late-night revelers looking for cheap, not-so-healthy food to soak up the alcohol coursing through their veins. The staff is sassy and the vibe is energetic. A jukebox in the corner of this small space belts out everything from the Pet Shop Boys to Ethel Merman. The crowd is an even mix of local and tourist, straight and gay. The hamburgers are grilled under old hubcaps and the omelets are the fluffiest you'll ever find. The restaurant's motto: "We love to fry and it shows." Irreverent, quirky, and eclectic, the Clover Grill is pure New Orleans. The dress code is non-existent and during Mardi Gras and Southern Decadence, clothing, it seems, is optional. The opening scenes of the film were shot not far away in Jackson Square. Other scenes were shot at the Lanaux Mansion at 547 Esplanade Avenue. The group home where Button lived is located on Coliseum Street in the Garden District. **F, C**

Walk up Bourbon Street toward Canal Street three blocks and turn left on St. Peter Street. Walk a block and a half and look to your right.

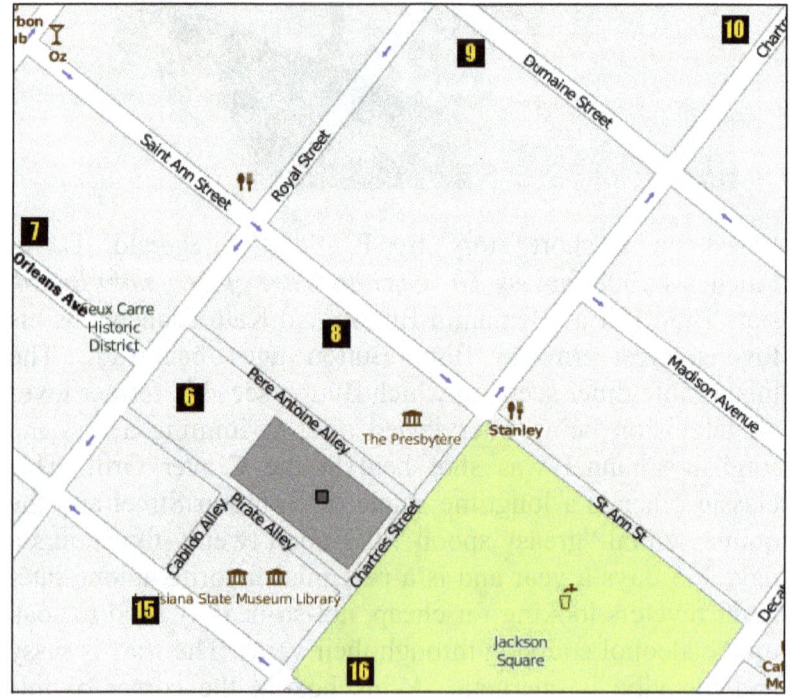

15. 632 St. Peter St.—*A Streetcar Named Desire*

Preeminent American playwright Tennessee Williams lived here when he wrote his masterpiece, *A Streetcar Named Desire*. From his writing room on the third floor, Williams could hear the Desire streetcar as it rumbled down Royal Street. In 1951, Elia Kazan, who had directed the play on Broadway, came to New Orleans to adapt the Pulitzer Prize winning play for the screen. The film starred Marlon Brando, Vivien Leigh, and Kim Hunter. The plot centers on Blanche DuBois who comes to New Orleans to stay with her sister and her husband as she descends into madness. Stanley and Stella lived on Elysian Fields, just downriver from the French Quarter. Blanche's favorite restaurant, Galatoire's, is located at 209 Bourbon Street. The opening scenes of the film were shot on Canal Street. The Desire streetcar no longer runs. Like most of the streetcars that once crisscrossed New Orleans, the Desire line has been replaced with bus service. Tennessee Williams considered New Orleans his spiritual home. **F, L**

Walk along St. Peter Street toward the river half a block and turn into Jackson Square.

16. Jackson Square—*This Property is Condemned*

Perhaps the most poignant scene between Robert Redford and Natalie Wood in Sydney Pollack's *This Property is Condemned* (1966) was shot at the fountain just inside Jackson Square in front of St. Louis Cathedral. In the film, Redford's character (Owen Legate) travels from New Orleans to a fictional Mississippi town on business where he meets and falls in love with Wood's character (Alva Starr). The screenplay, written by Francis Ford Coppola, was adapted from a one-act play by Tennessee Williams. **F, G**

Walk up Chartres Street toward Canal Street two blocks and turn right onto St. Louis Street. Walk six blocks to Basin Street.

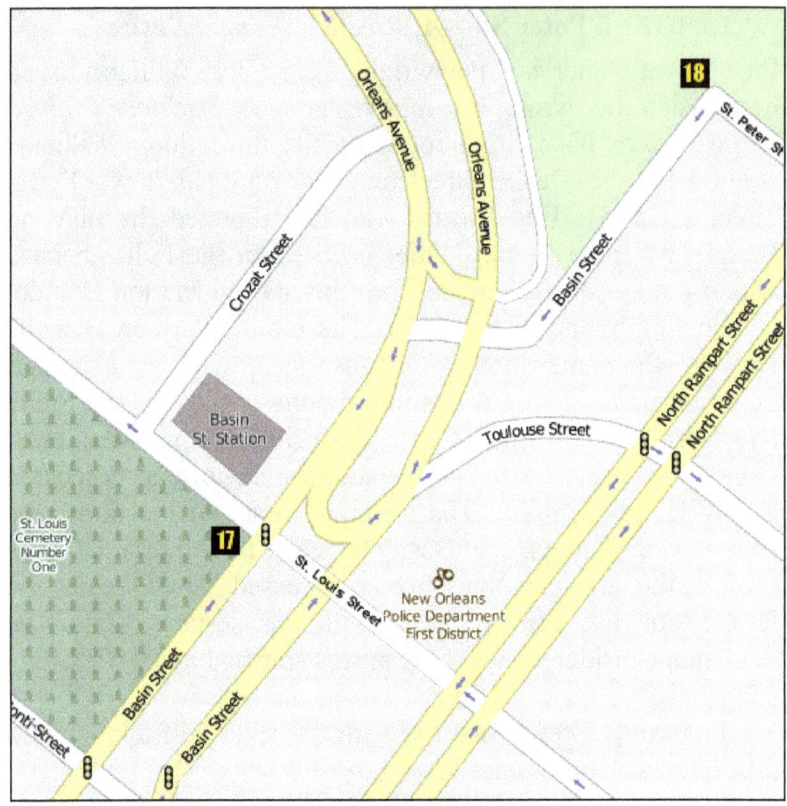

17. 425 Basin Street—*Easy Rider*

One of the most memorable scenes in Dennis Hopper's 1969 counter-culture classic, *Easy Rider*, takes place here at St. Louis Cemetery Number One. The movie is about two disillusioned young men, Billy and Wyatt, played by Dennis Hopper and Peter Fonda respectively, who travel by motorcycle from California to New Orleans in time for Mardi Gras. After arriving in town, the two hippies pick up two prostitutes, go to the cemetery to ingest LSD and proceed to have a very bad trip. After the film was released, the Roman Catholic Church, which owns the cemetery, was not amused and has not allowed any other movies to be filmed there. This cemetery was founded in 1789 and is the oldest cemetery in

New Orleans. Notable residents of the cemetery include Marie Laveau, the famous nineteenth century Voodoo Queen, and Homer Plessy of *Plessy v. Ferguson* legal fame. **F, G**

Walk down Basin Street away from Canal Street two blocks to the intersection of St. Peter Street. Look beyond the fence to your left.

18. St. Peter Street and Basin Street—*Ray*

Taylor Hackford's 2004 film *Ray* traces the life of legendary musician Ray Charles. This location was used in the scene where Ray, played by Jamie Foxx, encounters a group of demonstrators protesting segregation. Ray sides with them and declares he will not perform if his audience is segregated. Foxx won an Academy Award for Best Actor for his portrayal of Charles. **F, M**

19. Suggestions for Further Reading

Leonhard, Allan T. *New Orleans Goes to the Movies: Film Sites in the French Quarter and Beyond.* Margaret Media, Inc., 2008.

Jazz and Musical Heritage Walking Tour

"On Sabbath evening the African slaves meet on the green, by the swamp, and rock the city with their Congo dances."
— A visitor to New Orleans in 1819

Because New Orleans is a deeply emotional city, music has always been a vital thread in the fabric of life here. New Orleans is one of the most musical cities in the world and understanding a little of its history explains why. The original French colonists were, for the most part, street people—peasants and criminals who brought to the city the traditional French *joie de vivre*. Dancing has always been a favorite pastime here. From the city's earliest colonial years, everyone danced—the poor in the streets and later in rudimentary taverns and saloons; the aristocratic classes at elaborate masked balls. The first opera performed in what is now the United States (Andre Ernest Gretry's *Sylvain*) was staged in New Orleans at the Theatre St. Pierre in 1796. For most of the nineteenth century, there were several musical theatres throughout the city but none was more revered than the Theatre d'Orleans and later, the French Opera House. For over a century, opera was all the rage in New Orleans until it was supplanted in popularity by jazz. The birth of jazz was the inevitable musical expression of several cultures converging in New Orleans, primarily the coalescing of European and African musical traditions. Because of French legal precedents, slaves in New Orleans were afforded much more freedom than their counterparts in the rest of the nation. By law, slaves had Sundays off and many of them gathered on that day in the *Place de Negres*, or as it was later called, Congo Square. There they kept their African musical roots alive by making music and dancing. Polyrhythms, call and response, and blue notes—all prominent features of jazz—are all derived from

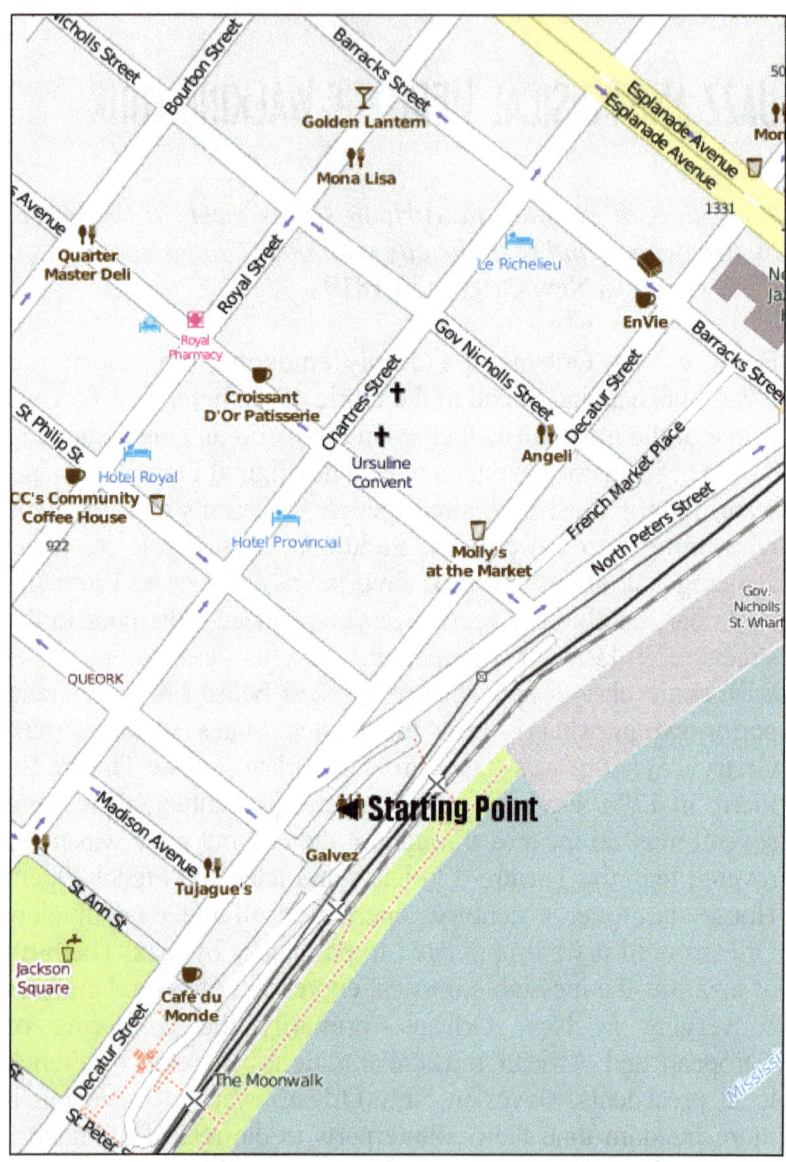

an Afro-centric sensibility. In addition to European and African musical customs, New Orleans music was also influenced by Caribbean rhythms brought to the city by thousands of refugees from the Haitian Revolution as well as by American vernaculars brought downriver by the thousands more after the Louisiana Purchase. It is impossible to say precisely when and where jazz originated; it was bubbling up from the streets all over town around the turn of the last century. We can point to Storyville as an incubator for early jazz. Decades later, New Orleans would serve as a cradle to an infant version of rock-n-roll and rhythm and blues. Fats Domino, Little Richard, and many others recorded their early work at Matassa's Recording Studio on the edge of the French Quarter. Still later, the city would give rise to hip-hop and rap stars such as Juvenile and Lil Wayne.

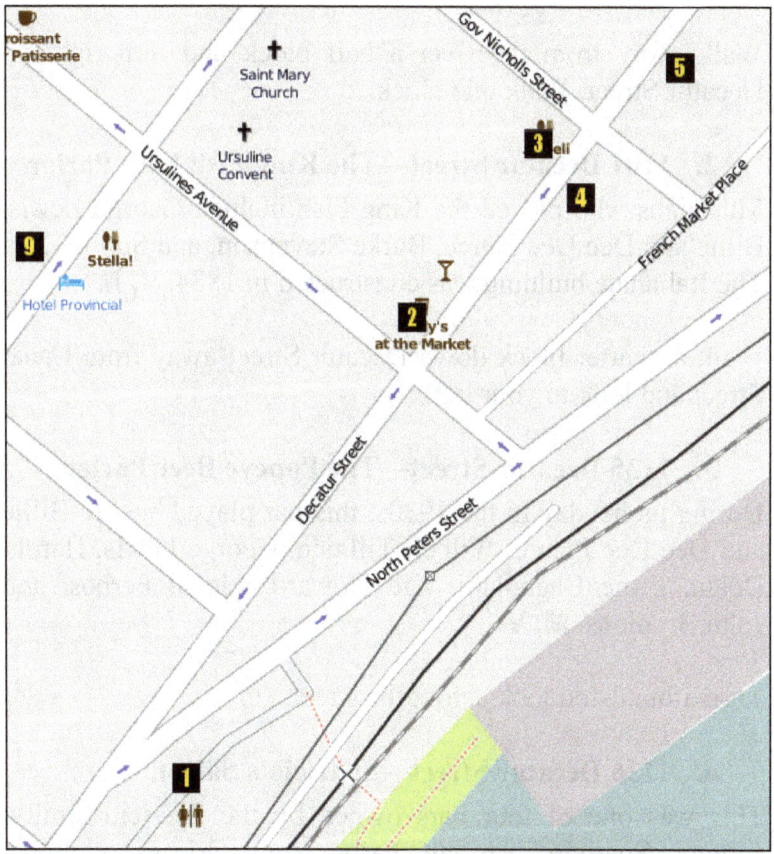

This tour begins in Dutch Alley in the French Market between N. Peters Street and the Mississippi River, about a block downriver from Café du Monde.

1. 916 N. Peters Street—The New Orleans Jazz National Historic Park

Part of the National Park Service, The New Orleans Jazz National Historic Park offers a performance area, a small exhibit, an information desk, and a bookstore. The park also sponsored an oral history project in which over 200 New Orleans musicians were interviewed. Open Tuesday through Sunday, 9:00 a.m. to 5:00 p.m. **M**

Walk away from the river a half block and turn right on Decatur Street. Walk one block.

2. 1101 Decatur Street—The King Fish Beer Parlor

Musicians who played the King Fish include George Lewis, Billie and Dee Dee Pierce, Burke Stevenson, and Smilin' Joe. The Italianate building was constructed in 1884. **V, M**

Walk a quarter block down Decatur Street away from Canal Street and look to your left.

3. 1135 Decatur Street—The Popeye Beer Parlor

During its heyday in the 1930s, this bar played host to Billie and Dee Dee Pierce, Wilbert Tillman, George Lewis, Harold Dejan, Ernie Cagnolatti, Kid Howard, Lionel Ferbos, and John Brunious. **M, V**

Turn around and look across the street.

4. 1136 Decatur Street—Sparicio's Saloon

This was one of four bars owned by the Sparicio family. Johnny Sparicio was an early New Orleans violinist. Bandleader Jack Laine and clarinetist "Yellow" Nunez used to frequent this bar. **V, M**

Walk one block down Decatur Street away from Canal Street and look to your right.

5. 1204 Decatur Street—Palm Court Jazz Café

If you're looking for some traditional, live jazz over dinner, the Palm Court Jazz Café is the place for you. Although it's only been open twenty-four years, the Palm Court has achieved the ambience of classic New Orleans restaurants from a grander age. Housed in a restored nineteenth century building, the restaurant features a mahogany bar, tiled floors, ceiling fans, and live jazz music each night beginning at 8:00pm. It's not uncommon to find owner Nina Buck dancing from table to table. Dress code is casual. **M, C**

Walk one block down Decatur Street away from Canal Street and look to your right.

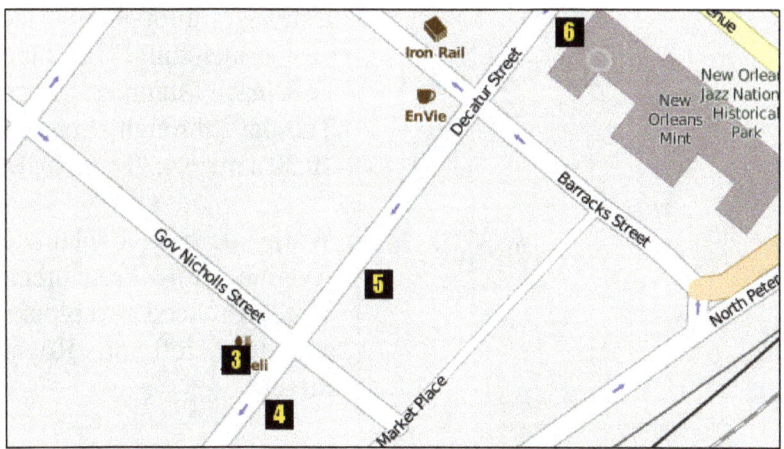

6. 400 Esplanade Avenue—The Old U.S. Mint and Jazz Museum

The Old U.S. Mint was built in 1835 and holds the distinction of being the only facility to mint both U.S. and Confederate money. It was here that General Andrew Jackson inspected the troops before marching ten miles downriver to the Battle of New Orleans in 1815. During the Civil War, after New Orleans fell to the Union, a Confederate sympathizer named William Mumford scaled the wall of the Mint and tore down the American Flag. General Butler, the Union governor, had him arrested and promptly executed. The Mint is now used as a jazz museum and is home to the New Orleans Jazz Club Collections of the Louisiana State Museum. One of the most prized artifacts in the museum is Louis Armstrong's first cornet. The Old U.S. Mint also hosts numerous festivals throughout the year, including Satchmo Fest each summer. Open Tuesday through Sunday, 10:30 a.m. to 4:30 p.m. **G, M**

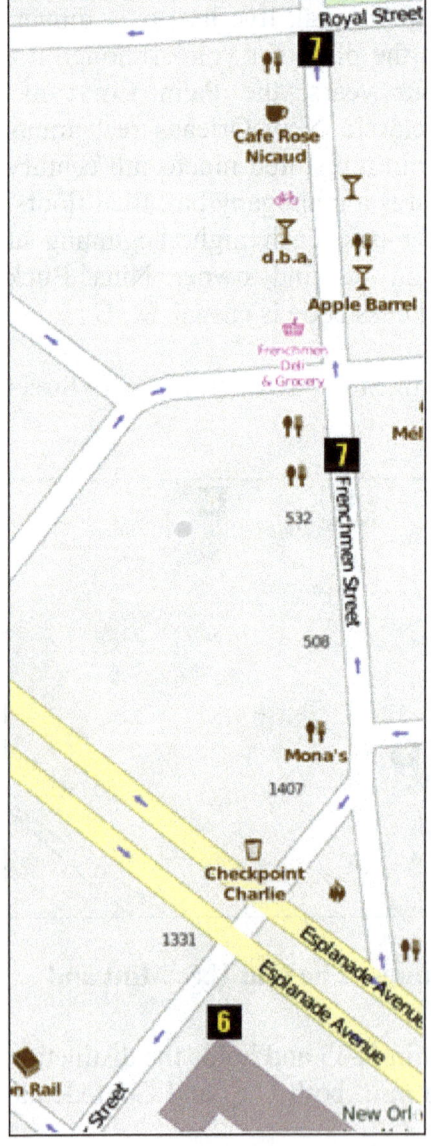

Walk across Esplanade Avenue to Frenchmen Street. Proceed two blocks and turn left on Royal Street.

7. Frenchmen Street

Just across Esplanade Avenue is Frenchmen Street. The first two blocks of the street constitute one of the hottest musical enclaves in New Orleans. This entertainment district hosts a dozen or so bars, all of which feature live music nightly, and several eateries. Cover charges are minimal and the street vibe is eclectic. It also tends to be less touristy (read less expensive) and more authentic than Bourbon Street. Some say Frenchmen Street has become what Bourbon Street used to be—a haven for genuine New Orleans music. **G, M**

Walk along Esplanade Avenue one block away from the river. Look to your right.

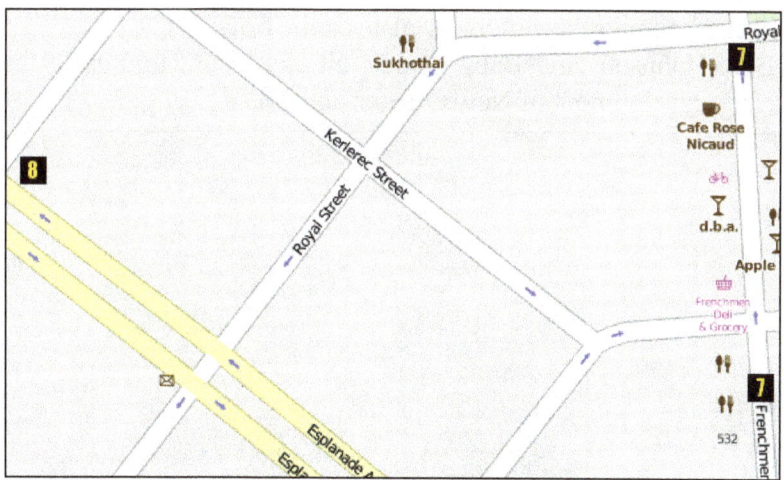

8. 741 Esplanade Avenue—Storyville and Tony Jackson

In the late 1800s, this was the home of City Alderman Sidney Story. It was Story who proposed the creation of a red-light district to confine prostitution to one area. Storyville lasted from 1897 to 1917 and was located not far from here behind the French Quarter closer to Canal Street. Storyville featured opulent mansion bordellos as well as shabby rooms, which could be rented for 50 cents. The larger bordellos featured live music and the district as a whole served as an incubator for an infant form of jazz. Tony Jackson was one of the district's most popular musicians. Jackson's piano-playing style was dynamic and mesmerizing. One of his signature moves was to do a high stepping "cake-walk" while pounding the keys. He also dressed to the nines, usually wearing an ascot tie and a diamond pin. Jackson's impeccable sartorial style set the standard for other performers. In addition to being an amazing pianist, he also composed and sang. His repertoire included ragtime, early jazz, pop, opera, blues, and some classics. His musical genius, incredible versatility, electric style and theatrical performances earned him the praise of his fellow musicians. Jelly Roll Morton called Jackson "the outstanding favorite" musician of New Orleans and jazz great Clarence Williams said, "We all copied Tony." Similar testimonials also came from Johnny St. Cyr, Bunk Johnson, and Baby Dodds, all significant figures in the early development of New Orleans jazz. **M, V**

Walk across Esplanade onto Bourbon Street. Walk three blocks to Ursulines Avenue and turn left. Walk two blocks to Chartres Street and turn right. Walk a half block and look to your right.

9. 1027 Chartres Street—Birthplace of Danny Barker

Famed jazz musician Danny Barker was born here on January 13, 1909. In addition to playing with Jelly Roll Morton, Charlie Parker, Cab Calloway, and others, Barker founded the Fairview Baptist Church Brass Band, out of which later came Wynton and Branford Marsalis, Shannon Powell, and many others. **M**

Walk half a block up Chartres Street toward Canal Street and turn right on St. Phillip Street. Walk two and a half blocks away from the river and look to your right.

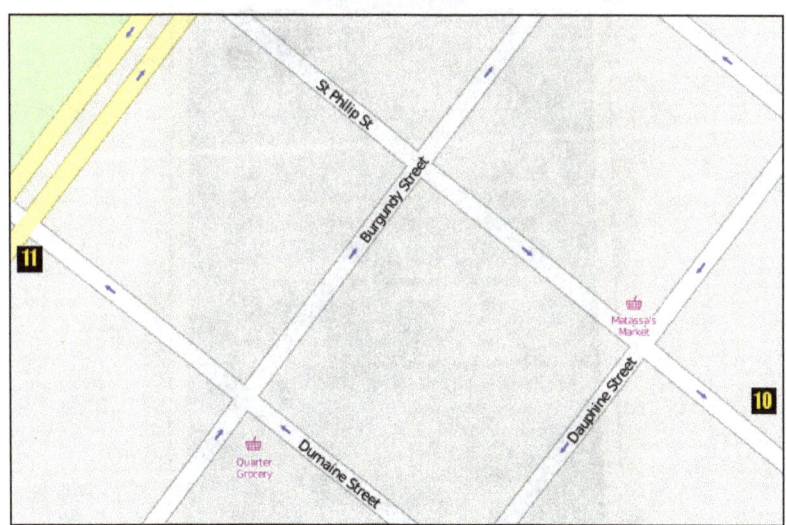

10. 827 St. Phillip Street—George Lewis Home

George Lewis was an early jazz clarinetist who played with such luminaries as Kid Ory, Buddy Petit, Chris Kelly, and

Bunk Johnson. In the 1950s, Lewis was a regular fixture at a number of clubs on Bourbon Street and later, in the 1960s, at Preservation Hall. Many jazz historians consider Lewis' music a prime example of what early New Orleans jazz was before it became commercialized in the 1930s and 1940s. **M**

Walk away from the river two and a half blocks and turn left on North Rampart Street. Walk one block to the corner of Dumaine Street. Cross Dumaine Street and look immediately to your left.

11. 840 N. Rampart Street—Cosimo Matassa's Recording Studio

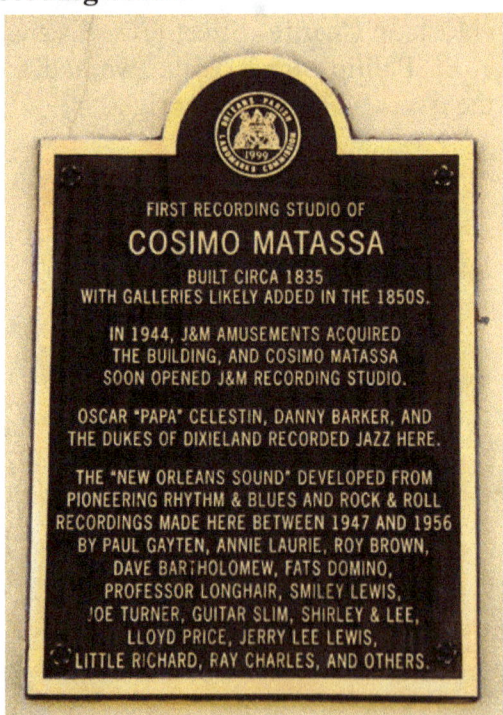

It was here in 1945 that Cosimo Matassa opened his J&M Recording Studio. Within a few years, the studio recorded some of rock-n-roll's earliest hits including Little Richard's

"Tutti Frutti," Roy Brown's "Good Rockin' Tonight," and Fat's Domino's "The Fat Man." Other artists to record here include Ray Charles, Sam Cooke, Jerry Lee Lewis, Irma Thomas, Allen Toussaint, Lloyd Price, Professor Longhair, and many others. Twenty-one gold records and over 200 nationally charting singles were recorded here. This site has been designated a historic Rock and Roll Landmark by the Rock and Roll Hall of Fame and Museum. In 2012, Cosimo Matassa was inducted into the Rock and Roll Hall of Fame. Photos of the studio's glory years are on display in the rear right corner of this laundromat. **M**

Walk one block up North Rampart Street to St. Ann Street and look to your right.

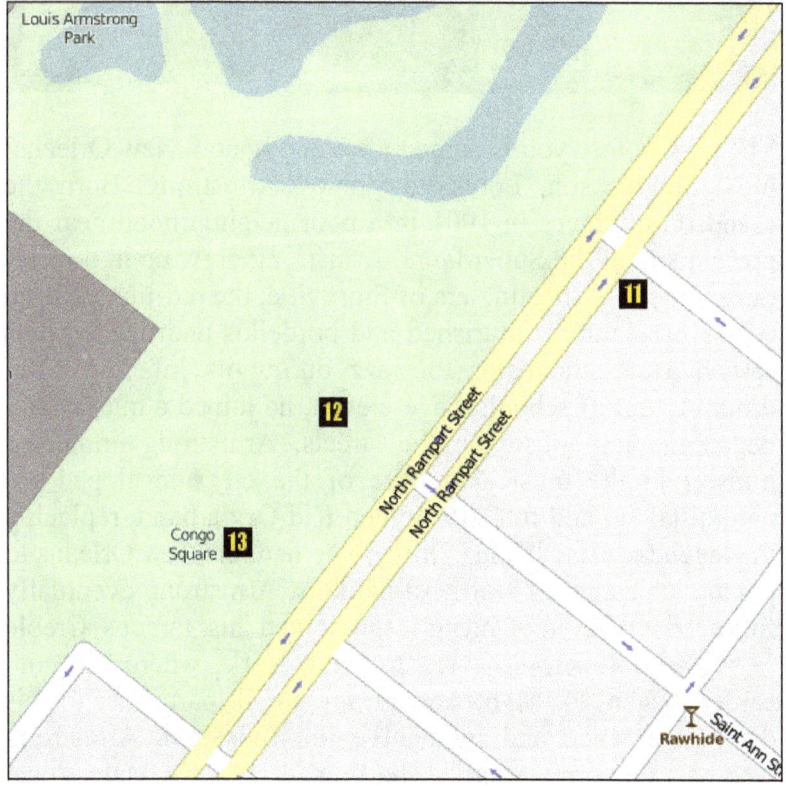

12. 800-900 Blocks of N. Rampart Street—Armstrong Park

The park before you is named after and honors New Orleans' most famous son, Louis "Satchmo" Armstrong. Born the grandson of slaves in 1901 in a poor neighborhood near the present site of the Superdome, Armstrong grew up in poverty during the freewheeling era of Storyville, the red-light district where prostitution flourished and bordellos and music clubs served as an incubator for jazz during its infancy. After dropping out of school at age eleven, he joined a quartet and began playing music on the streets. Armstrong immersed himself in the musical culture of the city, developed his natural talent, and in 1919, joined Kid Ory's band, replacing the legendary Joe "King" Oliver who had left New Orleans to pursue his career in Northern markets. Armstrong eventually followed Oliver to Chicago and joined his famous Creole Jazz Band. Later, he went to New York, where his solo career began to skyrocket in no small part due to his distinctive voice and innovative improvisation. Armstrong won two Grammy Awards: the first in 1964 for Male Vocal

Performance ("Hello Dolly"), the second for Lifetime Achievement, awarded posthumously in 1972. Louis Armstrong died in 1971. This park contains Congo Square, the Municipal Auditorium, the Mahalia Jackson Theatre for the Performing Arts, and a section of the New Orleans Jazz National Historic Park. Elizabeth Catlett sculpted the statue of Armstrong at the park's entrance. **G, M, AA**

Walk across North Rampart Street and look to your left.

13. 700 Block N. Rampart Street—Congo Square

The *Code Noir*, a set of rules governing the treatment of slaves in French colonial Louisiana, stipulated that slaves were not to work on Sundays, or if they did, they had to be paid. On their Sundays off, many of the slaves would gather here at the *Place de Negres*, or as it was commonly called, Congo Square. Here the slaves would play music, sing and dance, and trade goods with each other. These Sunday gatherings became the means by which many slaves kept the culture, especially the music and dance, of their African ancestors alive. Visitors to New Orleans in those days often visited Congo Square. Americans from the North and East were shocked not only that so many slaves (sometimes as many as 500-700) were allowed to gather without supervision, but also at the music they produced because African music had been outlawed in the American colonies. The preservation of African music through the weekly gatherings at Congo Square became crucial in the development of jazz. For this reason, Congo Square is considered sacred ground, not only by African Americans, but also by jazz enthusiasts. **G, M, AA**

Walk three blocks along St. Ann Street toward the river. Look to your left.

14. 800 Bourbon Street—Pete Fountain's Club

Now home to the popular gay dance club, Oz, this was Pete Fountain's Jazz Club in the 1960s and 1970s. The club attracted celebrities such as Frank Sinatra, Robert Goulet, Brenda Lee, Jonathan Winters, Cliff Arquette, Carole Lawrence, Phil Harris, and Robert Mitchum. Fountain became something of a celebrity himself, appearing on "The Tonight Show" with Johnny Carson fifty-six times. **M, Q**

Walk one block along St. Ann Street toward the river. Cross Royal Street and look to your right.

15. 638 St. Ann Street—The Crescent City Tour Booking Agency

This is an excellent place for information about the city and its attractions. Unlike most visitor centers, this booking agency is not owned by a specific tour company and offers unbiased recommendations. It also happens to be owned by the author of the book you now hold in your hands. Please feel free to pop in with any questions or just to say hello. **G**

Walk one block back to Bourbon Street and take a left. Walk one block (two if you count Orleans Avenue) to St. Peter Street and look to your right.

16. 701 Bourbon Street—Dixie's Bar of Music

Dixie's Bar of Music moved to this location in 1949 from its former St. Charles Avenue location and quickly became one of the trendiest bars on Bourbon Street. Dixie Fasnacht, whose last name means Mardi Gras in German, was an accomplished clarinetist who traveled in the 1930s with several all-girl bands including *The Harmony Maids*, *The Smart Set*, *Sophisticate of Swing*, and *The Southland Rhythm Girls*. Although she didn't advertise it as such, Dixie's was essentially a gay bar. In the 1950s and 1960s, it was a common police practice to raid gay bars and arrest gay patrons. Miss Dixie could always be counted on to pay bail for the release of her customers. **M, V, Q**

Walk a quarter block along St. Peter Street toward the river and look to your right.

17. 726 St. Peter Street—Preservation Hall

In 1961, Allan and Sandra Jaffe opened Preservation Hall as a sanctuary for traditional New Orleans jazz. At the time, modern jazz had become very popular and traditional New Orleans jazz was in danger of going extinct. Preservation Hall is open nightly. Doors open at 8:00pm. **M**

Walk three-quarters of a block along St. Peter Street and turn right onto Royal Street. Walk half a block and look to your right.

18. 627 Royal Street—Adelina Patti Home

Nineteenth century operatic superstar Adelina Patti lived here briefly in 1860. She became a local hero in that year when she was a last-minute stand-in lead soprano for *Lucia di Lammermoor*—a performance that saved the local opera company from financial disaster. **M**

Walk half a block up Royal Street toward Canal Street and turn right on Toulouse Street. Walk one block away from the river. Stop at Bourbon Street and look across the street to your left.

19. 541 Bourbon Street—The French Opera House

From 1859 to 1919, this site was home to the French Opera House. At the turn of the century, New Orleans was the theatre capital of the South and the French Opera House was its crown jewel. Throughout the nineteenth century, New Orleans had a love affair with opera and was considered the "opera capitol of North America." The French Opera House served as the epicenter of Creole society during a time when the city was becoming more and more Americanized. When the venerable old building burned to the ground in 1919, local writer Lyle Saxon tearfully watched the destruction and lamented in his newspaper column the next day, "The heart of the old French Quarter has stopped beating." **M**

Walk up Bourbon Street one block toward Canal Street and look to your right.

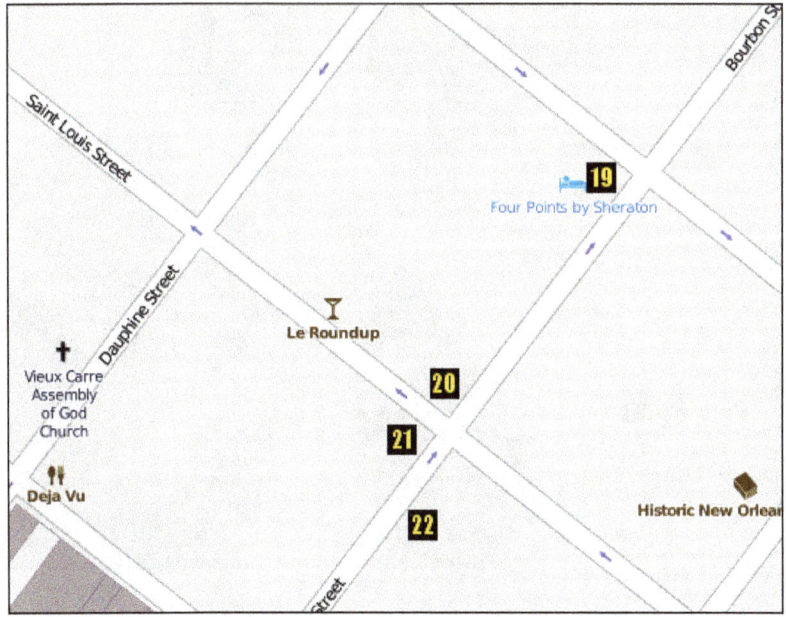

20. 501 Bourbon Street—Al Hirt's Club
Grammy award-winning trumpeter Al Hirt owned this club from 1962 to 1983. His albums *Honey in the Horn* and *Cotton Candy* made the top-ten list in 1964. Also that year,

Hirt scored a hit with his cover of Allen Toussaint's "Java." **M, V**

Walk across St. Louis Street and look to your right.

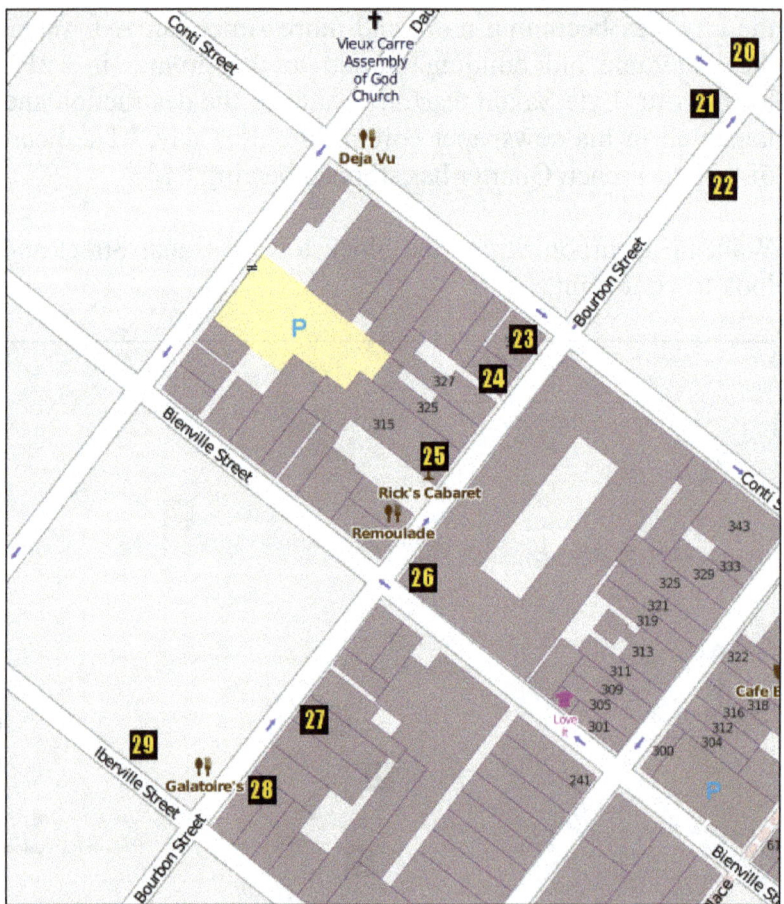

21. 441 Bourbon Street—The 500 Club

Owned by Leon Prima, brother of Louis, this club was one of the first jazz bars on Bourbon Street. In addition to jazz, the club also featured exotic dancers and burlesque shows in the 1950s, the most famous of which starred Lily the Cat Girl.

Her signature number was "the voodoo love potion dance." After the Cat Girl's death, Linda Brigette, better known as The Cupid Doll, replaced her. Noted for her enhanced breasts and big blonde hair, her routines involved dancing in a giant champagne glass, eating fire and using animals in her act. She was arrested during a performance in 1966 on obscenity charges. **V, M**

Walk up Bourbon Street toward Canal Street a quarter block and look to your left.

22. 426 Bourbon Street—The Dream Room

In the 1950s and 1960s, this dance hall played host to musicians such as Tony Parenti, Jules Bauduc, Merritt Brunies, Peter Bocage, Sharkey Bonano, and Jack Teagarden. This site was also the home of the Silver Slipper and Your Father's Mustache. **V, M**

Walk up Bourbon Street toward Canal Street toward the corner of Conti Street and look to your right.

23. 339 Bourbon Street—The Famous Door

Having opened in 1934, the Famous Door is the oldest music club on Bourbon Street. The names of the famous people who entered the door are listed on the wall next to the door. **V, M**

Walk a quarter block up Bourbon Street toward Canal Street and look to your right.

24. 333 Bourbon Street—The Mardi Gras Lounge

Sid Davilla owned this nightclub, which featured Freddie Kohlman and his New Orleans Jazz Band. The club also hosted a burlesque show starring Wild Cherry, whose style of exotic dancing ranged from Oriental to Cuban. **V, M**

Walk a quarter block up Bourbon Street toward Canal Street and look to your right.

25. 315 Bourbon Street—The Paddock Lounge

Opened in 1925 by equestrian Steve Valenti, the Paddock Lounge stayed opened for decades and had a horseracing theme. Regular performers included Oscar "Papa" Celestin and Octave Crosby. It closed in the early 1980s. **V, M**

Walk up Bourbon Street to the corner of Bienville Street and look to your left.

26. 240 Bourbon Street—The Old Absinthe House

Built in 1806, this building was first used as a store for an importing firm and later became a saloon in 1815. The Absinthe House Frappe was invented here by bartender Cayetano Ferrer. During Prohibition, the Absinthe House refused to close and openly served alcohol in defiance of federal law. For many years, the bar and the attached restaurant were owned and operated by legendary Mafia figure Diamond Jim Moran, so named because he occasionally had his chef insert a diamond into the desserts of pretty women. According to legend, this is one of several places where the pirate Jean Lafitte met General Andrew Jackson to plan strategy for the Battle of New Orleans. Jean Lafitte's ghost is said to haunt the building. In the early 1900s, jazz was a fixture here with musicians such as Steve Lewis, Frank Froeba, Burnell Santiago, and "Fats" Pichon. **G, V, C, H, M**

Walk half a block up Bourbon Street toward Canal Street and look to your left.

27. 228 Bourbon Street—The Sho Bar

Legendary jazz trumpeter Sharkey Bonano was a regular fixture at this bar when it offered live jazz music. Later, the bar hosted burlesque shows featuring the infamous Tee Tee Red, who billed herself as an "acrobatic-comedienne-contortionist." **M, V**

Walk a quarter block up Bourbon Street toward Canal Street and look to your left.

28. 200 Bourbon Street—El Morocco

In the 1940s and 1950s, Phil Zito and George Lewis played here. **M**

Turn right onto Iberville Street. Walk a quarter of a block away from the river and look to your right.

29. 811 Iberville Street—The King's Room

Pianist Armand Hug played here in the 1960s.

Go back to Bourbon Street and turn right. Walk one block to Canal Street and turn right. Walk three blocks and look across North Rampart Street to your right.

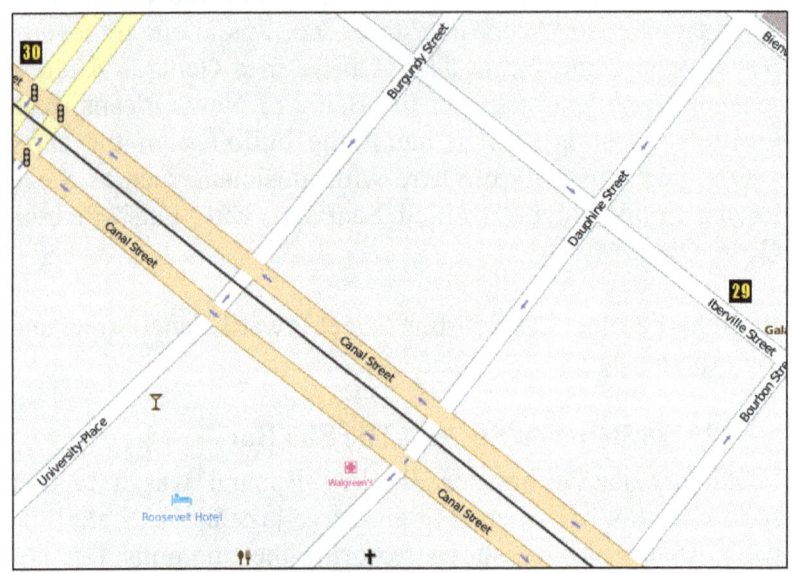

30. 1111 Canal Street—The Saenger Theatre

When it opened in 1927, The Saenger Theatre was heralded as the grandest theatre in the South. In addition to hosting live concerts and theatrical productions, the venerable old theatre also featured film screenings. The Saenger was undergoing minor renovations in 2005 when Hurricane Katrina flooded the city. Since the storm, The Saenger has been completely restored and re-opened in 2013. In 1977, The Saenger Theatre was placed on the National Register of Historic Places.

31. Suggestions for Further Reading

Hannusch, Jeff. *I Hear You Knockin': The Sound of New Orleans Rhythm and Blues.* Ville Platte, LA: Swallow Publications, 1985.

McCusker, John. *Creole Trombone: Kid Ory and the Early Years of Jazz.* University Press of Mississippi, 2012.

Spera, Keith. *Groove Interrupted: Loss, Renewal, and the Music of New Orleans.* New York: Picador, 2011.

LITERARY WALKING TOUR

"If New Orleans went into the memorial plaque business for all the writers who ever lived here they would have to brass-plate the whole town."
— Andrei Codrescu

New Orleans is often associated with food and music and to a lesser extent with literature. Most people are familiar with Tennessee Williams or Anne Rice but many do not realize that New Orleans has been inspiring writers since its founding. The first book published in Louisiana was a collection of letters written in the late 1720s from an Ursuline nun, Marie Hachard, to her family back in France. At various times in the 1800s, the city boasted no less than a dozen newspapers, one of which employed the great American poet Walt Whitman for a while. In 1845, Armand Lanusse edited and published *Les Cenelles*, a collection of poems all written by free men of color, which is generally regarded as the most important African American literary work of the Antebellum era. Some of the writers New Orleans has inspired include Kate Chopin, George Washington Cable, Grace King, Katherine Anne Porter, Mark Twain, Oscar Wilde, William Faulkner, Zora Neale Hurston, Tennessee Williams, Lillian Hellman, O. Henry, James Lee Burke, Truman Capote, and Walker Percy. In the 1920s, something of a writers' colony coalesced around Lyle Saxon, and the French Quarter played host to many of the twentieth century's greatest writers. *The Double-Dealer*, a local literary journal, published works by Sherwood Anderson, Ezra Pound, John Dos Passos, Carl Sandburg, Gertrude Stein, and the very first published works of William Faulkner and Ernest Hemmingway. In the 1960s, the bohemian Loujon Press published Allen Ginsberg,

Langston Hughes, Charles Bukowski, and William S. Burroughs. In more recent years, James Lee Burke, Anne Rice, and a host of others have captured the criminal and spiritual underworld of the city while others such as Tom Piazza and Andrei Codrescu have given voice to the resilience and unique character of New Orleans. Literacy may not be the first thing that comes to mind when most people think of Louisiana but the literary arts have a long history in New Orleans. Independent bookstores and reading salons, long extinct in much of the nation, continue to thrive in New Orleans.

This tour begins on Canal Street between Bourbon and Dauphine Streets.

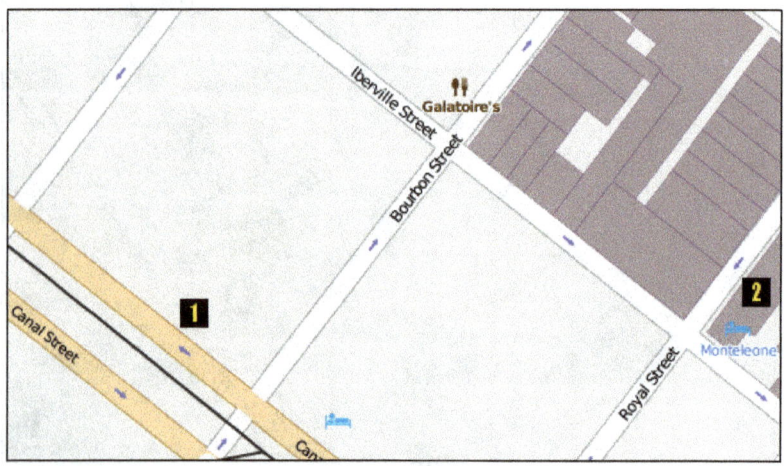

1. 800 Canal Street—Statue of Ignatius J. Reilly

This statue honors the main character of John Kennedy Toole's comic masterpiece *A Confederacy of Dunces*. This building was once the D.H. Holes Department Store, the opening scene of the novel. Set in 1963 New Orleans, Toole's masterpiece is widely regarded as the best fictional work to capture the unique idioms and dialects of New Orleans as well as the city's eccentric characters. In his lifetime, Toole was unsuccessful in getting his novel published. After his suicide in 1969, his mother found a carbon copy of the manuscript and persuaded Walker Percy, who was on the faculty at Loyola University, to read it.

Impressed, Percy used his influence to have the book published in 1980. *A Confederacy of Dunces* won the Pulitzer Prize in 1981. Much of the novel is set in the French Quarter, including Officer Mancuso's precinct at Conti and Royal Streets and Dorian Greene's apartment in the 700 block of St. Peter Street. **L**

Walk a block and a half along Canal Street toward the river and turn left onto Royal Street. Walk down Royal Street a block and a half and look to your right.

2. 214 Royal Street—The Hotel Monteleone

Step inside the lobby and look immediately to the right. There, a glass case displays this grand hotel's literary heritage. Among the writers who made the Monteleone home while they visited New Orleans were Ernest Hemmingway, Truman Capote, Rebecca Wells, William Faulkner, Richard Ford, Eudora Welty, Tennessee Williams, John Grisham, and Winston Groom. The Monteleone is home of the annual Tennessee Williams Literary Festival, held each March in honor of the playwright's birthday. The festival concludes with a "Stella!" yelling contest in Jackson Square. The Monteleone also hosts the annual Saints and Sinners Literary Festival, one of the largest LGBT literary festivals in the nation. **L, Q**

Walk down Royal Street away from Canal Street half a block

and turn right on Bienville Street. Walk one block to the corner of Chartres Street and look across the street to your right.

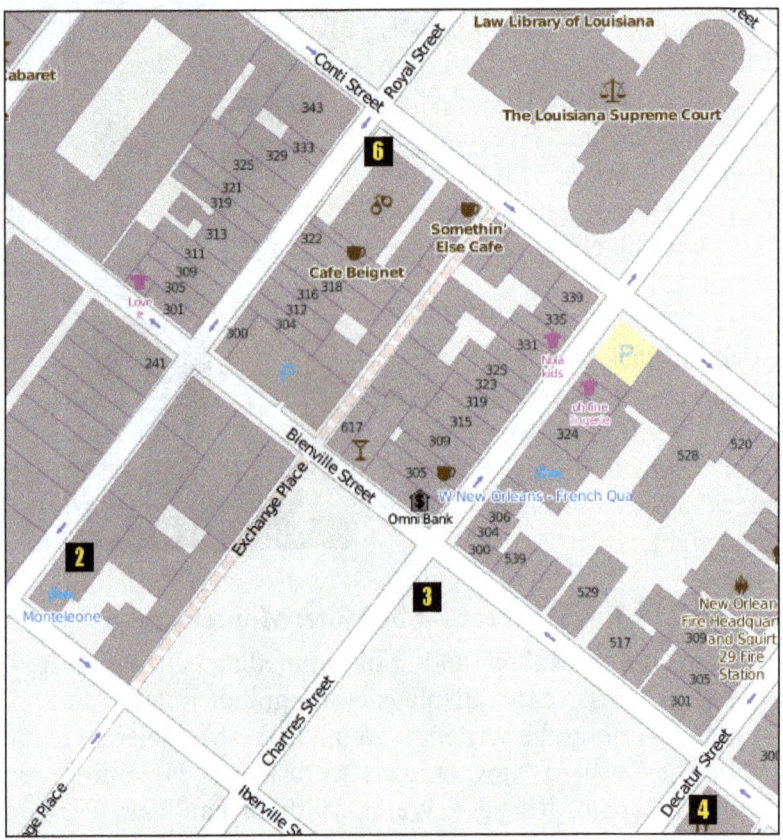

3. 230 Chartres Street—Crescent City Books

This shop is just one of several independent bookshops in the French Quarter. In addition to new and used books, the store also has a fine selection of prints and rare books. **L**

Walk along Bienville Street toward the river one block to the corner of Decatur Street and look across the street to your right.

4. 228 Decatur Street—Beckham's Book Shop

Here is another fine, independently owned bookstore featuring a tremendous selection of not only books but also classical music. **L**

Walk along Bienville Street away from the river one block and turn right on Chartres Street. Walk two blocks away from Canal Street and look to your right.

5. 500 Chartres Street—The Napoleon House

This popular bar and café has been a favorite haunt of writers throughout the twentieth century, including Richard Ford, Robert Olen Butler, Julie Smith, Tom Piazza, and Andrei Codrescu, among others. The building dates back to the early 1800s and was once the home of the first elected mayor of New Orleans, Nicholas Girod. Legend holds that when the French Emperor Napoleon Bonaparte went into exile, a plot was hatched here in New Orleans to rescue the emperor and bring him here to New Orleans. Mayor Girod graciously offered his home as refuge but Napoleon died before the daring plan could be completed. Since 1914, the Napoleon House has been a popular restaurant and bar. Its signature cocktail is the Pimm's Cup. **L, C**

Walk along St. Louis Street away from the river one block and turn left on Royal Street. Walk one block to the corner of Conti Street and look across the street.

6. 300 Royal Street—Patrolman Mancuso's Police Station

This beautiful, old building is home to the New Orleans Police Department's 8th District Station. This was the station out of which Officer Mancuso worked in John Kennedy Toole's Pulitzer Prize winning *A Confederacy of Dunces.* **L, A**

Walk along Conti Street away from the river two blocks and turn right on Dauphine Street. Walk a quarter block and look to your right.

7. 410 Dauphine Street—Dauphine Street Books

Here is yet another amazing, independent bookstore literally brimming with books. **L**

Walk down Dauphine Street away from Canal Street three-quarters of a block and turn right on St. Louis Street. Walk one block and turn left on Bourbon Street. Walk half a block and look to your right.

8. 516 Bourbon Street—Lafcadio Hearn

Lafcadio Hearn lived here in the 1880s during his tenure as a book critic and literary editor for two daily newspapers. Hearn wrote articles about New Orleans for *Harper's Weekly* and *Scribner's Magazine*. In writing about New Orleans for a national audience, Hearn was largely responsible for creating the mystique with which New Orleans is identified in the national mindset. Hearn stayed in New Orleans ten years before moving to Japan, where he earned great fame as a travel writer. **L**

Walk down Bourbon Street away from Canal Street half a block and turn right on Toulouse Street. Walk half a block and look to your left.

9. 719 Toulouse Street—Roark Bradford

Novelist Roark Bradford acquired this home in 1928 and lived here through the 1930s and 1940s. During that time, the home served as a meeting place for the city's literati, including William Faulkner and Sherwood Anderson. Bradford's favorite topic was African American culture. His major works include *Old Man Adam an' His Chillun*, *This Side of Jordan*, and *John Henry*. **L, C**

Walk along Toulouse Street toward the river half a block and turn left on Royal Street. Walk one block and turn right onto St. Peter Street. Walk one block to the corner of Chartres Street and look to your right.

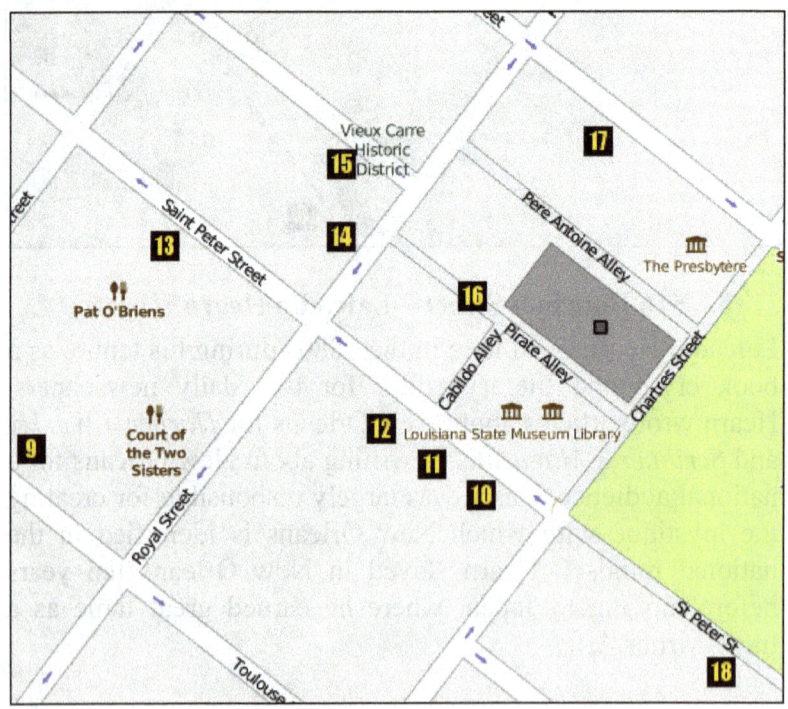

10. 616 St. Peter Street—Le Petit Theatre

On the corner of the Square, at the corner of St. Peter and Chartres Streets is Le Petit Theatre. In 1916, a group of local theatre lovers began producing plays in the drawing room of one of its members. Audiences grew and the Drawing Room Players began renting space in the lower Pontalba Building before opening Le Petit in 1919. The building you see today dates to 1922 and is a reproduction of Spanish colonial-style architecture. **A, SC, L**

In the same block, behind Le Petit Theatre are the next two stops.

11. 620 St. Peter Street—Le Petit Salon

This was the home of a women's literary group founded by Grace King. King, a New Orleans native, achieved some fame as a local-color author and was widely considered the voice of the patrician class of the Old South during the Reconstruction period. She began writing after an editor, tired of her complaints about George Washington Cable, challenged her to "write something better." **L, G**

Walk a quarter block along St. Peter Street away from the river and look to your left.

12. 632 St. Peter Street—Tennessee Williams

Preeminent American playwright Tennessee Williams lived here when he wrote his masterpiece, *A Streetcar Named Desire*. From his writing room on the third floor, Williams could hear the Desire streetcar as it rumbled down Royal Street. Williams also lived at 722 Toulouse, 710 Orleans, and 1014 Dumaine. **L, Q**

Walk along St. Peter Street away from the river onto the next block.

13. 700 Block St. Peter Street—Dorian Greene's Apartment

This block is the setting of Dorian Greene's apartment in John Kennedy Toole's *A Confederacy of Dunces*, site of the ill-fated peace party / cocktail soiree at which Ignatius Reilly's "Save the World Through Degeneracy" speech goes over like a lead balloon. **L**

Walk back to Royal Street and turn left. Walk half a block and look to your left.

14. 711 Royal Street—Truman Capote

New Orleans native Truman Capote lived here in 1945 while he was writing *Other Voices, Other Rooms*. **L**

Walk down Royal Street away from Canal Street half a block and turn left on Orleans Avenue. Walk a quarter block and look to your left.

15. 714 Orleans Avenue—Arcadian Books

Here is one more independent bookstore. **L**

Look to your left. The alley on the right side of the garden is the next stop.

16. 624 Pirate's Alley—The Faulkner House

This townhouse was once home to William Faulkner and it was here that he penned his first novel, *A Soldier's Pay*. Today, the Faulkner House is one of America's leading independent bookstores specializing in fine literature, rare editions, New Orleans literature, and of course, William Faulkner. The building adjacent to the bookstore was once used as a prison. L, A

Walk down Royal Street one block and turn right on St. Ann Street. Look to your right.

17. 638 St. Ann Street—The Crescent City Tour Booking Agency

This is an excellent place for information about the city and its attractions. Unlike most visitor centers, this booking agency is not owned by a specific tour company and offers unbiased recommendations. It also happens to be owned by the author of the book you now hold in your hands. Please feel free to pop in with any questions or just to say hello. **G**

Walk along St. Ann Street toward the river and turn right at Jackson Square. Walk one block then turn left on St. Peter. Walk half a block and turn right.

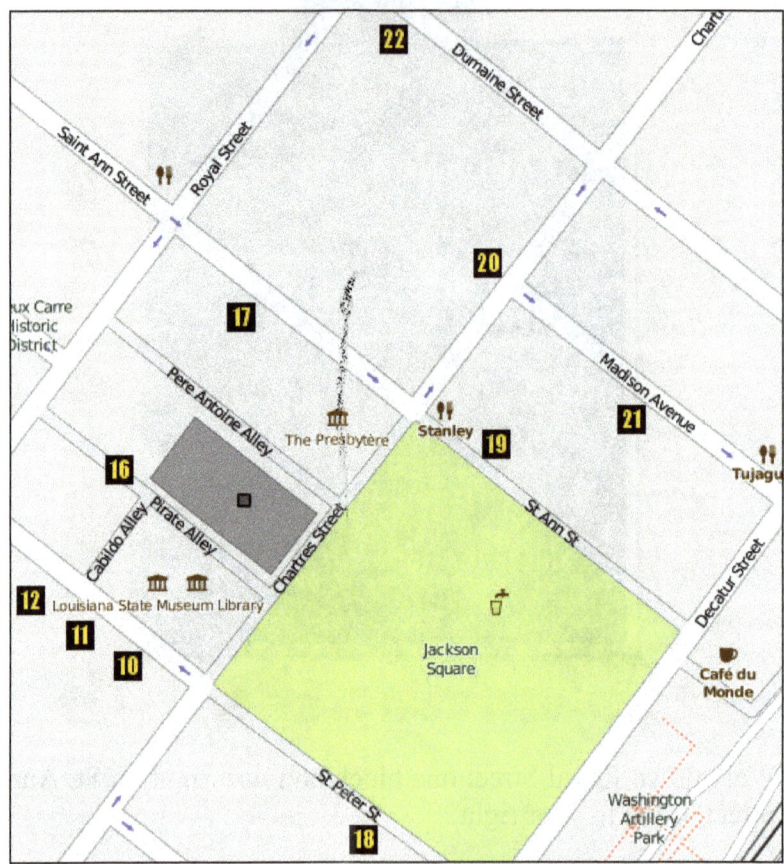

18. 540 St. Peter Street—Sherwood Anderson

Sherwood Anderson lived here in 1924. While here, he wrote *Dark Laughter* and helped William Faulkner, who lived around the corner, publish *A Soldier's Pay*. Anderson and Faulkner would later have a falling out over Faulkner's 1926 parody, *Sherwood Anderson and Other Famous Creoles*. **L, A**

Walk across the Square to the other red brick building.

19. 543 St. Ann Street—Katherine Anne Porter

Short-story writer Katherine Anne Porter lived here in the late 1930s. Her *Collected Stories* won a Pulitzer Prize in 1966. **L, G, A**

Walk to the lakeside, downriver corner of the Square and walk down Chartres Street half a block. Look to your left.

20. 823 Chartres Street—The Librairie

Yet another independent bookstore.

The small street behind you is the next stop. Walk along Madison Street toward the river half a block and look to your right. **L**

21. 536 Madison Street—Lyle Saxon

Here is the home of Lyle Saxon, writer, French Quarter preservationist, and perhaps the most influential gay New Orleanian of the last century. By the early 1900s, the French Quarter had deteriorated into a slum neighborhood consisting mostly of Sicilian immigrants. In the 1920s and 1930s, Lyle Saxon began restoring dilapidated homes in the French Quarter and promoting the area to other writers and artists as a haven of artistic inspiration. He also directed the Louisiana Writer's Project, which was a part of FDR's Works Progress Administration. As a result, the Quarter became something of a writer's colony that attracted the likes of William Faulkner, Sherwood Anderson, Ernest Hemmingway, Roark Bradford, John Dos Passos, Zora Neale Hurston, O. Henry, Katherine Anne Porter, Grace King, and others. It was here at this home that John and Gwen Steinbeck were married. Saxon galvanized the preservation and restoration of the French Quarter and thus ensured the Quarter's survival as one of America's most historic neighborhoods. Books by Saxon include: *Fabulous New Orleans*, *New Orleans City Guide*, *Gumbo Ya-Ya*, and *The Friends of Joe Gilmore*. **L, A, Q**

Walk back to Chartres Street and turn right. Walk half a block to Dumaine Street and turn left. Walk three-quarters of a block and look to your left.

22. 632 Dumaine Street—George Washington Cable

This French Colonial home, known as Madame John's Legacy, is named after a character in "Tite Poulette", a story by George Washington Cable. This story, along with several others, were originally published in *Scribner's Monthly* in the 1870s and would eventually be brought together in *Old Creole Days*. This work, together with Cable's masterpiece novel *The Grandissimes*, enraged both Creole and American society. The Creoles did not care for Cable's unflattering portrayal of them, and the Americans took issue with his anti-slavery stance. Cable is not widely read today, but when he died in 1925, he was considered a major American author. **L, G, FC, A**

Walk back to Chartres Street and turn left. Walk five blocks to Esplanade Avenue and turn right. Walk half a block and look to your right.

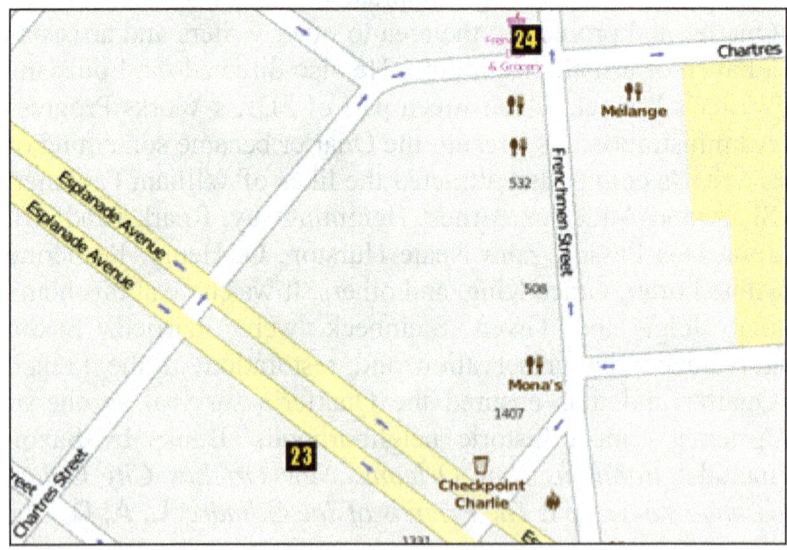

23. 510 Esplanade Avenue—John Dos Passos

John Dos Passos lived here briefly in 1924 while he was wrapping up *Manhattan Transfer*. This book is often regarded as a blueprint for his later masterpiece *U.S.A. Trilogy*. **L**

Walk along Esplanade Avenue toward the river half a block to Decatur Street and cross Esplanade Avenue. Walk one block and look to your left.

24. 600 Frenchman Street—Faubourg Marigny Arts and Books

Although technically not in the French Quarter (but very close to it), this store merits a stop as the South's oldest gay- and lesbian-themed bookstore. **L, Q**

Walk along Decatur Street back across Esplanade Avenue. Walk three blocks and turn right on Ursulines Avenue. Walk a block and a half and look to your left.

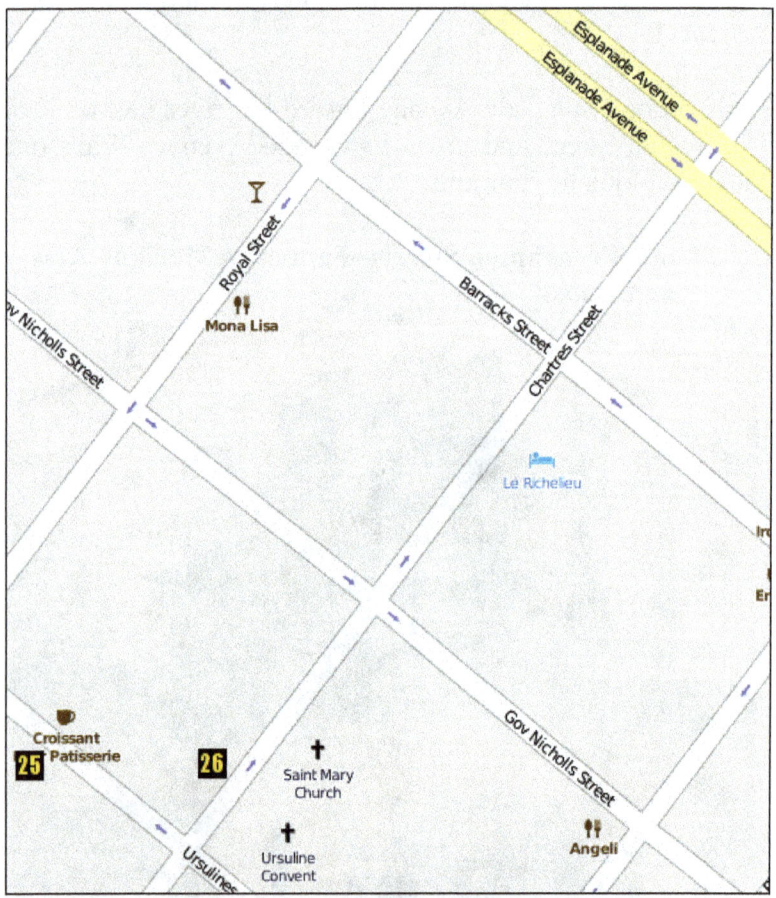

25. 618 Ursulines Avenue (and 638 Royal Street)—Loujon Press

Founded in 1960, the Loujon Press quickly became one of the most important small presses of its day and its avant-garde journal, *The Outsider*, featured writers such as Allen Ginsberg, Robert Creely, Charles Bukowski, Henry Miller, Lawrence Ferlinghetti, Langston Hughes, Amiri Baraka,

William S. Burroughs, and others. Press founders Jon and Louise "Gypsy Lou" Webb lived in the apartment upstairs where they set the type for the books. By day, "Gypsy Lou" sold artwork on the street corner. **L**

Walk back to Chartres Street and turn left. Walk a quarter block and look to your left.

26. 1113 Chartres St.—Frances Parkinson Keyes

This home, formerly the residence of Confederate General P.G.T. Beauregard, was also the home of novelist Frances Parkinson Keyes. Keyes wrote several books about New Orleans, the most famous of which is the murder mystery, *Dinner at Antoine's*. Keyes began renting this house in 1945 and later restored it after she purchased it. Keyes died in 1970. **L, G, A, V**

27. Suggestions for Further Reading

Kennedy, Richard S. *Literary New Orleans: Essays and Meditations*. Baton Rouge, LA: Louisiana State University Press, 1998.

Larson, Susan. *The Booklover's Guide to New Orleans*. Baton Rouge: Louisiana State University Press, 1999.

Long, Judy, and Patricia Brady, eds. *Literary New Orleans*. Athens, GA: Hill Street Press, 1999.

Miller, John. *New Orleans Stories: Great Writers on the City*. San Francisco: Chronicle Books, 1992.

Reed, John Shelton. *Dixie Bohemia A French Quarter Circle in the 1920s*. Baton Rouge: Louisiana State University Press, 2012.

Vice and Crime Walking Tour: Bars, Brothels, and Bad Boys

"New Orleans was founded by thieves and prostitutes and named after a cross-dresser."
— Jeffrey Holmes

New Orleans' reputation for letting the good times roll is well deserved. When the city was founded and colonists were needed, French officials looked to the streets and prisons of Paris. Loose women, convicted thieves, degenerate gamblers, and ne'r-do-wells were sent to build and populate New Orleans. But the French propensity for fun and frivolity was not limited to the lower classes; colonial governors instituted lavish feasts and elaborate masked balls. The general depravity and debauchery that characterized King Louis XIV's royal court was successfully transplanted to the New World in the form of New Orleans. The French Quarter has always been home to a thriving whorehouse industry, and crime, both petty and organized, has always been at home here. Because of imperial neglect and restrictive trade regulations during the city's colonial period, New Orleans has always relied on smuggling and piracy for its survival. The pirate Jean Lafitte was revered all over town and easily more popular than the territory's American governor. When the Americans acquired New Orleans in 1803, the city had already been around for almost a hundred years; consequently, American Puritanism and morality has never really taken hold here. The laborious Protestant work ethic has always given way to the spirit of *joie de vivre* in New Orleans. The city's culture of carnal indulgence—in food, in drink, and in sex—is legendary and derives from a

Mediterranean / Latin tradition. For this reason, New Orleans is often described as the most distinctive city in the United States, which, for the most part, is descended from a Protestant, Anglo-Saxon cultural tradition. This is not to say New Orleans is more sinful or immoral than other American cities. Human nature varies little regardless of geographical location. What makes New Orleans unique is that unlike other

U. S. cities, it is not burdened with the moral imperative to suppress its carnal impulses. In fact, to do so is so unnatural to New Orleans that the city prepares for the penitent season of Lent by celebrating Mardi Gras, which is the climax of the Carnival season. The word carnival, of course, comes to us from the Latin and means "farewell to the flesh."

This tour begins at the French Market, just downriver from Jackson Square.

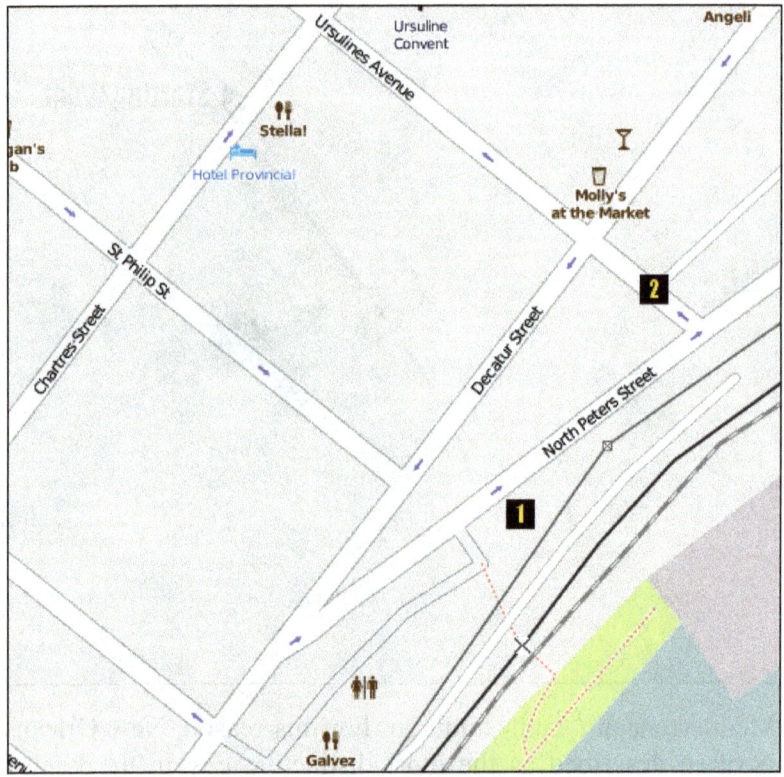

1. 1008 N. Peters Street—The Sicilian Mafia

The Mafia in New Orleans dates back to the 1860s and can be traced to three Sicilian immigrants—Raffaele Agnello, Joseph Macheca, and Giuseppe Esposito. These men laid the foundation of an organized crime syndicate that would give rise to two rival crime families: the Provenzanos and the Matrangas. Early Mafia activity was centered on the waterfront docks and the fruit imports from South America which were sold here at the French Market. Racketeering, extortion, prostitution and gambling were also staples of the crime operation. A street war erupted between the two families and in 1890 produced a casualty that remains infamous in New Orleans, the murder of Police Chief Hennessy. Hundreds of Sicilians were arrested but only nineteen were indicted. A sensational trial ended in acquittals for all the defendants. Shocked and infuriated by the verdicts, a public mob stormed the prison and lynched and or shot eleven of the defendants. The Matrangas eventually won the war and went on to control the New Orleans underworld well into the Twentieth Century. Noted boss Sam "Silver Dollar" Carolla was succeeded by the infamous Carlos Marcello, who is widely believed to have been the mastermind behind the John F. Kennedy assassination. Marcello, who described himself as a "tomato salesman," was reputed to have a sign on the wall behind his desk that read, "Three can keep a secret if two are dead." The Mafia in New Orleans predates the rise of Mafia families in New York and Chicago. **V**

Walk one block down North Peters Street away from Canal Street to the corner of Ursulines Avenue and turn left. Walk half a block and look down French Market Place Street.

2. 1000-1200 Blocks of French Market Place St.— Gallatin Street

From the mid-1800s well into the twentieth century, this strip was one of the roughest, seediest parts of town, rife with prostitutes and other criminals. It pre-dated Storyville as a red-light district and featured a host of brothels, the most notorious of which was the Lion's Den. It was common for prostitutes to pick the pockets of their clients during sexual interludes. Theft and murders were common in the 18th Century, as were street gangs, notably the Live Oak Boys, a group of Irish youths so named because their weapons of choice were clubs made of oak. Jazz legend Johnny Wiggs memorialized the area in his song, "Gallatin Street Grind." **V, M**

Walk along Ursulines Avenue away from the river three blocks and turn right on Bourbon Street. Walk three blocks to the corner of Esplanade Avenue and look across the street.

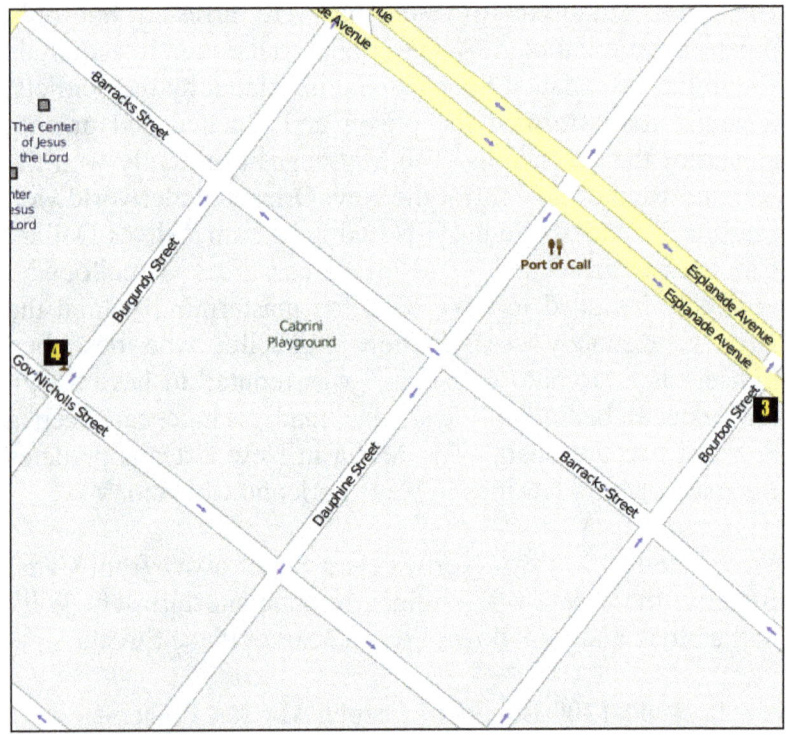

3. 741 Esplanade Avenue—Sidney Story and Storyville

In the late 1800s, this was the home of City Alderman Sidney Story. It was Story who proposed the creation of a red-light district to confine prostitution to one area. Storyville lasted from 1897 to 1917 and was located not far from here behind the French Quarter closer to Canal Street. Storyville featured opulent mansion bordellos as well as shabby rooms, which could be rented for 50 cents. Some of the bordellos were owned by lesbians and some even offered live lesbian sex acts. The larger bordellos featured live music, and the district, as a whole, served as an incubator for an infant form of jazz. The District, as it was called, even featured a directory of prostitutes; the notorious Blue Book not only listed the names and addresses of hookers, it also gave vivid descriptions of the various brothels and the precise nature of the services each offered. **V**

Walk along Esplanade Avenue away from the river two blocks and turn left on Burgundy Street. Walk two blocks to the corner of Gov. Nicholls Street and look to your right.

4. 1201 Burgundy Street—Clay Shaw and the JFK Assassination

Cosimo's, the bar on this corner, has managed to carve out a niche in the vast network of conspiracy theories surrounding the assassination of President John F. Kennedy. It was here that New Orleans District Attorney Jim Garrison was tipped off that Clay Bertrand was an alias for Clay Shaw. Garrison would later indict Shaw for conspiring to assassinate the president. The indictment and subsequent trial shocked New Orleans for Clay Shaw had long been one of the city's most successful businessmen and a respected citizen. In addition to directing the International Trade Mart, Shaw had also restored several properties in the French Quarter and was considered a leading historical preservationist. Several prominent figures in the lore surrounding the assassination had New Orleans associations. Lee Harvey Oswald lived in New Orleans for a while, as did David Ferrie and Guy Bannister. **V**

Walk up Burgundy Street toward Canal Street two blocks and turn left on St. Phillip Street. Walk two blocks to the corner of Bourbon Street and look to your left.

5. 1003 Bourbon Street—Home of Jean and Pierre Lafitte.

On this site in the early 1800s stood the residence of the infamous pirate brothers, Jean & Pierre Lafitte. The Lafitte brothers arrived in New Orleans around 1870 and based their pirate / smuggling operations out of Barataria Bay, south of New Orleans. Preying on the merchant ships of Spain and whatever other ships they came across, the brothers Lafitte afforded Creole society luxury items and slaves at cut-rate prices. Jean, the more flamboyant of the two brothers, was so beloved in the city that when the new American governor W. C. C. Claiborne nailed a wanted poster in the *Place d' Armes* (now Jackson Square) offering a $500 reward for Lafitte's capture, there appeared the next day another wanted poster offering $1000 for Claiborne's capture! Lafitte eventually won a pardon for his crimes from the U. S. government after he aided General Andrew Jackson in defeating the British in the Battle of New Orleans. The bar across the street, Lafitte's Blacksmith Shop, is often associated with Jean Lafitte, but there is also no historical evidence linking the two. **G, V**

Walk up Bourbon Street toward Canal Street one block to the corner of Dumaine and look to your right.

6. 901 Bourbon Street—Café Lafitte in Exile

Café Lafitte in Exile is the oldest gay bar in New Orleans and arguably the oldest continually operating gay bar in North America. Founded in 1933, the bar was originally located down the street where Lafitte's Blacksmith Shop now is. Back then, gay bars as we know them now did not exist as homosexuality was illegal, but the owners of Café Lafitte were open-minded and welcomed their gay clientele. The bar was as gay friendly as the times would permit. In 1953, the building came under a new owner who did not want gay people in the bar. The bar owners signed a lease on a new place and called it Café Lafitte in Exile, the "In Exile" referring to the regular patrons' status as being "in exile" from their former bar home. According to legend, on the night the bar opened, several regulars from the old bar went there to have one drink and then picked up their barstools and marched down the street to the new bar. Tennessee Williams was a regular at this bar when he lived in New Orleans. By the 1960s, the bar had a notorious reputation as a cruise bar; that is, a place for gay men to have anonymous sex. Because of this notoriety, the U.S. Navy sent a letter to the bar declaring it off limits to personnel of the U.S. Armed Forces. The letter is on permanent and proud display on the wall just inside the front door. **Q, V, L**

Walk along Dumaine Street toward the river one block and turn right on Royal Street. Walk one block to St. Ann Street and look to your left.

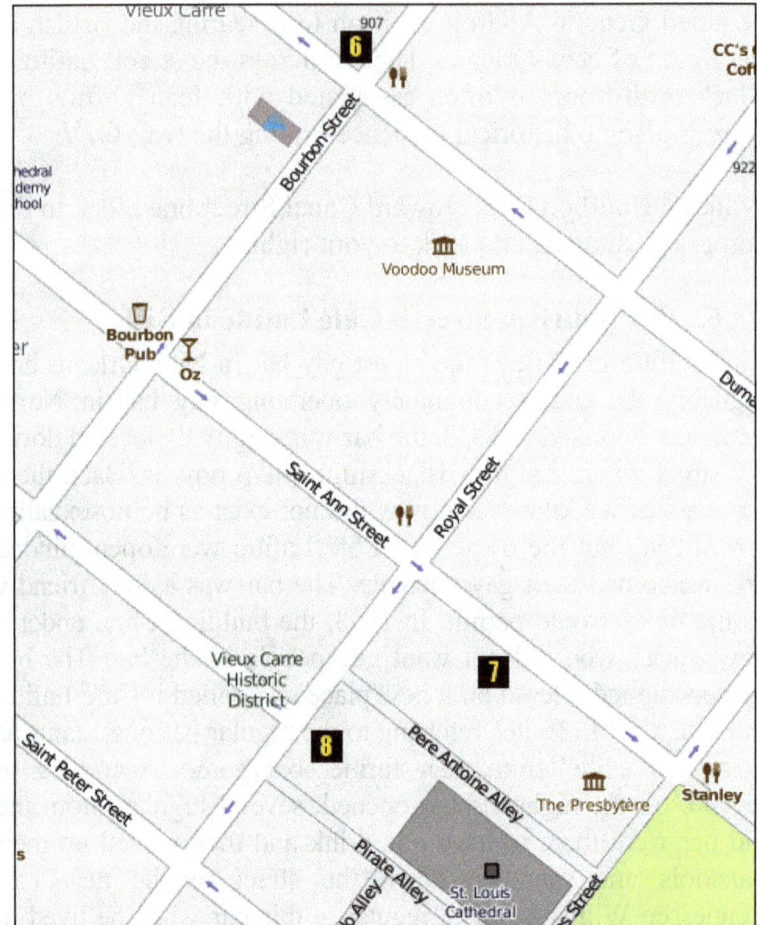

7. 638 St. Ann Street—The Crescent City Tour Booking Agency

This is an excellent place for information about the city and its attractions. Unlike most visitor centers, this booking agency is not owned by a specific tour company and offers unbiased recommendations. It also happens to be owned by the author of the book you now hold in your hands. Please feel free to pop in with any questions or just to say hello. **G**

Walk up Royal Street toward Canal Street half a block and stop at the little garden behind the cathedral.

8. 700 Royal Street—Dueling

During the Creole era, it was common for men to settle matters of honor by dueling. The slightest insult could result in the donning of swords. Dueling was so common that a number of fencing masters offered classes in dueling, especially in Exchange Place Alley. Many duels took place here in St. Anthony's garden behind the cathedral. By 1855, guns had replaced swords and the church put an end to dueling in the little garden. The new favorite place to duel became City Park then on the outskirts of town. Dueling was finally outlawed in New Orleans in 1890.

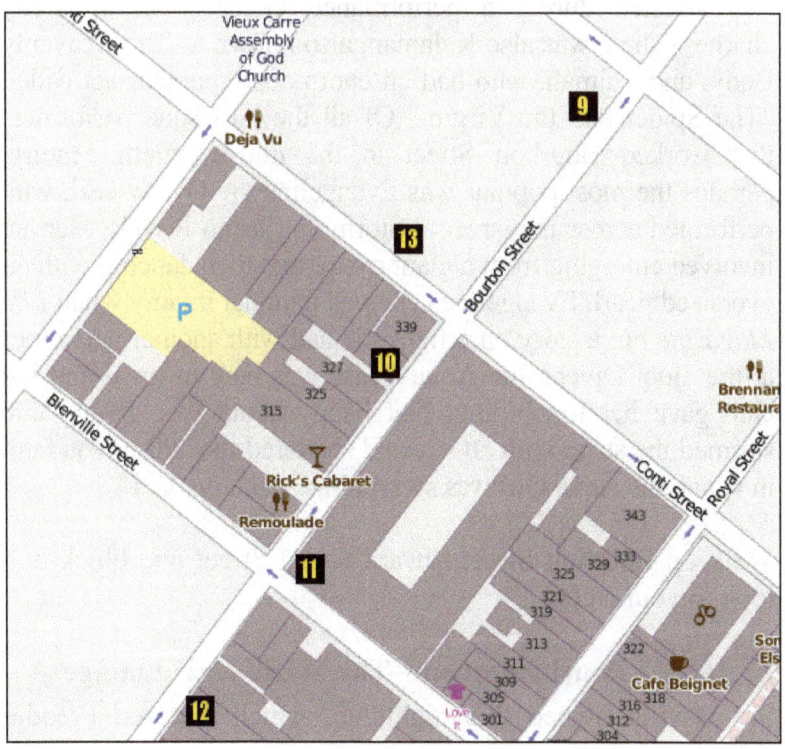

Walk up Royal Street toward Canal Street two and half blocks and turn right on St. Louis Street. Walk one block and turn left on Bourbon Street. Look to your right.

9. 441 Bourbon Street—Burlesque

Owned by Leon Prima, brother of Louis, the 500 Club was one of the first jazz bars on Bourbon Street. In addition to jazz, the club, like many others, also featured exotic dancers and burlesque shows in the 1950s, the most famous of which starred Lilly Christine the Cat Girl. Her signature number was something called "the voodoo love potion dance." After the Cat Girl's death, Linda Brigette, better known as The Cupid Doll, replaced her. Noted for her enhanced breasts and big blonde hair, Cupid Doll's routines involved dancing in a giant champagne glass, eating fire, and using animals in her act. She was arrested during a performance in 1966 on obscenity charges. There was also Kalantan, also known as The Heavenly Body, and Tajmah, who had an enormously popular act called "The Spider and the Virgin." Of all the burlesque performers that worked Bourbon Street in the mid-twentieth century, perhaps the most popular was Evangeline the Oyster Girl, who performed across the street at Stormy's Casino Royale. Her act involved emerging from a giant oyster and then dancing with an oversized pearl. Evangeline achieved national infamy when *Life Magazine* ran a story on a fight she had with another performer at the club. Divena the Aqua Tease was new in town and the club gave her top billing. Not happy about this, Evangeline stormed the stage with an axe and shattered the 300-gallon tank in which the Aqua Girl was swimming / dancing. **V, M**

Walk up Bourbon Street toward Canal Street one block and look to your right.

10. 333 Bourbon Street—The Mardi Gras Lounge

Sid Davilla owned this nightclub, which featured Freddie

Kohlman and his New Orleans Jazz Band. The club also hosted a burlesque show starring Wild Cherry, whose style of exotic dancing ranged from Oriental to Cuban. **V, M**

Walk up Bourbon Street toward Canal to the next corner and look to your left.

11. 240 Bourbon Street—The Old Absinthe House

Built in 1806, this building was first used as a store for an importing firm and later became a saloon in 1815. Bartender Cayetano Ferrer invented the Absinthe House Frappe here. During Prohibition, the Absinthe House refused to close and openly served alcohol in defiance of federal law. For many years, the bar and the attached restaurant were owned and operated by legendary Mafia figure Diamond Jim Moran, so named because he occasionally had his chef insert a diamond into the desserts of pretty women. According to legend, this is one of several places where the pirate Jean Lafitte met General Andrew Jackson to plan strategy for the Battle of New Orleans (but bear in mind that legend has that meeting taking place in a dozen locations throughout the French Quarter). Jean Lafitte's ghost is said to haunt the building. In the early 1900s, jazz was a fixture here with musicians such as Steve Lewis, Frank Froeba, Burnell Santiago, and "Fats" Pichon. **G, V, C, H, M**

Walk up Bourbon Street toward Canal Street half a block and look to your left.

12. 228 Bourbon Street—The Sho Bar

Legendary jazz trumpeter Sharkey Bonano was a regular fixture at this bar when it offered live jazz music. Later, the bar hosted burlesque shows featuring the infamous Tee Tee Red, who billed herself as an "acrobatic-comedienne-contortionist." **M, V**

Walk down Bourbon Street away from Canal Street two

blocks and turn left on Conti Street. Walk a quarter block and look to your right.

13. 811 Conti Street—The Erin Rose Bar

This excellent neighborhood Irish Pub's enduring popularity among locals and tourists alike is a testament to the legacy of longtime Quarter character Jim Monaghan. Over the course of three decades, Monaghan owned thirty bars in the French Quarter. Monaghan founded the French Quarter St. Patrick's Day Parade as well as the enormously popular Krewe de Vieux. Today, the Eric Rose has a loyal local following and is extremely visitor friendly. Killer Po-Boys is housed in the back of the bar and serves excellent food. This is a great place to relax and meet locals. **V, C**

Walk along Conti Street away from the river two blocks and look to your right.

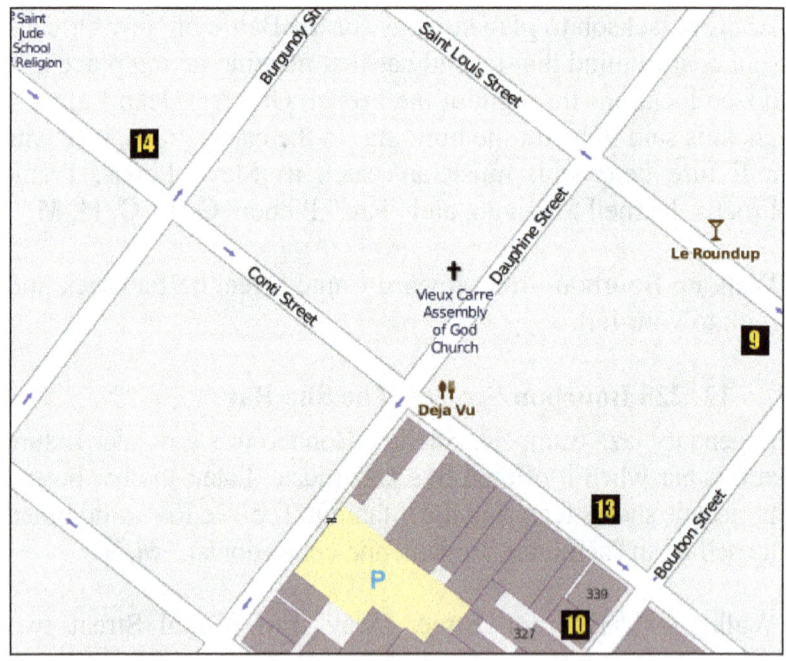

14. 1026 Conti Street—Norma Wallace

This building, which was constructed in 1830, was once home to Ernest J. Bellocq, the famed photographer who pictorially documented the working women of Storyville. Twenty years after the closing of Storyville, the infamous Norma Wallace, who turned the place into a thriving brothel, purchased the home. Norma was a savvy woman, and for twenty-five years, she discreetly entertained the city's business and political elite. Governors, gangsters and celebrities all graced 1026 Conti. For local boys, a visit to Norma's was a rite of passage. Norma Wallace died in 1974 and is fondly remembered by locals as New Orleans' "Last Madam." **V**

15. Canal Street to St. Louis Street / N. Rampart Street to Dauphine Street—The Tango Belt

The corner of the French Quarter bounded by Canal, North Rampart, St. Louis, and Dauphine Streets was at one time known as the Tango Belt because of all the clubs where the Tango dance was popular. In the first two decades of the twentieth century, the area was adjacent to Storyville and featured nightclubs, cabarets, theatres, restaurants, and a number of jazz clubs. When Storyville was closed in 1917, many of the brothels and freelance sex workers moved their operations into the Tango Belt. During prohibition, the moniker Tango Belt fell out of fashion but the area continued to host much of the French Quarter's sex tourism, the most famous bordello being Norma Wallace's at 1026 Conti Street, which was open from 1938 to 1963. Even today, prostitution still thrives in the Tango Belt in several gay bars, which feature male hustlers as well as transgendered prostitutes.

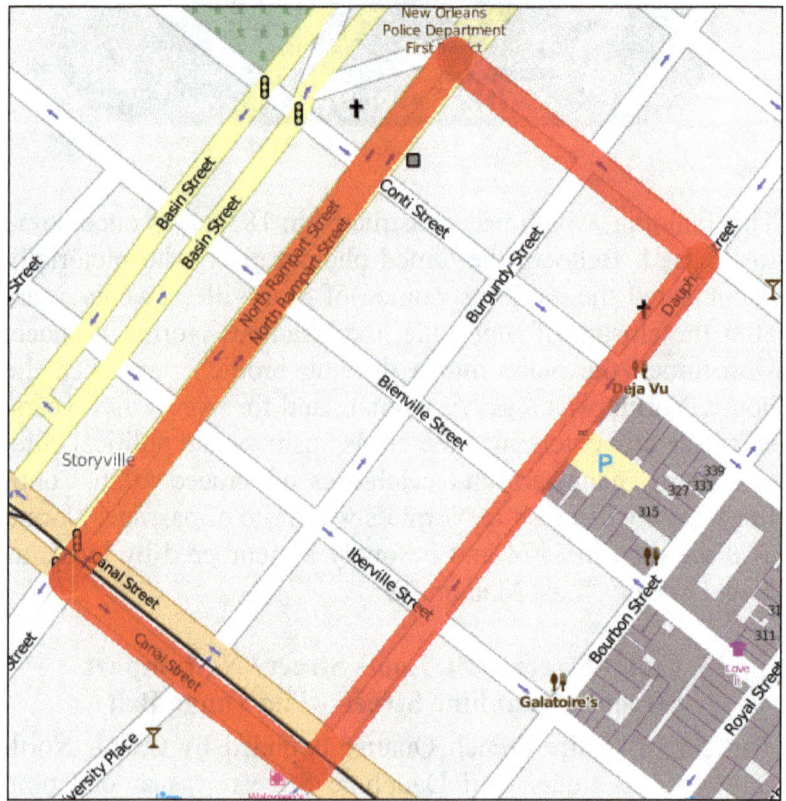

16. Gambling

These days, just about every bar in the French Quarter, and even many restaurants, offer customers video poker machines, but in years gone by, slot machines were all the rage. In 1934, New York Mayor Fiorello LaGuardia busted up gambling in New York. This created a dilemma for the Mafia, which needed a new market for its slot machines. In 1935, Huey Long, Louisiana's U. S. Senator and still de facto governor, met with mobster Frank Costello, the "Prime Minister" of the New York underworld, and cut a deal to have the slot machines brought in to Louisiana. New Orleans was delighted with the deal, and soon, slot machines were everywhere.

17. Suggestions for Further Reading

Asbury, Herbert. *The French Quarter: An Informal History of the New Orleans Underworld.* New York: Alfred A. Knopf, Inc., 2003.

Brouillette, Frenchy, and Matthew V. Randazzo. *Mr. New Orleans: The Life of a Big Easy Underworld Legend.* Beverly Hills: Phoenix Books, Inc., 2009.

Rose, Al. *Storyville, New Orleans: Being an Authentic, Illustrated Account of the Notorious Red Light District.* 1978.

Wiltz, Christine. *The Last Madam: A Life in the New Orleans Underworld.* De Capo Press, 2001.

Recommendations for Guided Tours

There are literally dozens of tour companies currently operating in New Orleans offering everything from customized walking tours to standard bus tours of the city. Searching online for tours or just perusing a brochure rack can be overwhelming. Asking hotel personnel for recommendations does not always yield the best response because many (but not all) are paid commissions by tour companies and most (but not all) concierges work for specific tour companies. There are a number of tour kiosks and visitor centers in the French Quarter but specific tour companies also own the overwhelming majority of them.

When I founded the Crescent City Tour Booking Agency, one of my desires was (and remains) to offer visitors unbiased suggestions based on visitors' specific interests and personalities. For that reason, the Crescent City Tour Booking Agency is an independent entity. We are able to book just about any tour company in the New Orleans area. In addition, we are also able to offer discounted prices on most of the tours we sell.

Please visit the agency's website at http://www.neworleanstourssightseeing.com/ for specific recommendations. You can also give us a call or stop by our office. In addition to booking tours, we also offer the following services: itinerary planning, transportation arrangement, and restaurant reservations. As a licensed tour guide, I am also available for private walking tours.

Crescent City Tour Booking Agency
638 St. Ann Street (near Royal St.)
504-568-0717
http://www.neworleanstourssightseeing.com/

About the Author

Frank Perez is a writer and licensed tour guide in New Orleans, Louisiana. A former college professor, Perez has a B.S. in Criminal Justice and a M.A. in English. He is also a graduate of the Delgado Community College Professional Tour Guiding Course as well as the Friends of the Cabildo Tour Guiding Course. He is the co-author of *In Exile: The History and Lore Surrounding New Orleans Gay Culture and Its Oldest Gay Bar.* He also writes a history column for *Ambush Magazine.* Perez lives in the French Quarter where he observes, writes, and manages his small business, the Crescent City Tour Booking Agency.

Index

1850 House, 87
500 Club, 196, 230
A Confederacy of Dunces, 204, 212
A Message from Khufu, 133
A Soldier's Pay, 212, 214
A Streetcar Named Desire, 130, 141, 161, 175, 211
Acme Oyster House, 102
Agnello, Raffaele, 222
Alciatore, Antoine, 112
Almonester y Roxas, Don Andreas, 32, 34, 86
Ambush Magazine, 137
American Institute of Architects, 98
Anderson, Sherwood, 19, 27, 114, 128, 202, 210, 214, 215
Anthony, Susan B., 134
Antoine's, 111, 163, 168
Arcadian Books, 212
Armeinius, 138
Armstrong, Louis, 70, 95, 184, 190
Arnaud's, 105, 107, 158
Arquette, Cliff, 192
Asbury, Herbert, 235
Ashley the Traffic Tranny, 10
Atakapa, 11
Audubon Institute, 80
Austin, Alice, 134
Baby Dodds, 186
Banderas, Antonio, 169
Bank of Louisiana, 164
Bank of the United States, 41
Bannister, Guy, 225
Baptandiere, Joseph, 156

Baraka, Amiri, 218
Barker, Danny, 187
Barkin, Ellen, 164
Barkus Parade, 10
Barney, Natalie Clifford, 134
Baron, Pierre, 91
Battle of New Orleans, 16, 31, 48, 51, 95, 98, 184, 199, 227, 231
Bauduc, Jules, 197
Baxter, Anne, 170
Bayona, 112
Bayou St. John, 12
Bayougoula, 11
Beals, Jennifer, 169
Beauregard, Pierre Gustave Toutant, 49, 93, 151, 219
Beauregard-Keyes House, 91
Beckham's Book Shop, 207
Begere, Maurice, 160
Begue, Madame, 118
Belle Reve, 130
Bellocq, Ernest J., 233
Bellow, April, 106
Beluche, Renato, 46, 90
Beluche, Rene, 46, 90
Beresford, Bruce, 167
Bernhard, Scott, 99
Bienvenu, Marcelle, 123
Bienville, Jean-Baptiste Le Moyne, Sieur de, 11, 29, 100, 126
Biloxi, 11
Blanchet, Kate, 173
Blassingame, John W., 77
Blue Book, 225
Bocage, Peter, 197
Boggs, Hale, 83
Boggs, Lindy, 83
Boggs, Luther, 143

Bonano, Sharkey, 197, 199, 231
Bonaparte, Napoleon, 15, 106, 110, 166, 208
Booker, James, 74
Bore, Etienne de, 97
Bottom of the Cup Tearoom, 39
Boudreaux, Cam, 106
Bouligny, Dominique, 96
Bourbon Street Awards, 137, 138
Bradford, Roark, 113, 128, 210, 215
Brady, Patricia, 219
Brando, Marlon, 175
Breakfast at Tiffany's, 139
Brennan, Owen, 107
Brennan's, 107, 108
Brigette, 197
Brigette, Linda, 197, 230
Brouillette, Frenchy, 235
Broussard, Joe, 105
Broussard's, 105
Brown v. Board of Education, 63
Brown, Roy, 74, 189
Brunies, Merritt, 197
Brunious, John, 182
Buck, Nina, 120, 183
Bukowski, Charles, 203, 218
Bullock, Sandra, 162
Burke, James Lee, 202, 203
Burroughs, William S., 203, 219
Butler, Benjamin, 18, 51, 95, 184
Cabildo, 14, 17, 31, 34, 86, 148, 150
Cable, George Washington, 46, 90, 98, 170, 202, 211, 216
Café du Monde, 31, 32, 116
Café Lafitte in Exile, 124, 136, 139, 140, 227
Cagnolatti, Ernie, 182
Calloway, Cab, 187
Calvo, Alberto A., 140

Camors, Bertha, 114
Camors, Emma, 114
Campanella, Richard, 56
Capote, Truman, 40, 139, 205, 212
Capucine, 170
Caracci, Vic, 113
Carey, Albert, 138
Carlos II, 13
Carolla, Sam, 223
Carson, Johnny, 192
Castro, Fidel, 164
Cat People, 171
Catlett, Elizabeth, 72, 191
Cazenave, Arnaud, 105, 107, 158
Celestin, Oscar, 198
Central Grocery, 118
Charity Hospital, 39, 140
Charles III, 150
Charles, Ray, 74, 178, 189
Cheval, Louison, 67
Chitimacha, 11
Choctaw, 11
Chopin, Kate, 202
Citizen's State Bank, 40
City Park, 129
Civil War, 16, 37, 51, 57, 93, 95, 134, 151, 152, 184
Claiborne, W. C. C., 226
Clover Grill, 10, 121, 138, 173
Code Noir, 15, 57, 67, 70, 191
Codrescu, Andrei, 145, 202, 208
Collin, Richard H., 123
Commander's Palace, 100, 109
Company of the Indies, 59
Company of the West, 12
Comus, 18
Confederacy of Dunces, 208

Congo Square, 58, 70, 71, 179, 191
Cooke, Sam, 189
Coop's Place, 119
Coppola, Francis Ford, 175
Cordeviolle, Etienne, 65
Correjolles, Francois, 93
Cosimo's, 225
Costello, Frank, 235
Cottman, Herman S., 133
Court of the Two Sisters, 115
Creely, Robert, 218
Creole Jazz Band, 71, 190
Crescent City Books, 206
Crescent City Tour Booking Agency, 44, 76, 88, 115, 139, 169, 193, 213, 228, 236, 237
Crosby, Octave, 198
Cruise, Tom, 169
Cucullu Row, 91
Curtiz, Michael, 172
Customs House, 66, 80
Dagobert, Father, 150
Dakin, James, 78
Dark Laughter, 214
Dauphine Street Book Shop, 10, 208
Davilla, Sid, 198, 230
Dawdy, Shannon Lee, 56
Dayries, Provosty, 124
de la Ronde, Pierre Denis, 48, 91
de La Tour, Pierre Le Blond, 79
de Soto, Hernando, 11
Decatur, Stephen, 24
Degas, Edgar, 41
Dejan, Harold, 182
Delehanty, Randolph, 99
Delille, Henriette, 44, 60, 65
Denis, Henry Raphael, 94

Desdunes, Rodolphe Lucien, 67
Dinner at Antoine's, 49, 93, 152, 219
Divena the Aqua Tease, 230
Dixie's Bar of Music, 138, 141, 193
Dmytryk, Edward, 170
Dodds, Baby, 132
Domino, Fats, 74, 181, 189
Dorsey, Thomas, 73
Dorsier, Eugene, 25
Dos Passos, John, 19, 128, 202, 215, 217
Double Jeopardy, 167
Drawing Room Players, 148
Dream Room, 197
Drennan, David P., 140
DuBois, Angelique, 156
DuBois, Blanche, 130, 175
Ducayet, Marie Odalie, 154
Dufilho, Louis Jr., 35, 157
Dumas, Alexandre, 66
Dunst, Kirsten, 169
Dupas, James, 157
Durel, Jean Florent, 137
Dwyer, Jeff, 160
Easy Rider, 161, 176
Eat, 122
El Morocco, 199
Ellis, Scott S., 56
Erin Rose, 10, 106, 232
Esposito, Giuseppe, 222
Evangeline the Oyster Girl, 230
Evans, Freddi Williams, 77
Fabulous New Orleans, 27, 89, 128, 215
Fairview Baptist Church Brass Band, 187
Famous Door, 198
Farragut, David, 18
Farrell, John, 140

Fasnacht, Dixie, 138, 141, 193
Faubourg Marigny Arts and Books, 132, 217
Faulkner House, 170
Faulkner, William, 19, 114, 128, 202, 205, 210, 212, 214, 215
Federal Writers Project, 89
Fein, Joe, 114
Felix's, 102
Ferbos, Lionel, 182
Ferlinghetti, Lawrence, 218
Ferrer, Cayetano, 198, 231
Ferrie, David, 225
Fincher, David, 173
Fitzgerald, F. Scott, 173
Fitzmorris, Tom, 123
Fleder, Gary, 165
Flynn, Tenney, 104
Fonda, Jane, 170
Fonda, Peter, 176
Ford, Richard, 205, 208
Fort Jackson, 18
Fort Rosalie, 13
Fort St. Philip, 18
Fountain, Pete, 10
Foxx, Jamie, 178
Fremiet, Emmanuel, 47
French 75 Bar, 105
French Indian War, 13
French Market, 11, 50, 111
French Opera House, 10, 179, 194
French Revolution, 15
Froeba, Frank, 199, 231
Galatoire, Jean, 104
Galatoire's, 10, 103, 175
Gallagher, Peter, 169
Gallier, Irene, 171

Gallier, James, 78, 97
Garrison, Jim, 132, 163, 225
Garvey, Joan B., 56
Gauche, John, 96
Gayarre, Charles, 97
Giancona, Pietro, 50, 93, 152
Ginsberg, Allen, 202, 218
Girod, Nicholas, 36, 110, 166
Glapion, Louis Christopher Dominick Duminy de, 75
Gleises, Paul Joseph, 154
Golden Lantern, 130
Goodman, John, 162
Goulet, Robert, 192
Green Goddess, 108
Greenwood, Bruce, 167
Gretry, Andre Ernest, 179
Grisham, John, 165, 168, 205
Groom, Winston, 205
Gross, Steve, 99
Gumbo Ya-Ya, 89, 128, 215
GW Fins, 9, 104
Hachard, Marie, 49, 202
Hackford, Taylor, 178
Haitian Revolution, 15, 180
Half Fast Walking Club, 10
Hall, Gwendolyn Midlo, 77
Hannusch, Jeff, 201
Harper's Weekly, 209
Harris, Phil, 192
Harvey, Laurence, 170
Heard, Malcolm, 99
Hearn, Lafcadio, 10, 209
Hellman, Lillian, 202
Hemmingway, Ernest, 40, 128, 202, 205, 215
Hennessy, David, 223
Henry, O., 128, 202, 215

Hermann-Grima House, 82, 167
Hirsch, Arnold Richard, 77
Hirt, Al, 195
Historic New Orleans Collection, 39, 43
Holmes, Jeffrey, 220
Hopper, Dennis, 176
Horowitz, Morton J., 100
Houma, 11
Howard, Henry, 88
Hug, Armand, 199
Hughes, Langston, 203, 218
Hugo, Victor, 66
Hunter, Kim, 175
Hurston, Zora Neale, 128, 202, 215
Iberville, Pierre Le Moyne d', 11, 23
In Cold Blood, 139
International Society for Paranormal Research, 147, 159
Interview With the Vampire, 170
J&M Recording Studio, 188
Jackson Square, 14, 17, 29, 31, 85, 126, 150, 166, 174, 175, 205
Jackson, Andrew, 16, 31, 51, 95, 97, 155, 184, 199, 227, 231
Jackson, Mahalia, 72, 73
Jackson, Tony, 124, 131, 185
Jaffe, Allan, 193
Jaffe, Sandra, 193
Jazz National Historic Park, 72
Jelly Roll Morton, 186, 187
Jezebel, 161, 166
JFK, 163
Jimani's, 142
Joan of Arc, 47
John Henry, 210
Johnny's Po-Boys, 110
Johnson, Bunk, 132, 186, 188
Johnson, Walter, 77

Johnston, Frances Benjamin, 134
Jolie, Angelina, 162, 170
Jones, Carolyn, 172
Jones, Doug, 138
Jones, Tommy Lee, 167
Jordan, Neil, 169
Jourdan, Pierre Antoine Lepardi, 115, 150
Judd, Ashley, 167
Juvenile, 181
Kalantan, 230
Katrina, Hurricane, 10, 19, 30, 39, 73, 122, 170, 201
Kazan, Elia, 175
Kein, Sybil, 77
Kelly, Chris, 187
Kennedy, John F., 73, 132, 163, 225
Kennedy, Richard S., 219
Keyes, Frances Parkinson, 49, 93, 112, 151, 152, 219
Kid Howard, 182
Kid Ory, 71, 187, 190
Killer Po-Boys, 106, 232
King Cake Queen Coronation, 137
King Creole, 161, 172
King Fish Beer Parlor, 182
King, Grace, 202, 211, 215
King, Jr., Martin Luther, 73
King's Room, 199
Kinski, Nastassja, 171
Klein, Victor C., 160
Kohlman, Freddie, 198, 231
K-Paul's, 109
Krewe de Vieux, 232
L'Ecole Centrale, 67
L'Union, 65
La Louisiane, 103
la Salle, Rene-RobertCavelier, Sieur de, 11
La Société des Dames Hospitalières, 96

La Tribune de la Nouvelle Orleans, 65
LaBranche, Jean Baptist, 84
Lacroix, Francois, 64
Lafitte, Jean, 31, 46, 90, 154, 199, 220, 226, 231
Lafitte, Pierre, 154, 226
Lafitte's Blacksmith Shop, 227
Lafon, Barthelemy, 98
LaGuardia, Fiorello, 235
Laine, Jack, 182
Lake Borgne, 12
Lake Pontchartrain, 12, 29
LaLaurie Mansion, 154
LaLaurie, Delphine, 154
Lanaux Mansion, 171, 174
Lanusse, Armand, 58, 202
Larson, Susan, 219
Latrobe Building, 40
Latrobe, Benjamin, 40, 79, 96
Latrobe, Henry, 96
Laveau, Marie, 75, 177
Lawrence, Carole, 192
Le Carpentier, Joseph, 93
Le Petit Salon, 211
Le Petit Theatre, 34, 147, 211
Leaves of Grass, 144
Lee, Brenda, 192
Leibovitz, Annie, 134
Leigh, Vivien, 175
Leonhard, Allan T., 178
Les Cenelles, 58, 202
Lewis, George, 182, 187, 199
Lewis, Jerry Lee, 189
Lewis, Steve, 199, 231
Life Magazine, 230
Lil Wayne, 181
Lilly Christine the Cat Girl, 230

Lily the Cat Girl, 196
Lion's Den, 223
Little Richard, 74, 181, 188
Little Vic's, 113
Live Oak Boys, 224
Long, Huey, 235
Long, Judy, 219
Louis IX, 23
Louis XIV, 23, 57, 220
Louis XV, 13, 24, 150
Louis, Jean, 39
Louisiana Purchase, 16, 25, 34, 80, 86, 109, 149, 166, 181
Louisiana State Bank, 40
Louisiana State Museum, 87, 90, 95, 149, 184
Louisiana Supreme Court Building, 163
Louisiana Writer's Project, 128, 215
Loujon Press, 202, 218
Lucia di Lammermoor, 194
Lupo, Salvatore, 46, 118
Luxembourg, Raphael de, 45
Macheca, Joseph, 222
Madame John's Legacy, 46, 90, 170, 216
Maestri, Robert, 88
Mahalia Jackson Theatre for the Performing Arts, 191
Make It Right Foundation, 170
Manhattan Transfer, 217
Manning, Taryn, 161
Marcello, Carlos, 223
Mardi Gras, 17, 121, 138, 176, 193
Mardi Gras Lounge, 198, 230
Marigny, Bernard de, 132
Marsalis, Branford, 187
Marsalis, Wynton, 187
Marti's, 141
Martin, Bennie, 111
Martin, Clovis, 111

Matassa, Cosimo, 74, 181, 188, 189
Matthau, Walter, 172
McCaffety, Kerri, 99
McCusker, John, 201
McDonogh, John, 126, 129
McNulty, Ian, 9
Medak, Peter, 169
Merieult, Jean Francois, 43
Merman, Ethel, 121, 174
Miller, Henry, 218
Miller, John, 219
Mills, Clark, 31
Mississippi River, 11, 29, 30, 67, 113
Mitchum, Robert, 192
Monaghan, Jim, 232
Monteleone, Antonio, 159
Montz, Larry, 160
Moran, Jim, 198, 231
Morton, Jelly Roll, 131
Moulon, Ruth, 47
Mumford, William, 51, 95, 184
Muriel's, 115, 150
Napoleon House, 36, 38, 62, 109, 110, 163, 165, 166, 208
Naquin-Delain, Marsha, 137
Naquin-Delain, Rip, 137
Natchez, 13
New Orleans African American Museum, 73
New Orleans City Guide, 89, 128, 215
New Orleans Jazz Band, 198, 231
New Orleans Jazz Club Collections, 184
New Orleans Jazz National Historic Park, 182, 191
Nicholas Girod, 208
Nunez, Don Vincente Jose, 35
Nunez, Rodger Dale, 143
Nystrom, Justin A., 77
O' Flaherty, Danny, 157

O' Flaherty's Irish Pub, 157
O'Reilly, Alejandro, 14, 51, 150
Old Absinthe House, 80, 108, 198, 231
Old Creole Days, 216
Old Man Adam an' His Chillun, 210
Olen Butler, Robert, 208
Oliver, Joe, 71, 190
Oswald, Lee Harvey, 163, 225
Other Voices, Other Rooms, 139
Our People Our History, 67
Oz, 192
Paddock Lounge, 198
Pakula, Alan J., 168
Palm Court Jazz Café, 120, 183
Palmquist, Jeffrey, 144
Panic in the Streets, 161
Parenti, Tony, 197
Parker, Charlie, 187
Patti, Adelina, 194
Pauger, Adrien de, 79
Pedesclaux, Pedro, 98
Percy, Walker, 202, 204
Perez, Frank, 144, 237
Perier, Sieur Etienne de, 114
Pet Shop Boys, 121, 174
Pete Fountain's Jazz Club, 192
Peters, Samuel J., 25
Petit, Buddy, 187
Petrie, Daniel, Jr., 164
Peychaud, Antoine, 42
Pharmacy Museum, 36
Philippe II, Duc d'Orleans, 23
Piazza d'Italia, 164
Piazza, Tom, 203, 208
Pichon, Fats, 199, 231
Pierce, Billie, 182

Pierce, Dee Dee, 182
Pinchback, P.B.S., 58
Pitt, Brad, 162, 169, 170, 173
Plessy v. Ferguson, 69
Plessy versus Ferguson, 58, 177
Plessy, Homer, 58, 63, 67, 69, 177
Pollack, Sydney, 175
Pontalba Buildings, 17, 31, 32, 87, 148
Pontalba, Celestin de, 87, 126
Pontalba, Gaston de, 126
Pontalba, Micaela Almonester de, 32, 87, 126
Pope John Paul II, 33, 86
Pope Paul VI, 33, 86
Popeye Beer Parlor, 182
Poree, Thomas, 97
Port of Call, 123
Porter, Katherine Anne, 128, 202, 215
Pouilly, J.N.B., 78, 82, 85
Pound, Ezra, 202
Powell, Lawrence N., 56
Powell, Shannon, 187
Poydras, Julien, 151
Presbytere, 14, 17, 31, 34, 86, 150
Preservation Hall, 54, 188, 193
Presley, Elvis, 172
Pretty Baby, 161
Price, Lloyd, 74, 189
Prima, Leon, 196, 230
Prima, Louis, 196, 230
Professor Longhair, 74, 189
Prudhomme, Paul, 100, 109
Quadroon Balls, 44, 169
Quaid, Dennis, 164
Randazzo, Matthew V., 235
Rasmussen, Buddy, 143
Ray, 178

Real-Marin, Elizabeth, 46, 90
Red, Tee Tee, 199
Redford, Robert, 175
Reed, John Shelton, 219
Reeves, Sally, 78
Reuben, Gloria, 169
Rex, 111
Rice, Anne, 169, 203
Richard, Robert, 169
Rigolets, 12
Rillieux, Norbert, 67
Rillieux, Vincent, 41
Rillieux-Waldorn House, 40
Rios, Fernando, 139
Roahen, Sara, 123
Roberts, Julia, 168
Roosevelt, Franklin D., 89, 215
Roosevelt, Theodore, 134
Rose, Al, 235
Roudanez, Louis Charles, 65
Runaway Jury, 165
Running of the Bulls, 9
Saenger Theatre, 200
Saint Domingue, 15
Saints and Sinners Literary Festival, 205
Sandburg, Carl, 19, 202
Santiago, Burnell, 199, 231
Saulay, Celie, 65
Saxon, Lyle, 18, 27, 89, 124, 127, 133, 195, 202, 215
Scarborough, Mike, 143
Schrader, Paul, 171
Scribner's Magazine, 209
Scribner's Monthly, 216
Sedella, Antonio de, 25
Seignouret, Francois, 42
Seven Years War, 13

Sevre, Mary Wheaton, 156
Shaw, Clay, 132, 133, 163, 164, 225
Shepard, Sam, 168
Sherwood Anderson and Other Famous Creoles, 214
Sho Bar, 199, 231
Silver Slipper, 197
Sinatra, Frank, 192
Sipprell, Clara, 134
Sisters of the Holy Family, 44, 60, 65
Slater, Christian, 169
Smilin' Joe, 182
Smith, Julie, 208
Smoller, Daena, 160
Snyder, Michael, 133
Sophisticate of Swing, 141, 193
Southern Decadence, 121, 124, 130
Southern Decadence Bead Toss, 137
Spanish War of Succession, 59
Sparicio, Johnny, 182
Sparicio's Saloon, 182
Spera, Keith, 201
Spicer, Susan, 112
St Mary's Church, 91
St. Anthony's Garden, 44, 168
St. Cyr, Johnny, 132, 186
St. Domingue, 65
St. Louis Cathedral, 14, 17, 31, 33, 86, 168, 175
St. Louis Hotel, 24, 37, 40, 41, 61, 62, 78, 85, 166
St. Louis IX, 33, 86
St. Peter Theatre, 54
Stanwyck, Barbara, 170
Starr, S. Frederick, 123
Stein, Gertrude, 19, 202
Steinbeck, Gwen, 128, 215
Steinbeck, John, 19, 128, 215
Stevenson, Burke, 182

Stokers, 133
Stone, Oliver, 163
Stormy's Casino Royale, 230
Story, Sidney, 131, 185, 224
Storyville, 58, 70, 124, 131, 185, 190, 223, 224, 233
Stowe, Harriet Beecher, 62
Sublette, Ned, 56, 57, 77
Submerged, 133
Suddenly Last Summer, 161
Sully, Susan, 99
Tajmah, 230
Takamine, Jokichi, 94
Tango Belt, 233
Tarzan of the Apes, 161
Taylor, Troy, 160
Teagarden, Jack, 197
Tee Tee Red, 231
Tennessee Williams Literary Festival, 205
The Big Easy, 161
The Buccaneer, 161
The Cincinnati Kid, 161
The Courage to Love, 61
The Cuckoo's Nest, 133
The Curious Case of Benjamin Button, 173
The Double-Dealer, 202
The Feast of All Saints, 169
The Friends of Joe Gilmore, 89, 128, 215
The Grandissimes, 216
The Harmony Maids, 141, 193
The Librairie, 215
The Outsider, 218
The Pelican Brief, 168
The Smart Set, 141, 193
The Southland Rhythm Girls, 141, 193
Theatre d'Orleans, 179
This Property is Condemned, 175

This Side of Jordan, 210
Thomas, Irma, 189
Tillman, Wilbert, 182
To Be Continued Brass Band, 10
Toledano, Roulhac, 99
Toole, John Kennedy, 204, 208, 212
Toussaint, Allen, 189, 196
Treaty of Ghent, 16
Treme', 68, 73, 130
Treme', Claude, 69
Tucker, Susan, 123
Tujague, Guillaume, 118
Tujague's, 118
Turner, Joe, 74
Turner, Richard Brent, 77
Twain, Mark, 134, 202
U.S. Army Corps of Engineers, 19
U.S. Mint, 51, 94, 183, 184
U.S.A. Trilogy, 217
Ulloa y de la Torre-Girault, Antonio de, 13
Ulloa, Antonio de, 149, 150
Uncle Tom's Cabin, 62
Upstairs Lounge, 124
Ursuline Convent, 48, 91
Ursuline Nuns, 24, 91
Valenti, Steve, 198
Vieux Carre Commission, 19, 79, 88
Vogt, Lloyd, 99
Von Reizenstein, Ludwig, 124
Wallace, Norma, 233, 234
War of 1812, 16, 31, 149
Warren Easton High School, 133
Washington Artillery Park, 31
Washington, Denzel, 168
Webb, Jon, 219
Webb, Louise, 219

Wells, Germaine, 105, 158, 159
Wells, Rebecca, 205
Welty, Eudora, 40, 205
Werlein, Elizabeth, 18, 88
White, Edward Douglas, 42, 63, 164
Whitman, Walt, 124, 143, 202
Wiggs, Johnny, 224
Wild Cherry, 198, 231
Wilde, Oscar, 202
Williams Research Center, 39
Williams, Clarence, 131, 186
Williams, L. Kemper, 44
Williams, Tennessee, 40, 136, 141, 175, 205, 211, 227
Wiltz, Christine, 235
Winters, Jonathan, 192
Wood, Alexander Thompson, 80
Wood, Natalie, 175
Works Progress Administration, 128, 215
Wyler, William, 166
Xiques, Angel, 82
Yellow Fever, 17
Yellow Nunez, 182
Your Father's Mustache, 197
Yuga, 124, 138
Zeringue, Jarred, 113
Zito, Phil, 199

www.ingramcontent.com/pod-product-compliance
Lightning Source LLC
Chambersburg PA
CBHW071621170426

43195CB00038B/1588